SCRIPTURE:
MEANING AND METHOD

Essays presented to
ANTHONY TYRRELL HANSON
for his seventieth birthday

Edited by
BARRY P. THOMPSON
Department of Theology
University of Hull

D1202795

HULL UNIVERSITY PRESS
1987

© Hull University Press

ISBN 0 85958 460 7

Phototypeset in 10 on 12 pt Times by Computape (Pickering) Ltd, Pickering, North Yorkshire, and printed by The University of Hull

SCRIPTURE: MEANING AND METHOD

Anthony Tyrrell Hanson

photo: Ieuan Ellis

Contents

PART TWO: METHOD

Foreword

It is well known that Anthony Hanson's drive and enthusiasm enable him to pursue a wide variety of interests both academic and otherwise. In addition to his scholarship in the field of Biblical Studies, his reputation as a teacher of Christian Doctrine, and his devotion and pastoral care as an Anglican priest, he also takes an active part in ecumenical affairs and encourages the study of non-Christian religions and Contextual Theology.

In this book, which has been planned by the Hull University Department of Theology where he was the professor until his retirement, it has not, of course, been possible to represent all aspects of Anthony Hanson's academic studies. We have thought it best, therefore, to single out his overriding interest in Biblical Studies and his particular concern for meaning and method in his approach to scripture. However, we have hoped to retain and reflect something of his wide-ranging theological pursuits in the way that the members of our Department have joined forces in the production of this book. Our biblical scholars, in addition to contributing articles in the usual way, have rendered invaluable help in the compilation of indexes. Others of us have made our contribution by way of editorial work. My own field of Social Ethics has a vested interest in the subject area of this book in terms of the use of scripture for approaching contemporary issues in Social Ethics. This interest has made my editorial work all the more enjoyable.

Particular thanks are due to three of my departmental colleagues, Elfride Bickersteth and Lester Grabbe, for sub-editing this book, and Lionel North for help with indexing. I would also like to thank our contributors for their readiness to submit articles. It is surely a mark of their esteem for Anthony Hanson that they should respond in such a way. Finally, I would like to thank Hull University Press for their patience and wise counsel: Professor Clement H. Dodd and Alan Best for their encouragement and help in overseeing the publication, Barbara Nield and Joyce Bellamy for their valuable editorial work on the manuscript, and Jean Smith for her help and care in seeing it through to completion.

Department of Theology   Barry P. Thompson
University of Hull
August 1986

ANTHONY TYRRELL HANSON

Curriculum Vitae

1916   Born 24 November, London, elder twin brother of R. P. C. Hanson.
1930–4   Cheltenham College.
1934–41   Trinity College, Dublin.
1938   B.A. in Literae Humaniores and Mental and Moral Sciences, Trinity College, Dublin.
1941   B.D., Trinity College, Dublin.
1941   Deacon.
1941–3   Curate of Bangor Abbey.
1942   Priest.
1943–7   Secretary, Student Christian Movement.
1945   Married Miriam Joselin.
1947–55   Tutor, Dornakal Divinity School, Hyderabad, India.
1953   D.D., Trinity College, Dublin.
1955–9   Tutor, United Theological College, Bangalore, Mysore, India.
1959–62   Canon Theologian of Belfast Cathedral.
1963–82   Professor of Theology, University of Hull.

List of Publications by A. T. Hanson

Books

The Revelation of Saint John the Divine (Torch Bible Commentaries) with R. H. Preston (London, 1949); reissued (The Christian Students' Library, Madras, 1954).

The Book of Job (Torch Bible Commentaries) with Miriam Hanson (London, 1953; reissued New York, 1962).

Prakatana Grundha Vyakhyanamu, being a translation of the above into Telugu by the author (Madras, 1955).

Jonah and Daniel (The Christian Students' Library, Madras, 1955).

Yona, Danielu Grundhamula Vyakhyanamu, being a translation of the above into Telugu by the author (Madras, 1957).

The Wrath of the Lamb (London, 1957).

The Church of the Servant (London, 1962).

The Facts about the Roman Catholic Church (Belfast, 1962).

The Pioneer Ministry (London, 1961; rev. ed. London, 1975).

Solomonu Gnyanagrandhamu, being a translation of the Book of Wisdom in the Apocrypha into Telugu (Madras, 1962).

A Commentary on the Book of Genesis (The Christian Students' Library), with Miriam Hanson (Madras, 1963).

Paul's Understanding of Jesus: invention or interpretation? (Hull, 1963).

Beyond Anglicanism (London, 1965).

Jesus Christ in the Old Testament (London, 1965).

The Pastoral Letters (Cambridge Bible Commentary on the New English Bible, Cambridge, 1966).

Studies in the Pastoral Epistles (London, 1968).

Studies in Paul's Technique and Theology (London, 1974).

Church, Sacraments and Ministry (London, 1975).

Grace and Truth (London, 1975).

The New Testament Interpretation of Scripture (London, 1980).

Reasonable Belief, with R. P. C. Hanson (Oxford, 1980).

The Pastoral Epistles (New Century Bible Commentary) (Grand Rapids, Michigan, and London, 1982).
The Image of the Invisible God (London, 1982).
The Living Utterances of God (London, 1983).

Articles

'Theophanies in the Old Testament and the Second Person of the Trinity', *Hermathena* 65 (1945) 67–73.
'The Interpretation of the Second Person Singular in Quotations from the Psalms in the New Testament', *Hermathena* 73 (1949) 69–72.
'The Interpretation of Phil.2:5', *Indian Journal of Theology* 7 (1958) 73–4.
'The Prayer Book: schoolmaster or cement?' in D. M. Paton (ed.) *Essays in Anglican Self-Criticism* (London, 1958).
'Symbolism and the Doctrine of God', *London Quarterly and Holborn Review* 189 (1964) 178–83.
'Christ in the Old Testament According to Hebrews', *SE* vol. 2, pt 1 (Berlin, 1964).
'Episcopacy in a United Church', *Biblical Theology* 15 (1965) 3–8.
'John's Citation of Psalm LXXXII', *NTS* 11 (1964–5) 158–62.
'John's Citation of Psalm LXXXII Reconsidered', ibid. 13 (1966–7) 363–7.
'Philo's Etymologies', *JTS* n.s. 18 (1967) 128–39.
'Teilhard de Chardin and Priesthood' *ExpT* 79 (1968) 308–10.
'Letting in Some Air', *The Churchman* 82 (1968) 184–6.
Introduction to reissue of R. C. Moberly, *Ministerial Priesthood* (London, 1969).
'The Great Form Critic', *SJT* 22 (1969) 296–304.
Articles on Christian Hope, Eschatology, Heaven and Hell, Invisible Church, Time and Eternity, Wrath, in A. Richardson (ed.), *A Dictionary of Christian Theology* (London, 1969).
'Ecclesia Quaerens' in A. T. Hanson (ed.), *Teilhard Reassessed* (London, 1970).
'A Survey of Theological Journals', *New Divinity* 2 (1971) 1–11.
'Was there a Complementary Initiation Rite in the First Two Centuries?', *Theology* 75 (1972) 190–7.
'Knowing God by Faith according to the Writers of the New Testament', *The Modern Churchman* 16 (1972–3) 111–17.

'The Old Testament Background to the Raising of Lazarus', *SE* vol. 6 (Berlin, 1973).

'The Oracle in Romans XI.4', *NTS* 19 (1973) 300–2.

'Episcopacy in Anglicanism and Beyond', *Anglican Theological Review* Supplementary Series no.2 (1973) 27–34.

'Hodayoth XV and John 17: a comparison of content and form', *Hermathena* 118 (1974) 48–58.

'Teaching Theology to Catholics in a Modern University', *Downside Review* 93 (1975) 77–82.

'Alan Richardson and his Critics in the Area of Hermeneutics', in R. H. Preston (ed.), *Essays in Theology and Change* (London, 1975).

'John I.14–18 and Exodus XXXIV', *NTS* 23 (1976–7) 90–101.

'Claude Montefiore', *The Modern Churchman* n.s., 20 (1976–7) 109–14.

'Rahab the Harlot in Early Christian Tradition', *Journal for the Study of the New Testament* 1 (1978) 53–60.

'The Ecumenical Crisis in the Western Church', *Doctrine and Life* 30 (1980) 137–49.

'The Midrash in II Corinthians 3: a reconsideration', *Journal for the Society of New Testament Studies* 9 (1980) 2–28.

'Has the Church of England changed its Doctrine?', in *The New Alternative Services Book of the Church of England* (Newland Papers, no. 4: Hull University, 1980), 18–28.

'The Domestication of Paul: a study in the development of early Christian theology', *Bulletin of the John Rylands University Library of Manchester* 63 (1980–1) 402–18.

'The Use of the Old Testament in the Pastoral Epistles', *Irish Biblical Studies* 3 (1981) 203–18.

'Vessels of Wrath or Instruments of Wrath? Romans IX.22–3', *JTS* n.s. 32 (1981) 433–43.

'Salvation Proclaimed: I.1 Peter 3^{18-22}', *ExpT* 93 (1981–2) 100–5.

'1 Corinthians 4^{13b} and Lamentations 3^{45}', ibid. 214–15.

'The Theology of Suffering in the Pastoral Epistle and Ignatius of Antioch', *SP* vol.18 (Oxford and New York, 1982).

'The Reproach of the Messiah in the Epistle to the Hebrews', *SE* vol. 7 (Berlin, 1982).

Review of J. Christian Becker, *Paul the Apostle: the triumph of God in life and thought*, in *Journal for the Society of New Testament Studies* 14 (1982) 123–5.

Articles on Communion of Saints, Descent into Hell, Eschatology, Parousia, Pre-Existence, The Risen Christ, Schism, in A. Richardson and J. Bowden, eds, *A New Dictionary of Christian Theology* (London, 1983).

Articles on Hermeneutics, Qumran Scrolls, in J. M. Sutcliffe (ed.), *A Dictionary of Religious Education* (London, 1984).

'Two Difficulties: an examination of basic Christian doctrine', *New Fire* 8 (1984–5) 198–202.

'A Resolution of our Difficulties', ibid. 272–5.

'Two Consciousnesses: the modern version of Chalcedon' in *SJT* 38 (1985) 471–83.

Pamphlet

The Effect of Church Union on the Ministry in South India (CMS, London, 1960).

Books Edited

Vindications (London, 1966).

Teilhard Reassessed (London, 1970).

List of Abbreviations

AV	Authorised Version
ch., chs	chapter(s)
C.M.S.	Church Missionary Society
col., cols	column(s)
ed., eds	editor(s), edition(s)
ET	English Translation
EvT	*Evangelische Theologie*
ExpT	*Expository Times*
frag., frags	fragment(s)
HUCA	*Hebrew Union College Annual*
JTS	*Journal of Theological Studies*
LCL	*Loeb Classical Library*
LXX	Septuagint
MM	J. H. Moulton and G. Milligan (eds), *The Vocabulary of the Greek New Testament* (1914–29)
MPG	Migne *Patrologia Graeca*
MPL	Migne *Patrologia Latina*
MS., MSS	Manuscript(s)
MT	Masoretic Text
NEB	New English Bible
NIV	New International Version
n.s.	new series
NT	New Testament
NTS	*New Testament Studies*
NovTSup	*Novum Testamentum, Supplements*
OT	Old Testament
p., pp.	page(s)
pt	part
RE	*Realencyclopädie der classischen Altertumswissenschaft*
rev.	revised
RSV	Revised Standard Version
SE	*Studia Evangelica*
SJT	*Scottish Journal of Theology*
SP	*Studia Patristica*
s.v.l.	*si vera lectio*
TWNT	*Theologisches Wörterbuch zum Neuen Testament*
v.l.	*varia lectio*
v.vv.	verse(s)
vol., vols	volume(s)
ZAW	*Zeitschrift für die Alttestamentliche Wissenschaft*

Dedication
to
Anthony Tyrrell Hanson

Διὰ τοῦτο πᾶς γραμματεὺς μαθητευθεὶς τῇ βασιλείᾳ τῶν οὐρανῶν ὅμοιός ἐστιν ἀνθρώπῳ οἰκοδεσπότῃ ὅστις ἐκβάλλει ἐκ τοῦ θησαυροῦ αὐτοῦ καινὰ καὶ παλαιά.

Matt. 13:52

Many scholars might merit that description, but it is particularly appropriate to your life and achievement. In a number of works you have shown how the old covenant and the new are related (the theme which prompted this verse in Matthew), how the exegesis of the New Testament is influenced by the Old, and how the unity of the two is thus demonstrated. We are thinking of *Jesus Christ in the Old Testament, Studies in Paul's Technique and Theology*, and *The New Testament Interpretation of Scripture*. But in a wider sense your bringing together of old and new, out of the treasury of your gifts and experience, may be demonstrated. You have been concerned to challenge a negative New Testament criticism which finds little that is historically reliable in the core documents of the New Testament. This has prompted discussion and debate both here and on the Continent, to which you have responded with warmth and enjoyment. You are a scholar with a respect for tradition – your criticism of trendy and fashionable theologies has been witty and pointed on many occasions (cf. *Vindications*) – but you are not afraid to revalue and reassess tradition in the light of new ideas and new reflection – an obvious example being your studies in Christology. In ecclesiology and liturgy also, you have avoided the enthusiasm of the moment, while pointing out the need for experimentation and openness. We instance here *Beyond Anglicanism*, and your introduction to the reissue of Moberly's *Ministerial Priesthood*, that classic Anglican statement. To this openness, your experience in the Church overseas, for twelve years in India between 1947 and 1959, has contributed much, and also led to your interest in Indian religion and in the wider revelation beyond Christianity. As a presbyter of the Church of South India, you found the contact with other communions an invigorating one, and your interest in ecumenical activity has been constant ever since. You have served the Church in various ecumenical enterprises and as theological adviser in various commissions. Your *Church, Sacraments and Ministry* is a text book used in Roman Catholic, Anglican and Free Church colleges and institutions, and studied by all with profit. You found especial sympathy for a scholar whose appeal transcended his own communion – Teilhard de Chardin (*Teilhard Reassessed*, edited by you in 1970, is evidence of this) – but perhaps such sympathy is not unexpected in one who was given his second baptismal name in memory of George Tyrrell.

You have also been aware of the wider ecumenism, of that unity of mankind, for which the Church's unity is a symbol and stimulus. You were converted to the Christian faith while at school, and you have not forgotten the need to bridge the divide between that old life and the new life in Christ in a number of works of apologetics, particularly *Reasonable Belief* in which you were the joint author with your brother Richard. You say in that work:

> Anselm's motto, 'Faith seeking understanding', is, if rightly under-stood, a sound one. If a Christian has found and experienced God and known him as true, it is entirely right and proper that he should examine with intelligence and with a good conscience the reasons which have led him to such a faith and approve them as sound or adjust them, rejecting some and allowing others. Faith and reason are not identical, but they are good partners.

That has been the keynote of a great deal of your activity as a university teacher and administrator.

The scholars from other universities who have contributed to this book acknowledge your standing in the world of biblical scholarship, and most have been associated with you in various capacities in your duties as Professor of Theology at Hull. Our original plan was to commemorate your work under three main headings, the biblical, the ecumenical, and the contextual, the latter including your contributions to Christian ethics and to the theological understanding of contemporary society. In the event, the cost of publishing such a very large book would have been prohibitive; and we are grateful to the scholars who would have contributed for their understanding in accepting the change in plans, and to those whose names are represented here who have adapted themselves so quickly to the changed format. They speak for all those who would have joined in this tribute.

Four of us in the Department of Theology are bold enough to add our own contributions – again as representative of the larger number of both past and present members of staff – and we know that you would wish this. You joined the Department in 1963, coming from the Cathedral Church of St Anne, Belfast, where you were canon theologian. Over the years the Department increased in staff numbers, in student population, and in the range of its activities. You came to the Department as the author of *The Wrath of the Lamb*, *The Pioneer Ministry*, a commentary on Job, and other books. Over the years you built on that reputation with works like *Grace and Truth*, *The Image of the Invisible God*, and commentaries on the Pastoral Epistles, to mention only a few, which have contributed much to the standing of the Department. You constantly encouraged us, and you proved a wise and resourceful Head of Department. You were a friend to students – and a formidable adversary to the more athletic of them on the squash courts, as your continued leadership of the Departmental squash ladder demonstrated.

One of the most fruitful new developments was our association with the Irish School of Ecumenics, which began in 1972 and resulted in a number of MA and diploma candidates whose examinations and theses we were glad to validate. We were grateful for the opportunity to assist in the launching of such an important ecumenical enterprise, and wished the ISE well when it finally became associated with Trinity College, Dublin, in 1982 – an augury of great hope for the future of Ireland and church unity generally. Other new developments have been the MA and diploma course in the Theological Understanding of Industrial Society, the part-time Certificate in Theology and the Bachelor of Theology. The two latter courses are the product of our belief – and yours – that the university of the 1980s must diversify its activities and make use of the great potential existing in those men and women who did not have the chance of university education at the normal age of eighteen but who would benefit from and appreciate the opportunity of studying alongside students in a Department such as ours.

We salute you on your seventieth birthday, Anthony. We honour you for your gifts of scholarship, for your vitality, and your sense of commitment. We thank God for your life and work, and we believe that you will still be astonishing and delighting us in years to come with the proof of your continued activity and zest for life.

Ieuan Ellis

PART ONE: MEANING

1

Eleutheria ('freedom') in the Bible

Birger Gerhardsson

We all love freedom, but when we say this we can mean very different things. It is possible to connect almost everything we consider good with the word 'freedom' (freedom to and freedom from). To write about freedom and liberation in the Bible, proceeding from our modern word 'freedom', would be the same as sketching a Bible theology. That is not my intention here. In this article, dedicated to my old and very dear friend Anthony Hanson,[1] I will stick to the Greek word-group ἐλεύθερος ('free'), ἐλευθερόω ('liberate'), and ἐλευθερία ('freedom') and present the biblical ideas about freedom which are covered by these terms. We can also explore the Hebrew and Aramaic material with the aid of these Greek concepts, taking both similarities and dissimilarities into consideration. This concentration of the subject makes it possible to perceive an important theme in its distinctiveness.

Greek Thinking

The Greek word *eleutheros* occurs for the first time in Homer. Its etymology is a matter of dispute. In Homer it seems to mean that someone is at home somewhere and has the right to be there.[2]

1. *Political Freedom*

The Greek thinking about freedom begins as a political reflection: its object is freedom within the free state (the πόλις)[3]. For the sake of clarity let me make a distinction between two aspects thereof: civil freedom (freedom as against slavery within the πόλις) and national freedom (the independence and autonomy of the state itself, in relation to other nations).

Slavery was ancient and common among the Greeks; people were constantly exposed to the difference between slave and free man. The *eleutheros*, 'free man', was the citizen who had full authority with rights and duties within the state. He was exempted from the restrictions which limited the life of the slave but he shared with other free men the duties that kept the state together. Free was the man 'who ruled himself', but in interaction with other free men. One of the basic civic rights was παρρησία, the right to 'say everything', i.e. freedom of speech. With the right to speak freely in public, one could take part in the governing of society: in appointing leaders, in law-making and in other common decisions. The free men put themselves under a common law and appointed common rulers whom they could also dismiss. From this law and rule they themselves were not free. Thinking men were also aware of the fact that the state, governed in this way, must be free itself from outer oppression, be independent and autonomous. Full civil freedom presupposes national freedom.

2. *Spiritual Freedom*

After the conquests of Alexander and the decay of many free states it became natural for thinking men to broaden their perspectives in the universal and cosmopolite direction and deepen their reflections about the individual; individualism and universalism usually belong together, as we know. Philosophers started an existential reflection on the nature of freedom. They asked themselves, who is the truly free human being in the cosmos? Even in the universe they saw a common rule and a common law – the natural law which no mortal has made and no mortal can change or abolish. True freedom is found, they said, where man lives in full harmony with this law. But the Stoic and Cynic philosophers pointed out that you can only live in this freedom – let me call it spiritual freedom – if you make clear to yourself what is yours and what is not yours, what is your concern and what is not. Greater forces than I, rulers of different kinds, can govern much in my life, hamper me and enslave me. But there is an area which really is mine and which I must never let anybody rule and enslave: my inner life, the life of my soul (τὰ ἔσω). I must learn to see this, to preserve my inner life intact and independent, and to keep control over it, letting everything else in the world pass. There is so much in this life – these thinkers said – which does not concern me in the final analysis, in a deeper meaning. These things of no real importance not only include my outer belongings but also my family and my body with its emotions and desires as well. Only if I liberate myself from false imaginations, learn to let everything irrelevant be irrelevant and to control that which truly is my own, only then am I free. The wise and good man experiences the true freedom in his complete self-discipline and tranquillity of mind (ἀπάθεια, ἀταραξία). In his harmony with natural law – that governs the whole universe – the wise man is sovereign, he is king. The examples referred to as ideals in this connection included Socrates and Diogenes.

This was a kind of salvation doctrine in a hard world. These visions opened new prospects for oppressed human beings, people in circum-stances which they could influence very little. And the same conditions applied to all, the slave and the emperor alike.

The Old Testament and Early Judaism

The Greek *eleutheria*-concepts provide us with interesting questions to ask in turning to the ancient Jewish sources written mostly in Hebrew or Aramaic. What do these sources reveal about the Jewish attitude to political freedom – national and civil freedom – and spiritual freedom?[4]

1. *Political Freedom*

In the Hebrew Bible there is no term corresponding to our word 'freedom'. The noun *ḥêrût* is not found in texts prior to the New Testament era; our earliest evidence is Jewish coins from A.D.70. Of course, there are words in the Hebrew Bible meaning 'free (man)' as opposed to 'slave' (*ḥopšî*, about twenty times),[5] and 'setting free' (*dĕrôr*, six times, and *ḥupšāh*, once);[6] it always applies to civil freedom. But we search in vain for a term meaning 'freedom'. The vocabulary shows that the very idea 'freedom' was not a matter of reflection in ancient Israel.

Slavery does not seem to have existed in Israel before the settlement in

Canaan, nor did it ever become as common among the Jews as it was among the Greeks. The Jews made a clear distinction between the Hebrew slave (*'ebed 'ibrî*) and the foreign slave. The position of the former was protected by many laws (see especially Exod. 21:1–11; Lev.25:39–55; Deut.15:12–18; Jer.34:8–22), including the regulation that he must regain his freedom in the seventh year. In these laws, a civil and national ideal finds expression: an Israelite shall be free. 'For they are my servants, whom I brought forth out of the land of Egypt; they shall not be sold as slaves. You shall not rule over him with harshness, but shall fear your God' (Lev.25:42–43, RSV).

National freedom was, of course, highly appreciated. This we can see not least in the numerous accounts of wars carried on in the name of God (*Yahweh's* wars) in order to secure the independence of the people and, above all, in the rich traditions concerning the liberation out of Egypt. In the Old Testament texts about this series of events there is no Hebrew word meaning 'free', 'freedom' or 'liberate'. Yet the central meaning of the exodus is liberation to national independence. Professor David Daube has shown that a long series of characteristic words in these narratives is borrowed from current legal language; these words are technical terms about the position of slaves and their liberation. That which is narrated is conceived of as a great act of deliverance in which the God of Israel redeems his first-born son Israel (cf. Exod.4:22–23) from slavery under Pharaoh, from the 'house of bondage', Egypt. The liberation means that Israel becomes free but at the same time becomes a slave or servant of God. Contemporary laws about the redeeming of slaves stated that the one who bought the freedom of a relative had the right to demand the service of the freed man for a stipulated time after his liberation.[7]

The exodus from Egypt is depicted as a political liberation to national independence: 'I am the Lord your God, who brought you forth out of the land of Egypt, that you should not be their slaves; and I have broken the bars of your yoke and made you walk erect' (Lev.26:13, RSV). Why do we always look in vain here for a word corresponding to the *eleutheria* of the Greeks? The answer is that the whole thing is not conceived of in democratic terms. The model is a different one; theocracy, the rule of God, the reign of God. Israel is liberated to a life as Yahweh's servant, God's slave, liable to live in accordance with Yahweh's will, God's law (see e.g. Lev.26:11–17, and Deut.6:10–25).

2. *Spiritual Freedom*

In numerous Old Testament texts we read that Yahweh promises his servant (slave) Israel all blessings, including deliverance from political oppression and victory over national enemies. And if the people be unfaithful, he threatens to punish them with curses, including defeat in war and slavery under the enemies (e.g. Deut.28 and Josh.23). Very telling are the texts in which Yahweh punishes his unfaithful people by selling them (as slaves) for some time to a foreign nation and its king (e.g. Judg.3:7–8, 41–42, 10:6–8) or simply giving them away to someone (Judg.6:1–2, 13:1, Ps.106:40–42). Such texts illustrate very concretely how political and spiritual freedom here make up a synthesis within a framework of a theocratic system.

It may be presumed that the exile made the Israelites especially aware of the fact that they could have a spiritual (religious) freedom without having national independence. In Babylon, Israel was enslaved as a nation but the people (the faithful among them) nevertheless preserved their fidelity toward Yahweh: they worshipped him and no other god and lived according to his law and no other god's law. Of course they longed for political freedom but they could see now that religious freedom was possible even in a situation of outer, national slavery.

From the time of Alexander on, Palestine was subjected to the foreign rule of the Ptolemies in Egypt, the Seleucids in Syria, and the Romans. These rulers were Hellenistically inspired, and Hellenistic culture had a great impact in Palestine during these centuries. We notice a development here which reminds us of the development in other parts of the Hellenistic world. Thinking men focused their reflection on a freedom independent of national freedom and civil freedom. This thinking was obviously inspired by Hellenistic popular philosophy which is easy to see in the Jewish world outside Palestine, e.g. in Philo. He wrote in his youth – in New Testament times – a book in which the Stoic view of spiritual freedom is not more than superficially judaised (*Quod omnis probus liber sit*). But Jewish thinkers even in Palestine – the Pharisees and after them the rabbis – received influences from the Hellenistic views of true freedom. They detected the freedom to be found in the will of God, in the Torah: 'You find no freeman excepting him who occupies himself with the study of the Torah' (M. Ab.6:2).[8] It is in this light we shall consider the words of 'the Jews' in John 8:33 (see below).

In spite of national catastrophies, Israel could look upon itself as the people Yahweh had liberated to freedom. Telling evidence for this may be mentioned. When at the synagogue services the Hebrew text of the books of Moses was read and translated into Aramaic, the language of the people, there were many instances where the exodus from Egypt was mentioned. There, words for 'freedom', 'free' and 'liberate' never occurred. But the translator felt free to interpolate the appropriate word. We find in the Aramaic targums, almost regularly (in the Targum Neophyti 1 to the Pentateuch more than fifty times), that the participle 'liberated' (*pĕrîqîn*, plur.) is inserted when Israel's exodus from Egypt is mentioned.[9] The almost 'Homeric' epithet of Israel in these texts is 'liberated'[10]. If we take as an example the famous introduction to the decalogue in Exod.20:2; Deut.5:6, the translation of the Palestinian targum (both recensions) runs: 'My people, children of Israel, I am the Lord, your God, who liberated you and brought you, liberated, out of the land of Egypt, out of the house of slavery'. The Jews emphasised quite generally and strongly that the exodus from Egypt meant liberation. This concrete example – the introduction to the decalogue – also shows that God's law, the Torah, in this way is presented as the law for a liberated people. We just miss the very expression 'the law of liberty'.

The ritual of the Jewish Passover meal – the Haggadah – has during the millennia become enriched with many elements from different epochs. Several of these elements show how the Jews have been able to look upon themselves as the 'free people', in spite of the fact that they have been forced to live as a politically oppressed nation or minority. One ancient rule is that the Passover meal should be eaten in a reclining position. The reason is that freemen recline when they eat. This is part of Hellenistic table manners, borrowed in Hellenistic times and referred to in the gospels (Mark 14:15, 18, and elsewhere).[11] The Haggadah also teaches that every Israelite must regard himself as if he himself had been delivered out of Egypt.[12]

In many ways we can see how the Jews, in their reflection on spiritual freedom, received important influences from Hellenistic – Stoic and Cynic – philosophy during the time from Alexander on. They did not want to be unfaithful to the God of the fathers; on the contrary. But in the struggle for their distinctive character in the covenant with Yahweh they were able to borrow patterns from the environment they braced themselves against.

On the other hand, the ancient holy scriptures kept alive the attitude that God's people ought to have national freedom as well. We see this for example in the Books of the Maccabees and in Josephus' accounts of battles of liberation and armed fighting. Oppositional, zealotic groups saw national freedom as an irremissible demand for God's people.[13] These movements of revolt could find better support for their attitude in numerous Old Testament texts than is usually thought. Even many Pharisees took this position. But the leading current among the Pharisees ascertained that Israel could serve God in (spiritual) freedom even if the people had to endure the supremacy of foreign political rulers.

The New Testament

In the New Testament writings we find words from the group ἐλεύθερος, ἐλευθερόω, ἐλευθερία, 41 times, 27 of them in the Pauline corpus, and 14 in all the other books together.[14]

The noun *eleutheria* is totally missing in the gospels. In the synoptics the adjective *eleutheros* occurs, but only once: Matt.17:26 (material peculiar to Matthew); the verb *eleutheroō* is lacking. In John the adjective and the verb occur twice each, but only in one text section: 8:31–40.

Nothing indicates that the very theme 'freedom' – *eleutheria, ḥêrût* – played any role in the teachings of Jesus. Matthew 17:26 does not take us very far, and John 8:31–40 is so strongly imprinted by the specifically Johannine way of thinking that it hardly permits conclusions about the vocabulary of the historical Jesus himself. I will return to that.

The central motif of the teachings of Jesus is expressed in the term βασιλεία τοῦ θεοῦ: 'Rule of God', 'Kingship of God', 'Kingdom of God'. It is presented as a sublime theocracy. God is depicted as the King of the world and the people of God as his faithful subjects, who may be called servants or slaves but who are, in fact, God's sons, the true Royal Children. They shall live in accordance with God's will, but they shall embrace his will from the depth of their innermost being: they shall will what God wills, governed by obedience and love for God. This is the cosmic order Jesus speaks about.

I cannot here discuss the question of the extent to which Jesus' own ideas about the Kingdom of God may have been inspired by Jewish thinking on true freedom. Let me, however, stress an important fact: if our sources give us sufficient information, Jesus of Nazareth did not show any real interest in what we call political freedom. He does not seem to have done anything in order to unify and liberate Israel politically, as a nation. Nor does he seem to have done anything about the fact that slavery existed as a social institution in Israel during his time. This was certainly of extreme importance for his adherents, when after his death they tried to interpret his mission and message.

The New Testament does not say very much about nations and how they shall be ruled. Nor has it much to say about national freedom. As for civil freedom, Paul and his school are the only ones who comment upon it, and then only briefly and in a way that is very revealing. The freedom the New Testament authors are interested in is the spiritual freedom that, according to their belief, Jesus Christ has brought about.[15] Let me now, against the background I have sketched in the foregoing, survey the New Testament texts where the group *eleutheros, eleutheroō, eleutheria* occur. I begin with the non-Pauline writings, where our theme is treated in a very fragmentary way, and then discuss the Pauline corpus somewhat more fully.

1. *The Epistle of James*

The Epistle of James stems from an early Christian author (1:1, 2:1) whose viewpoint does not have a very clearly Christian profile. It may be characterised as a superficially Christianised Judaism. In this tractate we do not find any polemics against the piety of the Jewish law. The author takes Abraham, 'our father', as a model when he writes about a faith completed by works (2:18–24); James can say without hesitation that Abraham was justified by works (ἐξ ἔργων, 2:21). Christians shall live according to God's law. In James this law is called 'the law of liberty' (νόμος ἐλευθερίας, 2:12) and the 'perfect law, the law of liberty' (1:25, RSV). Here in James, these designations have Christian connotations but they have hardly been coined within the church. They are certainly taken over from (Hellenistic) Judaism, albeit with a certain re-interpretation (centering on the demands of the Torah in accordance with the Sermon on the Mount). For James, 'freedom' is the same as faith in Christ and a life lived according to God's law (as interpreted by Jesus). But his conception of freedom has no specific Christological basis, and he does not say that 'the doers of the law' among the Jews lack freedom.

2. *The Gospel of Matthew*

In the synoptic gospels the word *eleutheros* occurs only at one place, in the pericope about the temple tax (Matt.17:24–27).[16] The main idea in this pericope is that Jesus and Peter, in the capacity of 'God's sons', are free from the duty of paying the tax to God's temple. They should nevertheless pay it, in order not to give offence – a way of reasoning we recognise even in Paul (e.g. Rom. 14:21, 1 Cor.8:13). The temple tax had been introduced by Nehemiah (Neh.10:32–33), but was usually connected with a regulation in the Mosaic law, a regulation dealing with a tax to the sanctuary (Exod.30:11–16). Matthew is certainly aware of the meaning and function of this tax. It had to be paid by every Jewish man aged twenty years or more, and was a ransom (*kōper*, λύτρον) for the one who paid it. This money paid for the offerings brought to God in order to make atonement for Israel's sin. Thus, the temple tax had a redeeming aim, a freedom-buying aim.

The Matthean Jesus bases his argument on the practice to be found among 'the kings of the earth'. These do not lay taxes on their own sons. The sons are free (ἐλεύθεροι), namely from taxation. The implication – a conclusion *a minore ad maius* – is that the King of Heaven cannot be less generous to his sons than the earthly kings are to their sons. Thus, 'God's sons' must be free. The expression βασιλεία τοῦ θεοῦ does not occur in this text, but obviously this teaching deals with one aspect of 'the Rule of Heaven': God's way of ruling his Kingdom.

Here, a concrete regulation in the traditional law is deprived of its validity with the aid of general reasoning about God's generosity and the high position of God's sons before God. Two things should be noticed here: (1) The sonship of Jesus and the sonship of the disciples (Peter) are brought together ('we' in 17:27) without the latter being derived from the former. This is unique to the New Testament. (2) 'Freedom' – concretely, the exemption from temple tax, but presumably having wider implications – is not Christologically derived (by way of reference to the person or work of Christ). The reasoning is carried out from a positive conception of God and from a high conception of 'Son of God' which is applied to Peter (the disciples) as well as to Jesus.

The Pharisees regarded themselves as 'Sons of God' and thought that they had freedom in and through the law; yet this condition did not authorise them to release themselves from a concrete command in the Torah. The Matthean Jesus has another opinion, but in this case he does not – as he generally does in the gospel of Matthew – criticise the Scribes and the Pharisees. He teaches and offers positive reasons for his own position. However, his opinion does not on this occasion introduce a new practice. Thus, we see that in this instance the Jewish men in the Matthean church neither polemicise against common Jewish practice nor provoke other Jews with an offensive practice of their own.

3. *The Gospel of John*

In the narrative about Jesus before Pilate in the fourth gospel (18:33–38), we see how clearly Jesus' Kingship (βασιλεία) is separated from political power. His Kingship is not of this world (18:36), he retains his Kingship – and thus his freedom – in spite of the fact that outwardly he is fettered and about to be condemned and executed. If his Kingship had been of a political nature his men would have defended him by violence when his enemies came to arrest him in Gethsemane (ibid., cf. 6:15).[17]

The subject of 'freedom' is, however, treated expressly in only one pericope: John 8:31–40.[18] Here 'the Jews' say to Jesus: 'We are descendants of Abraham, and have never been in bondage to any one. How is it that you say, "You will be made free?"' (8:33, RSV). This is no naïve attempt to deny that Israel has been in political slavery under foreign rulers many times. Here we meet the conviction that the Jews (the faithful among them) have a spiritual freedom which they have never given up. This time it is motivated with reference to the noble birth of the Jews, their descent from Abraham. Thus, they are spiritually free-born. But certainly this also implies that they are in a covenant with God and under his law.

The Johannine Jesus rejects their claims. He says that they would do what Abraham did, if they were Abraham's children, but they do not (8:39–40; cf. 41–47). They 'commit sin', and 'every one who commits sin is a slave to sin' (8:34; cf.44).

As the Son, Jesus can offer true and lasting freedom: 'If the Son makes you free, you will be free indeed (ὄντως ἐλεύθεροι)' (8:36). In this passage spiritual freedom is Christologically derived, not, it is true, from

Christ's atoning work here, but from Christ's person, his unique position as the Son of God. Liberation is effected by way of his mediating the divine 'truth' (ἀλήθειαν), the truth which will liberate (ἐλευθερώσει) (8:32). In the same way that Jesus before Pilate says that he has come into the world to bear witness to the truth (18:37), he says in chapter 8 that he mediates insight into the truth and that the truth makes men free (even from 'committing sin'). In this place, freedom is anchored in the unique Son, but at the same time we see that we are very close to the Hellenistic idea that the right insight gives humankind true freedom.

4. *Revelation and Peter*

In Revelation (6:15, 13:16, 19:18) the social categories 'free and slave' are mentioned, but only mentioned. In 1 Pet. (2:16), we meet an exhortation to 'live as free men, yet without using your freedom as a pretext for evil; but live as servants of God' (RSV). In 2 Pet. (2:19) it is said of false prophets that 'they promise ... freedom, but they themselves are slaves of corruption' (RSV). These passages I can leave without comment.

5. *The Pauline Corpus*

Unlike other New Testament authors, Paul and his school interpreted salvation in Jesus Christ in *eleutheria*-terms and tried to clarify what 'the freedom which we have in Christ Jesus' (Gal.2:4) is.[19] Certainly Paul already had a clear conception of true freedom during his time as a Pharisaic Jew, influenced by Hellenism. But he was forced into radical rethinking by his new situation – with the work of Jesus as a fresh point of departure – and his letters reveal how this happened. (In the following I shall not keep the deutero-Pauline writings apart from the genuine ones; for the sake of simplicity of expression I shall treat 'Paul' as the author of the whole Pauline corpus.)

Not for a second does Paul want to deny the privileges God has given Israel in the past: 'the sonship (υἱοθεσία), the glory, the covenants, the giving of the law, the worship, and the promises', the patriarchs, and Christ as 'according to the flesh' (Rom.9:3–5, RSV; cf. 3:1–4). But now the time has fully come, and God has 'sent forth his Son, born of woman, born under the law, to redeem those who were under the law, so that we might receive adoption as sons (*hyiothesia*). And because you are sons, God has sent the Spirit of his Son into our hearts, crying, "Abba! Father!" So through God you are no longer a slave but a son, and if a son then an heir' (Gal.4:4–7, RSV). The term 'sonship' (*hyiothesia*) can be used to refer both to Israel's traditional position in the covenant with God and to the qualified sonship Christ has now procured (cf. also Eph.1:5). This sonship will reach its fullness at the *parousia* (Rom.8:18–24), but it is a fact even now: the sons of God have the Spirit of God as a first fruit (Rom.8:23; Gal.4:5–7, and elsewhere).

Hyiothesia is one of the great words Paul uses for the position believers have obtained through Christ. *Eleutheria* is another (e.g. Gal.2:4, 5:1, 13). Paul describes this freedom in Christ using absolute terms: 'For all things are yours, whether Paul or Apollos or Cephas or the world or life or death or the present or the future, all are yours' (1 Cor.3:21–22, RSV). 'All things are lawful' (1 Cor.6:12), 'Nothing is unclean' (Rom.14:14), 'Everything is clean' (Rom.14:20). Negatively seen, this freedom is a freedom from sin (esp. Rom.6:17–23; cf. 5:15–21). It is a freedom from the law as well (Rom.7:4, 8:2, Gal.4:21–31, 5:1, 13, and elsewhere), the law that not only restricts man's freedom and enslaves him but also condemns the sinner to death (e.g. Rom. 7:9–11, 1 Cor.15:56). Thus, it is also freedom from death (ibid. and Rom.6:20–22, 1 Cor.15:21–22).

Humankind has in and through Christ been liberated from the greatest threats against his life. Sin, law and death can no longer break man's connection with the living and life-giving Lord. Man is now free from these enslaving powers and instead has become a 'slave' or 'servant' under God and Christ (e.g. 1 Cor.3:23, 6:19–20, 7:22–23; Gal. 3:13–14). This position is at one and the same time freedom and 'slavery', i.e. 'service' (Rom.6:22, 7:6; 1 Cor.7:22 and elsewhere).

The new freedom does not exist apart from Christ, not even for the Jews. Normally Paul seems to think that the Jews have received from God the offer and promise of freedom, but have not accepted it. Abraham did. He accepted freedom from God in faith, without trusting in his own works. According to Paul, Abraham believed in God's promise of Christ (Gal.3, Rom.4). Now that Christ has come, the true children of Abraham ought to accept Christ. The Jews have not done that, however, but tried to establish a righteousness of their own by putting their trust in the law (the Torah) and the works of the law (Rom.9–11). They have rejected Christ and the gospel of the salvation and freedom that God gives freely 'without law' (χωρὶς νόμου, Rom.1:16–3:26).

During his time as a Pharisee, Paul accepted a rich, holy heritage and could call it in its totality *Tōrāh*, 'teaching', 'law' (νόμος).[20] As a Christian he made – more clearly than before – a distinction between God's gifts and God's demands. And he saw that the decisive weight lies on that which God gives in divine sovereignty: the calling, the election, the promises and their fulfilment in Christ, and thus, also, sonship and freedom. To this freedom, humankind is called through the gospel (Gal.5:13) and it must be accepted and received by faith (Rom.1:16–3:26, and elsewhere).

The new experiences and insights forced Paul to give quite a new answer to the question: 'Why then the law?' (Gal.3:19). The new answer is that it had an interim task: during the time between Moses and Christ it had the mission of being a custodian over Israel until Christ would come and the rights of sonship would be realised (Gal.3:19–4:7). During this time the Torah gave knowledge of sin. Paul can say that the law was 'added because of transgressions' (Gal.3:19–20), and that it wakes sin to life, it even increases sin (Rom.4:15, 5:20, 7:1–25).

The apostle's restrictive words about the law are rather remarkable for a man who has earlier found his salvation and freedom in the law. The Christian Paul can no longer regard the Torah as a law of liberty. On the contrary, he calls it 'the law of sin and death' (Rom.8:2). Of the covenant on Sinai, where the law was given, he says that it is 'bearing children for slavery' (Gal.4:24). The law brings condemnation upon man, divine wrath (Rom.4:15) and curse (Gal.3:10–14); it brings death upon man (1 Cor. 15:56; Rom.7:9–11).

Thus the law is unable to give righteousness and freedom (Gal.2:21; cf. Rom.8:2–4). Yet, Paul cannot abandon the self-evident axiom that God's law must be 'holy and just and good' (Rom.7:12). The explanation of the negative effect of the law is to be found in the fact that it has been 'weakened by the flesh' (Rom.8:3). In a world where the flesh exists, with its desires, and sin as well, the law's 'You shall not' can do nothing but provoke sin and even increase it.

True freedom is only to be found 'in Christ', only with those who have accepted Christ in faith and died with him in baptism. 'For Christ is the end of the law and brings righteousness for every one who has faith' (Rom.10:4). Christians are free, but their freedom involves a service of

God and Christ (see above). They are no longer under the compelling force of sin; they can now yield their members to God as instruments of righteousness (Rom.6:12–23). Physical death still remains but it has lost its 'sting' and 'victory' (1 Cor.15:54–57); it cannot separate the believer from his liberator and Lord; it cannot cut off his citizenship in God's eternal Kingdom; it cannot end his sonship and freedom (cf. Rom.8:18–25, 31–39, and elsewhere).

Considering the fact that 'freedom' (ἐλευθερία) and 'law' (νόμος) generally belong together – such is the case both in Greek and in Jewish thinking – we would expect Paul to connect the word 'law' (νόμος) in some sense with the new spiritual freedom, for instance, by speaking about the 'law of Christ' over and over again in his discourses about freedom in Christ. The law was, after all, an important part of the very pattern of the *eleutheria*. But Paul on the whole avoids this usage. He uses the expressions 'the law of the Spirit of life in Christ Jesus' (Rom.8:2), 'the law of Christ', (Gal.6:2), 'Christ-regulated', ἔννομος Χριστοῦ, (1 Cor.9:21), and 'the law of faith' (Rom.3:27) but all these are occasional expressions with different meanings. None of them appears more than once in the Pauline literature and they are all difficult to interpret.[21] They are not standing, unconstrained elements of the pattern. This shows that Paul does not normally imagine that life 'in Christ' is ruled by some law.

What then? Is the Christian free to live as he likes? No, never! Paul says – over and over again – that existence in the new freedom is governed by the Spirit, Christ's Spirit, the Spirit of the living God. 'Where the Spirit of the Lord is, there is freedom' (2 Cor.3:17, RSV). The Spirit effects a life in accordance with the will of God in the same way as life in a fruit tree brings forth fruit (Gal.5:22–23). The law cannot produce such fruit, but it cannot have any objection against them either. Having listed the effects of the Spirit, Paul says: 'Against such there is no law' (ibid., cf. Rom.8:4). And it is very easy to see that the attitudes which Paul wants to see among the Christians – as 'fruit of the Spirit' – are the same sort as the central, ethical demands of the law, especially 'love' (ἀγάπη) (*passim*). But, of course, for Paul, the Spirit of God must be a much more perfect representative of the ethical will of God than any law can be. The Spirit comes from the heart of God and it both illuminates and gives strength.

I cannot here develop how Paul conceives the 'governing' of the

Christian life in freedom, but only give a hint.[22] The Christian is not thought of as an isolated individual, who lives for himself and does whatever he wants to do (Phil. 2:1–11, Gal.5:13–26, and elsewhere). Christians are 'citizens of Heaven' (Phil.3:20, NEB); together they make up a kingdom, a community: the body of Christ, the church. They are brothers and sisters in a spiritual family. They have all received the same Spirit (Rom.12, 1 Cor.12, Eph.4). Sometimes Paul seems to regard the Spirit as the true civil spirit in the Kingdom of God; it functions, of course, much better than any law would be able to do. In the fellowship of the congregation some typical attitudes emerge, are discerned, and encouraged, and are consolidated. A Christian way of life is developed, which the law, if it had the right to pass judgment upon it, would not be able to condemn.

At the same time, Paul is eager to stress that the individual must preserve an inner freedom and control of his own, an individual responsibility and authority, so that the new patterns of life do not become a new slavery. Paul warns the individual Christian against submitting himself to foreign yokes of different kinds. The spiritual freedom the Christians have in Christ must be maintained and guarded (e.g. Gal.5:1). The reader can easily imagine the persuasive tone in the apostle's exhortation: 'Do not become slaves of men' (1 Cor.7:23, RSV).

What about *civil* freedom? The Pauline corpus does contain exhortations addressed to slaves, but they never include advice to seek freedom. Nor are those who own slaves urged to free them and let them go, because the Lord has liberated them. To be sure, the lordship of Christ is actualized in these passages, yet the slaves are only exhorted to serve their owners with honesty, obedience and love, and the masters to treat their slaves justly and as brothers (Col.3:22–4:1, Philem.8–21; cf. Eph.6:5–9, 1 Tim.6:1–2, Titus 2:9–10; cf. also 1 Pet.2:18–25). We might expect that Paul and his school should have gone back to the ancient Jewish ideal that those whom God has liberated should also be free politically, nationally and civilly (cf. e.g. Lev.25:42–43, quoted above). But the apostle isolates the spiritual freedom in Christ in a way that resembles the Stoic way of thinking. The freedom in Christ lies on a plane where social differences become unessential – and national and sexual differences as well (Gal.3:28, Col.3:11). The dissimilarities *kata sarka* between Jew and Greek, free men and slaves, men and women, lose their weight. Yet they are not abolished. Paul has a principle which he imprints upon all his communities: everyone should remain in the social state in which he was when he became a Christian (1 Cor.7:17–24; cf. Gal.5:6, 6:15). This means that the apostle even exhorts the Christian slave who could gain freedom to remain in his servile status.[23] The reason given is: 'For the man who as a slave received the call to be a Christian is the Lord's freedman, and, equally, the free man who received the call is a slave in the service of Christ' (1 Cor.7:22, NEB). To be sure, declarations of this kind are calculated to relativise the differences between free and slave and must in the long run have far-reaching effects, but they also mean that the social order is allowed to go on as it is. The slave remains in civil respects a slave.[24]

In the same way, Paul also rejected claims to full equality made by Christian women, and instead inculcated subordination to men in accordance with the inherited Jewish custom, based partly upon Old Testament texts (1 Cor.11:2–16, 14:33–40; cf. 1 Tim.2:11–15, and the *Haustafel*-tradition). Paul accepts the fact that women do not have παρρησία, public freedom of speech; he allows this fact in the prevailing social order to be valid even within the Christian community, and he points out that this is a custom in 'all congregations of God's people' – the church everywhere at this time (1 Cor.14:34–38). Here we see that early Christianity paid respect to the prevailing social order that women did not have full civil rights in society (with public freedom of speech) but were under the guardianship of their husbands in some respects.[25]

It is striking that Paul does not use his view of spiritual freedom in Christ to motivate a struggle for civil freedom. Nor does he derive national freedom from it (Rom.13:1–7). Whatever else Paul was, he was not a zealot. In his expectation that God would soon change everything (Rom.8:18–24, and elsewhere), he saw limits for the specific mission of the church.

Overview and Commentary

The reader may have noticed that not all aspects of what we call freedom have come into the picture in this presentation, where I have stuck to the ideas covered by the word group *eleutheros, eleutheroō, eleutheria*. For instance, I have not touched upon liberation from plagues and ill-nesses.[26] The reason is that the *eleutheria*-ideas normally move within a certain pattern of thought, a kind of social model. As a rule, they concern the free man's position within society or the position of a free society in relation to other societies or the free man's position in existence, conceived as a universal society.

We have seen how undifferentiated the ancient Jewish view was, as compared with Greek ideas about *eleutheria*. Within a theocratic total view, no real distinction was made between national, civil and spiritual freedom. But such distinctions were forced on the Jews as time went by, during difficult periods of their lost national freedom. Then ideas developed about true freedom for human beings, even if they are enslaved nationally and civilly: freedom under the lordship of God, freedom in the law of God, which I have called spiritual freedom. This Jewish development was obviously stimulated by important impulses from popular Hellenistic philosophy.

The thinking about freedom in the New Testament certainly has this Jewish background; of course it also received additional influences directly from the Hellenistic milieu. But the decisive point of departure seems to be very clear: Jesus of Nazareth did not fight for the liberation of the Jewish nation, nor did he work for the abolition of civil slavery within the Jewish society. He preached and gave his life for freedom at a deeper level, for spiritual freedom – conceived as a prelude to an imminent liberation of the world in all respects (the Kingdom of God). The model is a sublime theocracy and it concerns freedom for all kinds of people, even those who find themselves in national oppression or civil slavery without being able to escape from this fate. The gospel offers and gives real lasting freedom at this level, while awaiting the rebirth of the whole world.

Elements from the *eleutheria*-theme are to be found at scattered places in the New Testament but the theme appears fully developed only in one group of writings, the Pauline corpus. Here we meet a grandiose picture of true freedom: 'the freedom we have in Christ'. Let me end this article with some reflections on the question of how we shall apply this view of freedom today.

Spiritually, Paul was a very strong man. His devotion and self-discipline gave him an almost Stoic elevation above the elementary needs and outer realities of life. Sometimes his way of reasoning resembles the attitude of the Stoics (1 Cor.7:29–31, Phil.4:11–13).[27] He did not interfere in the external order of society around himself, in spite of its terrible evils. His reasons were several. Let me mention three of them:

(1) an eschatological reason: he shared the conviction that the appointed time was near and that the church must therefore concentrate upon its central mission assigned by Christ: the preaching of the gospel;

(2) a tactical reason: obviously he meant that the church should not provoke the political authorities unnecessarily; this would hamper the rapid diffusion of the gospel;

(3) a common-sense reason: he knew that very few of his listeners had any real influence on the plane where international, national or civil order is settled.

How shall we deal with the New Testament legacy today? In desperation at the fact that the so-called Christian countries seem to be so uninterested in correcting the crying injustices prevailing in the world on the political plane – nationally and socially – many Christians today are groping for a new theology of freedom: 'liberation theology'. The risk they run in these strivings is the risk of blurring the gospel and, thus, the very point of the Christian message. At the centre of the New Testament stands the gospel of spiritual freedom in Christ presented as a gift from God to the world, a voluntary gratuitous gift, given without counter-demands, χωρὶς νόμου. We cannot procure this gift for ourselves, nor can we procure it for others. It is God that gives it. And it can be received in jubilant joy even by people who suffer under national and civil oppression without seeing any brightening in these respects; people who must – at least for the time being – be satisfied with a 'theology of captivity'.

We must not spoil this message, not even in a well-founded social zeal. Yet, I think we can adopt an attitude to the external realities of life other than the attitude Paul adopted in his time and his milieu. Let me return to the three reasons:

(1) Christianity has had more time than Paul thought it should get. Certainly we have the opportunity to do immensely much more about the evils on the political plane than Paul thought was possible, if only we try.

(2) In few places in the world today need the church fear that the political authorities can effectively stop an earnest preaching of the gospel. The usual thing is that Christians are much too obedient towards the worldly authorities.

(3) In almost all modern democratic countries, Christians take part in the governing of society. What Paul expected God to do through the emperor and other political rulers God does today in the democratic countries through us, as we have the right to vote and to elect representatives to carry out the tasks that were previously in the emperor's sphere. In this way a responsibility comes upon us which very few of Paul's listeners felt in his time. I cannot develop this theme here, but I think that the old Lutheran notion of God's 'secular realm' (*das weltliche Regiment*) can still be of some help in this connection.

What I mean is that we must draw much keener conclusions from 'the freedom we have in Christ' than Paul did in his situation.[28] I think we must say as follows: if the Kingdom of God means freedom, if the Spirit of the Lord creates freedom, if Christ wills freedom and voluntary obedience, then we have here a high ideal and an inspiring pattern for our human valuations and strivings. It is reasonable, and it is extremely pressing and urgent, that we let these visions of freedom have their impact on all planes. They ought to confirm the high appreciation we spontaneously have of national and civil freedom and they ought to inspire and motivate us to a resolute struggle against oppression of all kinds and for freedom in all dimensions of human existence. Freedom entails responsibility.

Notes

1. An early version of this paper was read at the Anglo-Scandinavian Theological Conference in York, 22–28 July 1983. I thank Anthony Hanson and the other participants for a very rewarding discussion.
2. D. Nestle, *Eleutheria*, vol. 1 (Tübingen, 1967). For literature on the theme of this article, see *TWNT*, vol. 10 part 2 (1979) pp. 1073–6.
3. M. Pohlenz, *Griechische Freiheit* (Heidelberg, 1955); see also idem, *Staatsgedanke und Staatslehre der Griechen* (Leipzig, 1923). For two brilliant surveys, see H. Schlier, ἐλεύθερος κτλ, *TWNT* vol. 2 (1935) pp. 484–92, and K. Niederwimmer, *Der Begriff der Freiheit im Neuen Testament* (Berlin, 1966) pp. 1–54.
4. A common weakness in presentations of *eleutheria* in the New Testament is that no or very little attention is paid to the Old Testament and early Jewish background: Schlier and Niederwimmer (see note 3) are typical. (C. Johansson, *Concepts of Freedom in the Old Testament* (New York, 1965) has not been available to me).

5. E.g. Exod. 21:2–6, 26, 27, Deut.15:12,13,18, Jer.34:9,10,11,14,16; see concordance and lexica. *Ben ḥôrîn*, in later Hebrew very common for 'freemen', seems to have a special meaning in most Old Testament instances: 'nobleman', 'one of the nobles', e.g. Neh.2:16,5:7.
6. *Děrôr*: Lev.25:10, Jer.34:8,15,17, Ezek.46:17, Isa.61:1. *Ḥupšāh*: Lev.19:20. None of the words for 'free' and 'setting free' is considered in E. Jenni and C. Westermann (eds), *Theologisches Handwörterbuch zum Alten Testament* (2 vols; 3rd edition, 1979). *Ḥopšî* and *děrôr* are treated, however, in the *Theologisches Wörterbuch zum Alten Testament* vol. 3 (1982) pp. 123–8 (N. Lohfink) and vol. 2 (1977) pp. 283–7 (R. North), with bibliography.
7. D. Daube, *The Exodus Pattern in the Bible* (London, 1963).
8. This saying is attributed to R. Joshua ben Levi (3rd century AD) but the motif is much older. For quotations of the same type, see A. Schlatter, *Der Evangelist Matthäus* (4th ed., Stuttgart, 1957) on Matt.17:26, and idem, *Der Evangelist Johannes* (2nd ed., Stuttgart, 1948) on John 8:32–37. In much Jewish thinking Torah is the law of the cosmos; see e.g. M. Hengel, *Judentum und Hellenismus* (2nd ed., Tübingen, 1973) pp. 307–18.
9. See R. Le Déaut's translation *Targum du Pentateuque* (5 vols, Paris, 1979–81) vol. 5, p. 72, the word 'libérés'.
10. 'Le mot *pěrîqîn* (= libérés) revient sans cesse, comme une épithète homérique, dès qu'il est fait mention de la sortie d'Egypte', Le Déaut, vol. 1, p. 365, note 9.
11. Mark 14:18: ἀνακειμένων αὐτῶν. Even the words ἀνάγαιον . . . ἐστρωμένον (14:15) reveal that the guests ate in a reclining position. I thank Dr Daube for drawing my attention to this fact.
12. M. Pes. 10.5, a conclusion from Exod.13:8: 'And you shall tell your son on that day, "It is because of what the Lord did for me [sic] when I [sic] came out of Egypt"' (RSV).
13. M. Hengel, *Die Zeloten* (2nd ed., Leiden, 1976) pp. 114–23.
14. Additionally, the word ἀπελεύθερος, 'liberated', in 1 Cor.7:22 should be mentioned. For literature on freedom in the New Testament, see notes 1, 2, 19, and 27 in this article, as well as the commentaries to the texts which are mentioned. Among the New Testament scholars who have analysed the freedom theme in a most penetrating way I want to mention, additionally, R. Bultmann, e.g. *Theologie des Neuen Testaments* (7th ed., 1977) pp. 331–53, and E. Käsemann, especially *Der Ruf der Freiheit* (5th ed., Tübingen, 1972), and *An die Römer* (3rd ed., Tübingen, 1974).
15. The expression 'spiritual freedom' is not entirely satisfactory, because bodily health is often closely connected with it; not always however. See below, note 26.
16. For literature, see – besides the commentaries to the pericope – R. Hummel, *Die Auseinandersetzung zwischen Kirche und Judentum im Matthäusevangelium* (2nd ed., München, 1966) pp. 103–6, W. G. Thompson, *Matthew's Advice to a Divided Community* (Rome, 1970) pp. 50–68, and J. D. M. Derrett, *Law in the New Testament* (London, 1970) pp. 247–65.

17. For literature, see R. E. Brown, *The Gospel According to John (xii–xxi)* (New York, 1970) p. 896.
18. Cf. Niederwimmer, *Der Begriff der Freiheit* (see note 3) pp. 220–34, and the commentaries ad loc.
19. The words occur as follows: ἐλεύθερος, Rom.6:20, 7:3, 1 Cor.7:21,22,39, 9:1,19, 12:13, Gal.3:28, 4:22,23,26,30,31, Eph.6:8, Col.3:11; ἐλευθερόω, Rom.6:18,22, 8:2,21, Gal.5:1; ἐλευθερία, Rom.8:21, 1 Cor.10:29, 2 Cor.3:17, Gal.2:4, 5:1,13. On the freedom theme in Paul, see – besides the works I have already mentioned – O. Schmitz, *Der Freiheitsgedanke bei Epiktet und das Freiheitszeugnis des Paulus* (Gütersloh, 1923), H. Schlier, *Das Ende der Zeit* (2nd ed., Freiburg, Basel, Wien, 1972) pp. 216–33, and F. Mussner, *Theologie der Freiheit nach Paulus* (Freiburg, Basel, Wien 1976).
20. On the law problem in Paul, cf. H. Hübner, *Das Gesetz bei Paulus: ein Beitrag zum Werden der paulinischen Theologie* (2nd ed., Göttingen, 1980), P. Stuhlmacher, *Versöhnung, Gesetz und Gerechtigkeit* (Göttingen, 1981), pp. 166–91, H. Räisänen, *Paul and the Law* (Tübingen, 1983), E. P. Sanders, *Paul, the Law, and the Jewish People* (Philadelphia, 1983).
21. For the different meanings of the term νόμος in Paul, cf. Räisänen, *Paul.* I would not, however, go as far as Räisänen.
22. For a somewhat broader treatment, see my book *The Ethos of the Bible* (London, 1981), pp. 63–92.
23. I think 1 Cor.7:21 must be interpreted in this fashion. See the commentaries.
24. See further my book *The Ethos*, pp. 84–8.
25. See ibid. pp. 87–8.
26. In Luke 4:18–19 Jesus quotes a prophetic word from Isaiah (61:1–2) to the effect that the Messiah shall 'proclaim release (ἄφεσιν) to the captives' and 'set at liberty (ἐν ἀφέσει) those who are oppressed'. In their New Testament setting these words do not aim at liberation of people under military oppression or in prison. Jesus did, as we know, nothing of that sort. The words in the programmatic sermon in Luke 4 aim at liberation from guilt, illness and obsession; see such passages as 5:17–26 and 13:10–17. It is interesting that the connection between spiritual liberation and bodily health seems to be quite self-evident in the synoptics, while Paul seems to be aware of the fact that the two do not always go together; see e.g. 2 Cor.12:7–10, Gal.4:13–14.
27. See Schmitz, *Der Freiheitsgedanke* (see note 19 above), and cf. H. Preisker, *Das Ethos des Urchristentums* (Gütersloh, 1949) pp. 167–95, 239–44.
28. We must also remember that in spite of all his radicalism in questions of individual ethic Paul seems to have been less radical in matters of *social* ethic than the apostles in Jerusalem; see B. Holmberg, *Paul and Power* (Lund, 1978).

2

'The Scripture' in John 17:12

Wendy E. Sproston

On behalf of those who, like myself, have been students of Anthony Hanson, I would like to take this opportunity to thank him for his inspiration and encouragement. I hope he will regard the paper which follows, read at the British New Testament Conference at Manchester on 22 September 1985, as a worthwhile extension of his interest in the New Testament use of Scripture.

In John 17:6 ff. Jesus prays for those whom the Father has given him out of the world. In 17:11–12 he asks that they may be kept in the Father's name as he himself has kept and guarded them, adding in 17:12 (RSV): 'and none of them is lost but the son of perdition, that the scripture might be fulfilled' (καὶ οὐδεὶς ἐξ αὐτῶν ἀπώλετο εἰ μὴ ὁ υἱὸς τῆς ἀπωλείας, ἵνα ἡ γραφὴ πληρωθῇ).

What is 'the scripture' that is here referred to as being fulfilled? It is the majority view in the commentaries and elsewhere that the relevant text lies outside 17:12 and its context, and the assumption is that John refers to Ps.41:9, already quoted with reference to Judas Iscariot in 13:18.[1] Yet 13:18 and 17:12 have nothing in common beyond a reference to the fulfilment of scripture (a feature by no means exclusive to our two texts[2]) and a reference to Judas, in the one instance by means of an Old Testament 'betrayal' text and in the other by the phrase ὁ υἱὸς τῆς ἀπωλείας ('the son of perdition'). There is nothing beyond this to connect the two texts. Indeed, for the evangelist to make a reference to an earlier text giving no verbal hint of its wording or context would be out of character with his usual explicit style of cross-referencing.[3]

A second possibility is that the scripture referred to is actually contained *within* 17:12. This has much to recommend it in that whenever

he uses γραφή (or its cognate verb) and πληρόω, as in 17:12, it is clearly
the evangelist's habit to ensure that the relevant quotation is immediately
to hand.[4] If 17:12 is no exception, it follows that the 'scripture' is actually
quoted there in some form. However, we are still left with the problem of
defining what the scripture is. On the one hand it may be contained in the
reference to Judas as ὁ υἱὸς τῆς ἀπωλείας. But then the whole clause
εἰ μὴ ὁ υἱὸς τῆς ἀπωλείας looks like a digression from the main
argument prompted perhaps by the presence of ἀπόλλυμι already in the
text. On the other hand there is the possibility that ἡ γραφή does not
here refer to an Old Testament text but to the words of Jesus, 'which
thou hast given me . . . none of them is lost.' These words are an obvious,
although imprecise, repetition of 6:39, and they reappear again in 18:9
accompanied by the evangelist's introductory words ἵνα πληρωθῇ ὁ
λόγος ὃν εἶπεν.[5]

The following is an attempt to clarify three points about ἡ γραφή in
17:12: first, that it is unlikely to be a reference to the scripture quoted in
13:18; second, that it does not refer to εἰ μὴ ὁ υἱὸς τῆς ἀπωλείας
which is a digression about Judas prompted by the verb ἀπόλλυμι; and
third, that it may be a reference to the Jesus-Logion quoted already in
6:39 and to reappear again in 18:9.

The Problem Posed by Judas Iscariot: 13:18 as Part of the 'Choosing and Foreknowledge' Theme.

It is one of the great affirmations of the Prologue to John's gospel that
those who come to believe in Jesus' name are born of God and
empowered to become 'children of God' (τέκνα θεοῦ) (1:12–13). As the
gospel proceeds this theme is elaborated and nuances are added.
Whoever believes in the Son will not perish (μὴ ἀπόληται) but will gain
eternal life (3:16). Those who come to Jesus are within the gift of the
Father (6:65, see 6:44,37) and what is so given him shall not perish (6:39)
and cannot be snatched out of his hand nor out of the Father's (10:28,29
see 3:35). Chapter 17 adds that these faithful are to be kept,[6] guarded,[7]
and protected from evil (17:11,12,15).

What is said in 17:12, notwithstanding certain textual difficulties,[8] is
well within this framework: the faithful have been kept, and none of
them is lost. Indeed the strong similarity between ᾧ δέδωκάς μοι . . .

οὐδεὶς ἐξ αὐτῶν ἀπώλετο (17:12) and ὃ δέδωκέν μοι μὴ ἀπολέσω ἐξ αὐτοῦ (6:39) is to be noted. Furthermore, we have in 18:9 the reappearance of this theme at the very point where Jesus does protect his disciples (18:8) so that the reference to 17:12/6:39 is unmistakable even though the wording is not identical: οὓς δέδωκάς μοι, οὐκ ἀπώλεσα ἐξ αὐτῶν οὐδένα.

To quote J. N. Birdsall's comment on 10:29, the overriding theme of passages such as these is 'the unassailability of the flock of God because of his guardian power'.[9] But John cannot maintain this theme unless he can account for the tradition that one of the 'flock', indeed one of the twelve, chosen by Jesus himself, was a betrayer. That he makes no attempt to deny this uncomfortable datum is to his credit; that he is able to turn it to his advantage is a measure of his theological ability.

How, then, does John deal with the problem posed by the tradition about Judas Iscariot? There are a number of ways in which he does this.

First, like Matthew and Luke, he is not slow in finding an explanation in terms of fulfilment of Old Testament scriptures (see Matt.27:9–10; Acts 1:16–20; John 13:18; note, too, the passing reference to Ps.41:9 in Mark 14:18).

Second, he makes of Judas a particular exception to the 'unassailability' theme and so he blackens Judas' character at every turn. Judas is identified as a devil (6:70). He is the one who complains about the waste of ointment (12:4–5 cf. Mark 14:4; Matt.26:8) not, the evangelist adds, because he cared for the poor but because he was a thief (12:6). Judas is Satan's pawn, subject to Satan's will (13:2), possessed by him (13:27 cf. Luke 22:3), and described in terms which refer to him (see 14:30 cf. 12:31; 14:31 cf. Mark 14:42; Matt.26:46). In distinguishing Judas by the eschatological phrase ὁ υἱὸς τῆς ἀπωλείας (17:12 cf. 2 Thess.2:3) John intends perhaps to indicate that he is to be seen as the agent of the final enemy who brings about the ultimate onslaught of evil before the eschaton. Thus Jesus' choice of Judas is woven into an overall eschatological scheme; he is the figure which symbolises the final apostasy before Satan's downfall at the crucifixion.[10]

Third, John draws some distinction between those who follow Jesus, in particular the chosen betrayer, and those who come to Jesus who are within the Father's gift (6:64–65). These last will not be cast out (6:37 cf. 12:31) nor will they perish (6:39) but are drawn by the Father and will be raised up (6:44 see 6:39).

Finally, he emphasises that Jesus' choice of Judas was not fortuitous, but that the choice was deliberately made in the full knowledge of what was to come. The argument is threefold:

(1) Jesus knows what is in man (2:24–25) and thus recognises Judas for what he is (6:70–71);

(2) He chooses Judas, therefore, in the foreknowledge that Judas will betray him (6:64; 13:10–11; 13:18; 13:21–22);

(3) This foreknowledge and the fulfilment of prediction are seen as grounds for faith (13:19).[11]

As indicated above, Jesus' statement in 13:18 lies within this final category. It refers to Judas as part of the 'choosing and foreknowledge' theme, the scripture having been placed alongside the statement in 'proof-text' manner.[12] Accordingly, the text of 13:18a: Οὐ περὶ πάντων ὑμῶν λέγω· ἐγὼ οἶδα τίνας ἐξελεξάμην, has as its direct antecedent the 'word' of Jesus in 6:70: οὐκ ἐγὼ ὑμᾶς τοὺς δώδεκα ἐξελεξάμην; καὶ ἐξ ὑμῶν εἷς διάβολός ἐστιν.[13]

In chapter 17, however, the theme of choosing is completely absent,[14] and the thought is wholly concentrated on the notion of giving[15]: the Father has given to the Son (vv. 2,4,7,8,11,12,22,24); the Son has given to the disciples (vv. 2,8,14,22); and the disciples are those given to the Son by the Father (vv. 2,6 (twice), 9,11,12[16],24). Thus the thought is wholly on the fortunes of the τέκνα θεοῦ who are given to Jesus by the Father (6:37,44,65). The promise of eternal life (3:16), of being raised up (6:39,44), neither perishing (3:16; 6:37,39) nor being snatched away (10:28–29), holds good because of the protecting power of the Father (17:11,12,15). The theme of Jesus' *choice* of Judas is far removed from the context of 17:12, and the text of 17:12 itself carries no notion of the 'choosing and foreknowledge' references of 6:70–71 and 13:18–19 which feature Judas, but rather addresses itself to the 'unassailability' theme pre-figured in 3:16; 6:39 and 10:28 and carried through to 18:9. It is unlikely, therefore, that when John writes here ἵνα ἡ γραφὴ πληρωθῇ, giving no verbal reference to Ps.41:9, that it is this scripture as quoted in 13:18 that he has in mind.

If, as argued above, 17:12 has no connection in thought with the 'Judas' references in 6:70–71 and 13:18–19, then the reference to Judas here begins to look like an apparently uncalled-for digression from the theme of the chapter.[17] It may be, after all, that the evangelist *has* chosen to pause here and remind us of this notable exception to his rule, but if it is a reminder, it does not come in the form of a reference to Ps.41:9, but in the form of a reference to Judas himself. Here it is important to note the wording. Judas is not named but referred to as ὁ υἱὸς τῆς ἀπωλείας, a phrase whose exact antecedents are difficult to trace.[18] However, that the evangelist does refer to Judas Iscariot at this point, and in this particular form has, I suggest, much more to do with the presence of the verb ἀπόλλυμι ('to destroy') already in his text than with thematic considerations.

Judas Iscariot and ἀπώλεια/ἀπόλλυμι in John's Gospel

Commentators generally accept that the phrase ὁ υἱὸς τῆς ἀπωλείας in John 17:12 is a reference to Judas Iscariot.[19] This being the case, it follows that the evangelist can use this phrase in the complete confidence that his readers will know to whom he is referring. It may be that the phrase, not used of Judas in any other New Testament writing, is already in his tradition as a form of description of the betrayer,[20] its presence in 17:12 prompted by a play on words (ἀπώλετο/ἀπωλείας).[21] What follows does not rule out these considerations, but is an attempt to show that the connection between the figure of Judas and the notion of perdition/destruction is already a part of the evangelist's thinking before he reaches 17:12, such that the digression εἰ μὴ ὁ υἱὸς τῆς ἀπωλείας would come naturally to his pen once he had used the verb ἀπόλλυμι.

The evidence comes from the Johannine version of the anointing of Jesus (12:1–8). It is drawn first by comparing this story in John with its Synoptic counterparts, and second by examining the significance of John's accusation that Judas was a thief (12:6).

The similarities between the Johannine and Markan accounts of the anointing of Jesus are sufficiently remarkable as to suggest, at the very least, strong connections in the tradition at the pre-canonical level.[22] In the main John appears to 'follow' the Markan sequence often to the point of close verbal correspondence.[23] When it comes to the matter of the complaint about the ointment, however, John's account specifies that it is Judas who speaks (12:4). At this point Mark simply makes some general reference (Mark 14:4). Matthew, however, does attribute the complaint to 'the disciples' (Matt.26:8).

Why is Judas featured at this point in John's narrative? John certainly wishes to vilify Judas and uses the anointing tradition as an opportunity to do so. However, apart from his identification of Judas as the one who makes the complaint and his own gloss on Judas' character added in 12:6, the similarity between his account and the Markan version continues to be striking (note that even the burden of the complaint is the same[24]). We should therefore allow the possibility that the 'Judas' references are a peculiarly Johannine contribution to the tradition. Why, then, has John chosen to draw Judas into the action? He may be familiar with the (Markan) setting of the incident which gives prominence to Judas (see Mark 14:1–2, 10–11), or have been motivated by Judas' known interest in obtaining money for himself (see Mark 14:11; John 12:6) to see his presence during the incident as particularly apt.[25] I suggest, however, that there is something more specific than this. In the Markan account, at precisely the point where the Johannine parallel introduces the presence of Judas, there is the question: εἰς τί ἡ ἀπώλεια αὕτη τοῦ μύρου γέγονεν; (Mark 14:4b, echoed in Matt.26:8: εἰς τί ἡ ἀπώλεια αὕτη;). The question is not reproduced by John, but his knowledge of it (and on other grounds he evidently knows the whole tradition well) may have suggested to him that the speaker should be Judas. After all, what could be a more fitting irony than that the complaint about loss (ἀπώλεια) should be made by the 'son of loss'? Thus, at precisely the point where ἀπώλεια (in Mark, the only instance) appears in the tradition, John sees the opportunity to introduce Judas into his own narrative. Thereafter, with a reference to money and a Passion setting already to hand, he found this story tailor-made for further vilification of the betrayer.

The second point involves John's accusation in 12:6, that Judas was a thief (ὅτι κλέπτης ἦν). That John shows a marked hostility towards Judas and takes every opportunity to blacken his character has already been noted,[26] and no doubt the accusation that Judas was a thief is no exception to this policy.[27] Yet this particular reference sits a little oddly. In other 'Judas' texts (6:70; 13:2,27;17:12) the intention is to imply that Judas is a creature of Satan whose fortunes are bound up with the train of events leading to the crucifixion and the collapse of the devil's schemes (see 12:31–32). In describing Judas as a mere thief, however, accustomed to stealing from the money-box, John seems to have stooped, untypically, to the level of petty spitefulness. It is difficult to see any reason for this particular accusation from within the Synoptic tradition.[28] However, what John himself has to say about the thief earlier in his gospel may well prove to be to the point.

In John chapter 10 the 'good shepherd' material is used to distinguish between Jesus as the true leader and others (variously depicted as the thief, the robber, and the hireling) who are false. It is difficult to define the source-material for this allegory whose basis seems to shift between presenting Jesus as the door of the sheepfold (vv. 1,7–9) and as the shepherd (vv. 2–3, 11–12).[29] What is important for our purposes, however, is what is said of the thief alone in verse 10.[30] In contrast to Jesus who comes to give life (ἐγὼ ἦλθον ἵνα ζωὴν ἔχωσιν) we read that the thief (ὁ κλέπτης) comes only 'to steal and kill and destroy' (ἵνα κλέψῃ καί θύσῃ καὶ ἀπολέσῃ). The verb ἀπόλλυμι ('to destroy') is applied only to the thief in this allegory and, I suggest, is the basis for John's describing Judas as a thief in 12:6. This would give to John's ὅτι κλέπτης ἦν a properly sinister ring.[31] Moreover, the similarity between οὐχ ὅτι περὶ τῶν πτωχῶν ἔμελεν αὐτῷ ('not that he cared for the poor') in 12:6 and οὐ μέλει αὐτῷ περὶ τῶν προβάτων ('he cares nothing for the sheep') in 10:13[32] is probably a further indicator that in 12:6 John had the 'good shepherd' material in mind.

The purpose of the above argument has been to demonstrate that there is good reason to assume a strong association in John's tradition between the figure of Judas and the notion of perdition/destruction. I have suggested that this association may account for the presence of Judas in 12:4 at a point where the tradition known to him (and as represented in Mark) features the word ἀπώλεια. I have also suggested that the association of ἀπόλλυμι with κλέπτης in John 10:10 lies behind John's statement in 12:6 that Judas was a thief.

When we turn to 17:12 we see that it is of a piece with this tendency. Here ἀπόλλυμι appears in the text (καὶ οὐδεὶς ἐξ αὐτῶν ἀπώλετο) and although the thought here concentrates on the unassailability of those in the Father's keeping (see 6:39), the association between Judas and ἀπόλλυμι naturally triggers the digression εἰ μὴ ὁ υἱὸς τῆς ἀπωλείας. What is more, this move may have gained further impetus by what the evangelist has written in 10:28. The passage 10:27–29 is a piece of 'good shepherd' material held over from the earlier part of the chapter.[33] Accordingly, 10:28, in contrasting the life-giving mission of Jesus with destruction (οὐ μὴ ἀπόλωνται), picks up the theme of 10:10 where destruction has already been associated with the thief (ὁ κλέπτης οὐκ ἔρχεται εἰ μὴ ἵνα . . . ἀπολέσῃ). However, 10:28 also shows connections with 17:12. Thus the καὶ οὐδεὶς ἐξ αὐτῶν ἀπώλετο in 17:12, prefigured in 10:28, may by this time carry the notion of the destruction wrought by the thief in 10:10. The thief is now known to be Judas (12:6), and thus a reference to him in the form of a play on ἀπώλετο is natural.

If this argument is correct, then ἡ γραφή which the evangelist has in mind in 17:12 has nothing to do with Judas either in the form of any known reference to ἀπώλεια, or in the form of the quotation of Ps. 41:9 in 13:18. The clause εἰ μὴ ὁ υἱὸς τῆς ἀπωλείας, whose presence is accounted for by the existence of ἀπόλλυμι already in the text, is strictly a digression from the main argument of the verse, and indeed from that of the chapter as a whole.

What, then, is ἡ γραφή in 17:12? It remains to explore one further possibility, namely, that it refers to the 'word' of Jesus himself, cited already in 6:39 (10:28) and to be repeated again with the formula ἵνα πληρωθῇ ὁ λόγος in 18:9.

'The Scripture' in 17:12 as a Reference to the 'Word' of Jesus

In the work of the fourth evangelist we see the emergence of an attitude whereby the word or command of Jesus comes to be placed alongside scripture and can be regarded as of equal weight. More recent studies in source criticism recognise that John preserves a collection of Jesus-Logia and uses it as the basis for his own midrashic style of composition.[34] While this treatment of the sayings of Jesus is not exclusive to John,[35] it is perhaps true to say that his readiness to treat the word of Jesus as he would a word of scripture is explicit.

In writing his account, the evangelist orientates the narrative tradition available to him around the Jesus-Logia and thus weaves it into his own exegesis of the sayings. He composes his gospel in this manner because he writes from a community in which there is a strong tradition of the preservation of Jesus' words (and deeds) later to be interpreted, which tradition he also records (2:22; 12:16; 15:20 see 13:16).[36] Accordingly, he is prepared to place the words of Jesus on a level with scripture (2:22; 5:47; 13:18), he emphasises that Jesus' words and commandments are to be kept (8:51(52); 14:15,21,23; 15:10),[37] and accepts that Jesus' words, like scripture, can be fulfilled (18:9; 18:32).[38]

I suggest that in 17:12 we have another instance of this concentration on fulfilment of a Jesus-statement. The statement first appears in recognisable form in 6:39, is partly referred to in 10:28, and then repeated in 17:12 and 18:9, in these last two instances accompanied by a fulfilment formula. In none of the instances beyond 6:39 is the quotation of the previous text precisely the same but the reference is unmistakable:

6:39　(πᾶν) ὃ δέδωκέν μοι μὴ ἀπολέσω ἐξ αὐτοῦ

10:28　[10:29 ὃ δέδωκέν μοι] οὐ μὴ ἀπόλωνται

17:12　(τῷ ὀνόματί σου) ᾧ δέδωκάς μοι ... οὐδεὶς ἐξ αὐτῶν ἀπώλετο

18:9　οὓς δέδωκάς μοι, οὐκ ἀπώλεσα ἐξ αὐτῶν οὐδένα.

The neuter ᾧ in 17:12 is to be preferred.[39] It has already been used in 6:39 (probably attracted by reference to the neuter τὰ ... κλάσματα, ἵνα μή τι ἀπόληται in 6:12), and in 17:12 it can also be made to refer to τὸ ὄνομα immediately preceding it. There is no doubt, however, that the statement in 18:9 refers to 17:12. That the two do not match in every detail does not seem to matter,[40] and the mention of τὸ ὄνομα in 17:12 probably anticipates what is to happen in 18:5 ff. where the protective power of God's name is seen in action.[41]

I suggest, therefore, that for John there is no difference in meaning between ἵνα ἡ γραφὴ πληρωθῇ in 17:12 and ἵνα πληρωθῇ ὁ λόγος in 18:9 since both refer to the same Jesus-Logion on the unassailability of those given him by the Father and in both cases the Logion is quoted.

If this case has been proven, then it means that John has used ἡ γραφή, normally reserved by him to refer to an Old Testament text, to describe a 'word' of Jesus. That he can do this is probably because he is accustomed to treating the Jesus-Logia as he would treat texts from αἱ γραφαί. Whether it can be said, however, that in this instance[42] John has in fact made a conscious move to call a Jesus-Logion 'scripture' is another matter. A looser rendering of ἡ γραφή here to convey something like 'tradition' or 'writing' may be more suitable.[43]

Notes

1.　See the following commentaries ad loc.: C. K. Barrett, *The Gospel according to St John*, 2nd ed. (London, 1978); J. H. Bernard, *The Gospel according to St. John*, 2 vols (Edinburgh, 1942); R. E. Brown, *Gospel according to John* (The Anchor Bible, vols 29 and 29A; New York and London, 1966,

1972); R. Bultmann, *The Gospel of John: A Commentary* (Oxford, 1971); E. C. Hoskyns, *The Fourth Gospel*, ed. F. N. Davey (London, 1947); M.-J. Lagrange, *Évangile selon Saint Jean* (Paris, 1948); B. Lindars, *The Gospel of John* (New Century Bible, vol. 16: London, 1972); G. H. C. MacGregor, *The Gospel of John* (Moffat New Testament Commentary, London, 1959); J. N. Sanders, *A Commentary on the Gospel according to St John*, (Black's New Testament Commentaries), edited and completed by B. A. Mastin (London, 1968); A. Schlatter, *Der Evangelist Johannes: wie er spricht, denkt und glaubt* (Stuttgart, 1960); R. Schnackenburg, *The Gospel according to St John*, 3 vols (London and New York, 1968–82). See also G. Reim, *Studien zum alttestamentlichen Hintergrund des Johannesevangeliums* (Studiorum Novi Testamenti Societas Monograph Series, vol. 22: Cambridge, 1974) pp. 45–7.

2. John uses a number of different formulae to introduce his quotations from scripture (see, for example, 7:38; 7:42; 10:34; 19:37). The formula common to 13:18 and 17:12 is ἵνα ἡ γραφὴ πληρωθῇ. It occurs twice more, in 19:24 and 19:36, but in neither case is there intended any connection with 13:18.

3. See, for example, 4:46; 4:53 cf. 4:50; 11:2, 37; 12:1; 18:9, 32.

4. Apart from 17:12, where γραφή and πληρόω are used together, a quotation is always made: see 13:18; 19:24; 19:36. The same applies (apart from the general reference in 5:39) where γραφή is used with other verbs: see 7:38, 42; 10:35(34); 19:28,37. For the use of γράφω with quotation (apart from the general references 1:45; 5:46) see 2:17; 6:31,45; 8:17; 10:34; 12:14–16; 15:25. The use of πληρόω and λόγος in conjunction also always involves a quotation: see 12:38; 15:25; 18:9,32. The single exception is οὐδέπω γὰρ ᾔδεισαν τὴν γραφήν in 20:9, but here a quotation would not be to the point since the interest is centred not on the scripture but on the fact that the beloved disciple 'saw and believed' (v.8) without the aid of scriptural proof. I am unable to agree with Freed that 20:9 may refer to the written record of the Passion in the Synoptics (cf. Luke 24:45–46), or that in general John quotes from the Synoptics (E. D. Freed, *Old Testament Quotations in the Gospel of John* (*NovTSup* vol. 11, Leiden, 1965) pp. 56–8). What may be a parallel tradition cannot be said to amount to a quotation.

5. I note that this possibility has been suggested by Freed (ibid. pp. 57, 96, 98). However, by confusing what is said in 6:39 with the reference to Judas in 6:70 (later shadowed in 13:18) he has, in my opinion, weakened the argument. Nevertheless, his case perhaps deserves more kindly treatment than it receives in Brown (op.cit., vol. 2, p. 760) and Reim (op. cit., p. 47 n. 84).

6. The verb τηρέω is always used before chapter 17 with reference to the keeping of words or commandments. Only here does it refer to people.

7. The verb φυλάσσω is used rarely before 17:12: see 12:25,47 where it has a slightly different meaning. Its use in 17:12 may be due simply to the need for an alternative to τηρέω.

8. See the helpful discussion in Lindars' commentary, pp. 524-5.

9. J. Neville Birdsall, 'John X. 29', *JTS* n.s. 11 (1960) 342–4 (p. 344). This is also quoted by Barrett (op.cit., p. 382).

10. See further W. E. Sproston, 'Satan in the Fourth Gospel', *Studia Biblica 1978*, 2 (Sheffield, 1980) pp. 307–11.
11. For the same theme but with different subject-matter see 14:29. Commenting on 13:19 Lindars remarks on the similarity between this theme in John and Deutero-Isaiah's pronouncements that 'Yahweh is known to be the real God . . . because his word uttered in prophecy comes true, and he has foreknowledge of the saving events' (op. cit., p. 455).
12. See M. Wilcox, 'The Composition of John 13:21–30', in E. Earle Ellis and Max Wilcox (eds), *Neotestamentica et Semitica* (Edinburgh, 1969) pp. 143–56 (pp. 145, 156).
13. This is not, of course, to deny the influence which the scripture cited in 13:18 has had on parts of ch. 6: see John's use of τρώγω in 6:54–58.
14. The verb ἐκλέγομαι ('to choose') reappears again in 15:16,19 but not thereafter.
15. This chapter alone accounts for almost one-third of the 76 instances of δίδωμι throughout the gospel.
16. There is some confusion in the text in 17:11,12 as to whether the ᾧ δέδωκάς μοι should read in both cases οὓς δέδωκάς μοι, and thus refer, not to τὸ ὄνομα immediately preceding it, but to the disciples. This confusion is understandable in the light of other similar references to the disciples in ch. 17 which use both masculine and neuter forms (see οὓς in v.6, ὧν in v.9, compare ὃ in vv.2,24). The neuter form is probably to be preferred as the harder reading (compare πᾶν ὃ δέδωκέν μοι in 6:39) despite the masculine reading in 18:9, which repeats 17:12 (see Lindars, op. cit., pp. 524–5). A double reference both to τὸ ὄνομα and the faithful may be intended in 17:12.
17. Schnackenburg (op. cit., vol. 3, p. 182 see n. 50) observes that 'this consideration of the "son of perdition" . . . seems to be superfluous in this context' and cites an article by J. Becker who suggests that it may be the work of an editor. Schnackenburg himself, however, is not completely convinced that this digression should be excluded.
18. See the discussions ad loc. in commentaries by Schnackenburg, Lindars, Schlatter, Bernard and Hoskyns. Bultmann suggests that εἰ μὴ κτλ may have been in the source already as a general reference but that the evangelist has particularised it to Judas (op. cit., p. 504 n. 2).
19. See ad loc. Schnackenburg, Brown, Lindars, Sanders and Mastin, Hoskyns, Schlatter, Macgregor, Bultmann, Barrett; also Freed (op. cit., p. 97).
20. It is Schlatter's view that the phrase was certainly not coined by John (op. cit., p. 322, see also Barrett, op. cit., p 508).
21. This feature is noted ad loc. by Lindars, Sanders and Mastin, Macgregor and Bernard; see Freed (op. cit., p. 98).
22. See the lengthy discussion in C. H. Dodd's *Historical Tradition in the Fourth Gospel* (Cambridge, 1963) pp. 162–73. See also commentaries by Brown and Barrett ad loc.
23. See Barrett, op. cit., p. 44. Note, however, that the detail of the actual anointing shows preference for Luke 7:38 over against Mark 14:3.
24. Compare τοῦτο τὸ μύρον πραθῆναι . . . δηναρίων τριακοσίων καὶ δοθῆναι

τοῖς πτωχοῖς (Mark 14:5) with τοῦτο τὸ μύρον . . . ἐπράθη τριακοσίων δηναρίων καὶ ἐδόθη πτωχοῖς (John 12:5).

25. See Brown (op. cit., vol. 1, p. 453).
26. See p. 26 above.
27. That Judas had been in charge of the money-box and thus occupied a position of trust (12:6) must have been a particularly sore point.
28. For κλέπτης see Matt.6:19,20; 24:43; Luke 12:33,39; for κλέπτω see Matt.6:19,20; 19:18; 27:64; 28:13; Mark 10:19; Luke 18:20. In Mark κλέπτης does not appear at all and the only instance of the cognate verb is in a reference to the Ten Commandments (10:19). Both κλέπτης and κλέπτω in Luke and Matthew appear in the sayings on heavenly treasure, the commandments, the *parousia*, and with reference (in Matt.) to stealing Jesus' body from the tomb.
29. See the discussions ad loc. in commentaries by Barrett, Bultmann, and Lindars.
30. It does not necessarily follow that what is said only of the thief in v. 10 must also apply to the λῃστής (see v. 1). R. E. Brown (op. cit., vol. 1, pp. 394–5) suggests that the evangelist has now moved on from the κλέπτης . . . καὶ λῃστής reference in v. 1 (plural in v. 8) so that the contrast in v. 10 between Jesus and the thief implies that this figure is 'a general representative of darkness who is a rival to the Son'. Lindars too, although he sees the mention of the thief in v. 10 as derived from v. 1, indicates here the beginning of 'a new line of exposition' where the description of the thief is 'virtually . . . a new subsidiary parable' (op. cit., pp. 359–60).
31. Both Lindars and Brown (op. cit.) suggest the reference to killing in 10:10 is connected in thought with John's description of the devil as a murderer in 8:44.
32. Noted by Brown (op. cit., vol. 1, p. 448). The expression in 10:13 is, however, used of the hireling.
33. So Lindars, op. cit., p. 354.
34. See B. Lindars. 'Traditions behind the Fourth Gospel', in M. de Jonge (ed.), *L'Évangile de Jean*, (Louvain, 1977) 107–24, and *Behind the Fourth Gospel* (London, 1971) pp. 43 ff.; P. Borgen, 'The Use of Tradition in John 12:44–50', *NTS* 26 (1979–80) 18–35; M. Wilcox, 'The Composition of John 13:21–30', pp. 155–6 (see n. 12).
35. Borgen (op. cit.) compares John and Paul in this respect; see also M. Wilcox, 'The Denial-Sequence in Mark XIV, 26–31, 66–72', *NTS* 17 (1970–71) 426–36 on Mark.
36. It seems that the members of the Johannine community regarded themselves as peculiarly fitted to interpret Jesus' words. The Beloved Disciple and the Paraclete, key figures with whom the community associates itself, are presented as gaining or imparting an intuitive grasp of the mission and significance of Jesus, see 13:23–24, 28; 20:8(9); 13:23(25), cf. 1:18 (the Beloved Disciple), and 14:26; 16:12–13 (the Paraclete). See further R. E. Brown, *The Epistles of John* (Anchor Bible vol. 30) pp. 94–6.
37. Brown, in his commentary on the Johannine Epistles (op. cit.), argues that

this oscillation between λόγος and ἐντολή is not merely fortuitous, but rather suggests a Semitic background where the Ten Commandments were the 'words' of God (see Exod. 34:28). Thus, to refer to Jesus' command as a 'word' is implicitly to equate it with the Decalogue (p. 252).

38. Compare the references to fulfilment of scripture (13:18; 19:24,36), the prophetic word (12:38), and the word in the law (15:25). For a discussion on the 'word' of Jesus as fulfilled in John's gospel see Freed, op. cit., p. 57.

39. See the discussion in commentaries by Barrett and Lindars on 17:11.

40. In 18:32, where the 'word' of Jesus is again fulfilled, the reference is obviously to Jesus' prediction of his crucifixion given in 12:32. However, merely the quotation of the gloss in 12:33 is here deemed sufficient to recall the Jesus-statement.

41. See Brown's commentary on the gospel, vol. 2, p. 764.

42. Freed, however, claims something like this for the references in 7:42 and 20:9 (op. cit., pp. 51,58).

43. Freed is careful to avoid the conclusion that γραφή in a case like this should be translated 'scripture' (op. cit., pp. 51,59).

3

Stephen's Apologia

F. F. Bruce

Hebrews and Hellenists

Anyone starting to read through the Acts of the Apostles for the first time is bound to be taken by surprise in moving from the fifth to the sixth chapter. To a reader who has had any experience in source criticism it becomes evident at once that the author has begun to draw upon a different source for the narrative starting at Acts 6:1 from the source or sources used for the first five chapters. We are now introduced abruptly to two rather sharply differentiated groups in the Jerusalem church – the Hebrews and the Hellenists – without any indication of the nature of the distinction between them.

Both groups were Jewish; the distinction between them, it seems, was mainly linguistic. The Hebrews were Aramaic-speaking and attended synagogues where the scriptures were read and the prayers recited in Hebrew; the Hellenists were Greek-speaking and attended synagogues where the whole service was conducted in Greek. Even in Jerusalem in the decades preceding AD 70 there were Hellenistic synagogues, such as the synagogue of the Freedmen mentioned in Acts 6:9 or the synagogue known from the Theodotus inscription[1] (it has been suggested by some that these were not two different synagogues but one and the same synagogue). As for bilingual Jews, those who attended a Greek-speaking synagogue were probably included among the Hellenists, but most Hellenists would be monolingual.[2]

If the basic difference between the two groups was linguistic, there would be other differences, both cultural and religious, giving each group a sense of separate corporate identity. Luke records one instance of alleged discrimination in the preferential treatment which the Hellenists believed the Hebrew widows were receiving over theirs when the poorer members of the fellowship received their daily allocation from the common fund. No doubt there were other points at issue between the two groups, some of them perhaps theological in character, but Luke concentrates (*more suo*) on a non-theological area of dispute. And rightly so: leaders of religious bodies may insist on points of theological disagreement, but the rank and file of the membership will begin to show an interest when the disagreement affects them in a practical way.

We have no information about the origin of the Hellenistic group in the primitive church. There may well have been Hellenists among Jesus' followers in Jerusalem before his crucifixion; if so, their number was augmented from Pentecost onwards. It was probably among such Hellenists, rather than in the ranks of the twelve apostles and their adherents, that Jesus' more radical utterances about the temple were cherished and repeated.

When Jesus was being judicially examined by the high priest and his colleagues, an attempt was made to convict him on a charge of speaking against the temple: more specifically, it was reported, he had undertaken to destroy the existing temple 'made with hands' and to replace it in three days with another, 'not made with hands' (Mark 14:58).[3] Those who bore this testimony are called false witnesses, and in any case their testimony was disallowed because of inconsistency in wording. But Jesus certainly said something about the destruction of the existing temple,[4] and the theme of a new one, 'not made with hands', entered into the thought and language of early Christianity in a way that leaves no doubt that it goes back to him.

The apostles and their associates, on the other hand, who continued to frequent the temple, could appeal to Jesus' description of it as 'my Father's house' (Luke 2:49; John 2:16) and to his endorsement of the prophetic estimate of it as 'a house of prayer for all the nations' (Isa.56:7, quoted in Mark 11:17).

In his attitude to the temple, Luke differs both from the apostles and from the Hellenists (if Stephen is regarded as their representative spokesman), but he has a lively sympathy with the Hellenists. It was Hellenists who, forced to leave Jerusalem because of the persecution that broke out after Stephen's death, carried the gospel north to Antioch. Antioch, according to tradition, was Luke's native city; whether it was or not, he was keenly interested in Antiochene Christianity and in the part it played in the further expansion of the gospel along the road that led to Rome.

Stephen's Début

When the Hellenistic complainants were invited to select seven men to take charge of the distribution of charity, they evidently selected men whom they already recognised as their leaders. Right from the outset they fulfilled a much wider ministry than that of *septem viri mensis ordinandis.*[5] Stephen in particular engaged in public proclamation and debate, arguing for a much more radical interpretation of the Christ-event than anything contemplated by the apostles. The apostles stressed the continuity between the work of Christ and God's earlier dealings with Israel; Stephen stressed the discontinuity. All that the temple order stood for had been rendered for ever obsolete by the work of Christ. The new order had come; the old had to go.

No wonder, then, that he was charged with blasphemy against Moses and against God: against Moses, by teaching the impermanence of the law, and against God, by announcing the abolition of his holy house. The latter was a capital offence, and one over which the Jewish authorities were allowed by Rome to exercise jurisdiction without reference to the governor. If convicted on this charge, Stephen was liable to death by stoning. But first the law required that he should have an opportunity to reply to the charges against him. It is his reply that is now to be considered.

The Nature of Stephen's Reply

What kind of speech is it? Not a forensic speech for the defence, although it is set in a forensic context. It is scarcely an answer to the high priest's question – 'Is this so?' – although it is closely related to that part of the accusation which alleged that Stephen kept on speaking 'against this holy place' (6:13). But it makes no attempt to refute that charge; it rather confirms it.

It can be recognised as an early sample of one type of Christian *testimonia adversus Iudaeos* – the type which fixes on some aspect of Jewish faith or practice and argues that it has departed from the divine intention. The aspect fixed on in this speech is the worship of God: it was never the purpose of God, it is argued, that his people should worship him in a permanent structure of stone and lime, tied to one spot.

This is not Luke's personal point of view: for most of his twofold history, from the angelic annunciation to Zechariah to Paul's last visit to Jerusalem, the temple occupies an honoured place. Nor can it be convincingly said (although it has been said by several scholars in recent years) that Stephen's speech expresses a Samaritan as against a Jewish attitude.[6] So far as the temple was concerned, the issue between Samaritans and Jews was whether Gerizim or Zion was the place where God was to be worshipped. But Stephen's argument would exclude the Samaritan viewpoint as emphatically as the Jewish.

The speech takes the form of a survey of Old Testament history, a form not unfamiliar in Jewish usage. The survey falls into four parts: (1) the patriarchal narrative (Acts 7:2–16), (2) the oppression in Egypt and call of Moses (7:17–34), (3) the exodus and wilderness wanderings (7:35–43), (4) tabernacle and temple (7:44–50). It is followed by a vigorous denunciation of the contemporary Jewish establishment for bringing to its climax the disobedience of earlier generations.

The speech is, no doubt, a manifesto of early Hellenistic Christianity, or, at any rate, of one segment of early Hellenistic Christianity, which took over and elaborated the critique of the temple and its sacrificial cult found in the ancient prophetic tradition of Amos, Isaiah and Jeremiah.[7] William Neil goes so far as to call the speech 'a vital manifesto of the breakaway of the Church from its Jewish moorings'.[8] Even if it represented the viewpoint of a minority in the church at that early date, it pointed towards the direction in which the church was to move, and Neil shares the perspective of Luke himself in saying that Stephen's critique 'was, under the guidance of the Spirit, the cause of the next great advance in the expansion of the Church'.[9]

1. *The Patriarchal Narrative*

The main point emphasised in the first division of the apologia is that the worship of God is not necessarily tied to any one locality, whether to a holy land, a holy city or a holy house. The patriarchs had no fixed abode;

they moved from place to place, and God was with them wherever they were. At the beginning of the patriarchal record God revealed himself to Abraham in Mesopotamia, in the land of the Chaldaeans; at the end of the record he was with Joseph in Egypt.

Some of the peculiarities of Stephen's treatment of the patriarchal narrative arise from its severe abridgement. When he says that Jacob and his sons, who went down to Egypt, were taken back nevertheless to Canaan for burial, he has them 'laid in a tomb which Abraham bought for a sum of silver from the sons of Hamor in Shechem' (7:16). This is a telescoping of the tomb near Hebron, in the field which Abraham bought from Ephron the Hittite, to which Jacob's body was taken for burial (Gen.23:16–20; 49:29–32; 50:13), with the piece of ground which Jacob bought from the sons of Hamor at Shechem, in which Joseph's body was eventually buried (Gen.33:19–20; Josh.24:32). It is unlikely that one should see here a Samaritan exaggeration of the importance of Shechem: in the Samaritan Bible Jacob's burial near Hebron is as clearly attested as in the Masoretic and Septuagint editions.

A point of contact with the Samaritan Bible may indeed be recognised in Acts 7:4, where Stephen says that Abraham left Harran for the promised land after his father's death. This is the *prima facie* impression given by the narrative of Gen.11:31–12:5, but it is apparently ruled out by the Masoretic and Septuagint chronology, according to which Terah's death at the age of 205 must have taken place sixty years after Abraham's departure from Harran.[10] However, in the Samaritan text Terah dies at the age of 145, when Abraham would have been 75, his exact age when he set out from Harran, according to Gen.12:4. But there is nothing distinctively Samaritan about this variant: it is a sample of the harmonising tendency of the popular Palestinian recension of the Pentateuch which lies behind the Samaritan text.[11]

Another deviation from the Masoretic text – and, for that matter, from the Samaritan and Septuagint editions – is the statement that the divine call first came to Abraham before he moved from the land of the Chaldaeans to Harran. According to the Genesis account, the departure from Ur of the Chaldees for Harran was undertaken on Terah's initiative (Gen.11:31). An account of the matter closer to Stephen's is presented in Nehemiah 9:7, where it is God who chose Abraham and brought him out of Ur of the Chaldees.

According to Samuel Sandmel, 'to see what the writer makes of

Abraham is often to see most clearly what the writer is trying to say.'[12] That was said with primary reference to Philo, but it is interesting to see how it applies to Stephen. Stephen emphasises God's promise to Abraham, and the faith and obedience shown in Abraham's response to the promise, both in his migration to the promised land and in his sojourn there without ever acquiring possession of it.

Although God does not restrict his presence to the promised land, there is quite a positive attitude to the land throughout Stephen's apologia. God brought Abraham into the land (7:4); he decreed that Abraham's descendants should worship him there (7:7); the patriarchs were buried there (7:16); in due course, with the Israelites' entry into the land under Joshua, the promise to Abraham that his posterity would possess it was ultimately fulfilled (7:45). Their worship of God in the land fulfilled the spiritual essence of the promise; the building of Solomon's temple had nothing to do with it. The negative thrust of Stephen's argument is directed against the idea that God's presence was confined to the land and that he was at his people's disposal there. The attitude which gave rise to this idea was encouraged beyond all measure by the building of the temple.

2. *Oppression in Egypt and Call of Moses*

Stephen's account of the oppression in Egypt and the birth and upbringing of Moses summarises the Exodus narrative (according to the Septuagint),[13] apart from the description of Moses as 'trained in all the wisdom of the Egyptians and . . . mighty in words and deeds' (7:22). The resemblance to the Emmaus disciples' description of Jesus in Luke 24:19 ('a prophet mighty in deed and word') may suggest that Acts 7:22 is redactional; nevertheless, it could be a remarkably moderate epitome of the picture of Moses given by a number of Jewish Hellenists, representing him as a master of all branches of knowledge and of the art of war.[14]

Stephen's speech is probably the earliest extant authority for making Moses forty years old when he left Egypt for the first time, with the corollary that his sojourn in Midian lasted a further forty years (7:23,30); it was, in any case, natural to bisect in this way the eighty years assigned to him at his return from Midian in Exodus 7:7. The story of his intervention in defence of an oppressed fellow-Israelite when he 'had grown up' (Exod.2:11) is filled out with an explanation of his conduct at that time: 'he thought', says Stephen, 'that his kinsfolk would have recognized that he was God's agent for their deliverance, but they did not' (7:25) – a highly probable account of the matter.

In due course the God who appeared to Abraham in Mesopotamia and was with Joseph in Egypt revealed himself to Moses in the 'wilderness of Mount Sinai' (7:30) and sent him back to Egypt. As neither temple nor sacrifice was required for those earlier theophanies, so neither was required for the theophany to Moses. The ground on which the theophany to Moses took place was holy because God manifested himself there. But again, God's presence called for no material shrine. Moses neither built an altar nor offered sacrifice on this holy ground.

3. *The Exodus and the Wilderness Wanderings*

The statement that Moses 'performed wonders and signs in Egypt and at the Red Sea, and in the wilderness for forty years' (7:36) is so similar to a passage in the *Assumption of Moses* that a literary relationship is probable.[15] If we are to think of direct borrowing, then Luke must be the borrower (since the *Assumption* is to be dated about AD 34), but the relationship may be less simple than that.

It is plain throughout the New Testament that, at a very early date in the history of the church, the Old Testament narrative of the exodus and the wilderness wanderings provided a model for the relating of the Christian story of redemption, with its practical implications for the life of the redeemed. As early as the date of 1 Corinthians, not more than a quarter of a century after the death and resurrection of Christ, Paul presents a fairly detailed series of analogies between the two.[16] The letter to the Hebrews and the letter to Jude show that the use of this pattern was not confined to Paul or his milieu.[17] Stephen, too, shows some knowledge of it and develops it distinctively.

Moses is portrayed as a counterpart to Jesus. Although he was at first rejected by his people, his title to be their leader and deliverer was vindicated by God. The locution ἄρχοντα καὶ λυτρωτήν (7:35) is synonymous with ἀρχηγὸν καὶ σωτῆρα, used of the disowned but vindicated Jesus in Acts 5:31. The 'angel who spoke to him at Mount Sinai' was with him and the people in the wilderness – the angel of Exodus 23:20–21, of whom God said, 'my name is in him.' Stephen does not (explicitly, at least) identify this angel with Christ, as Justin did in the following century.[18] What does clearly emerge is the identification of Christ with the prophet like Moses (7:37). This identification has already been made in Acts 3:22–23, where Peter in the temple precincts quotes more fully the promise about the prophet in Deuteronomy 18:15. Peter points to this promise as the primary instance of the way in which not only Moses but 'all the prophets from Samuel and his successors' foretold the day of Christ. The promise that God would 'raise up' a prophet was fulfilled when he 'raised up' his servant Jesus (Acts 3:26).

In the context of Stephen's speech the relevance of the angel (who was there when Moses received 'living oracles' to deliver to the people) is underlined in the peroration, where the nation is accused of not keeping the law, even if it was given by angelic administration (7:53).[19] This reference to angelic administration does not imply, as do the references to it in Galatians and Hebrews,[20] that the law is inferior to the gospel; but Stephen is far from suggesting that it was Christ who gave Israel the law.

Moses, rejected once in Egypt, was rejected again in the wilderness; so it was also with the prophet like Moses. Jesus, rejected during his earthly ministry, was rejected again when he was presented to the people as their leader and deliverer after his resurrection. The present generation was following the precedent of the wilderness generation. The repudiation of Moses by the wilderness generation took the form of open idolatry, in the worship of the golden calf. It could not be said, surely, that the present generation's repudiation of Jesus was at all bound up with idolatry, but Stephen somehow implies that it was. But how? Perhaps because by their devotion to the material temple they were 'rejoicing in the works of their hands' (7:41). If the people of the wilderness generation 'turned to Egypt in their hearts' (7:39), Stephen's hearers may be thought to have turned to Egypt in a spiritualised sense of that word.

Because the Israelites in the wilderness were guilty of idolatry in the matter of the golden calf, says Stephen, God's judgment on them took the form of their abandonment to even greater idolatry: 'he gave them over to worship the host of heaven' (7:42). For this conclusion confirmation is found in the oracle of Amos 5:25–27, reworded in the form (7:42–43):

> Did you offer slaughtered beasts and sacrifices to me
> forty years in the wilderness, O house of Israel?

No: you took up the tent of Moloch,
   the star of your god Raiphan,
the images which you made to worship them;
   and I will remove you beyond Babylon.

Apart from the detailed variations of this version (which for the most part follows the Septuagint) from the Masoretic text, the point of the oracle in this new context is quite different from that which it had in its original context. There the implied answer to Yahweh's question is (as though supplied by himself): 'No; you learned my will and undertook to do it.' The meaning is practically identical with that of Jeremiah 7:22–23: what Yahweh asked from his people in the wilderness was not burnt offerings and sacrifices but obedience to his will – righteousness and mercy, not ritual punctiliousness. Because Amos' contemporaries, for all their scrupulous observance of the cult, neglected righteousness and mercy, appropriate judgment would overtake them:

You shall take up Sakkut your king
   and Kaiwan your star-god,
your images which you made for yourselves;
   therefore I will exile you beyond Damascus.

But Stephen (following the Septuagint) pushes the star-worship which Israel began to practise under Assyrian influence (Sakkut and Kaiwan being Assyrian names for the planet Saturn) back into the wilderness period. Even then, it was not the God of their fathers that they worshipped, but Moloch and Raiphan (Raiphan being perhaps derived from an Egyptian name for Saturn). The idolatry which ultimately brought the nation into exile 'beyond Babylon' (this is a deviation from the Septuagint wording)[21] had its origin during the wilderness wanderings.

Yet the Israelites in the wilderness had at their disposal all the apparatus necessary for the pure worship of God. In addition to the resources available to the patriarchs they had the 'tabernacle of the testimony' made by Moses in accordance with divinely prescribed specifications (7:44). This was a movable shrine, appropriate to a pilgrim people. It served them not only in the wilderness but also, for some generations, in the land of Canaan, to which they brought it when they settled there under Joshua.

4. *Tabernacle and Temple*

The appropriateness of the movable tabernacle was underlined in the response given to David when he conceived the plan of building a more permanent house for Yahweh, something similar to the palace which he had built for himself. 'I have not dwelt in a house since the day I brought up the people of Israel from Egypt to this day', said Yahweh through the prophet Nathan, 'but I have been moving about in a tent for my dwelling. Did I ever say to any of the rulers of Israel, "Why have you not built me a house of cedar?"' (2 Sam.7:6–7). Nothing was farther from Yahweh's mind, it appears, than a permanent structure to accommodate him, as though such a thing were possible. David was content with the response from Yahweh; it was Solomon who built a house for him.

For all the commendation which Solomon receives for this enterprise from the Deuteronomists, the total emphasis of Stephen's survey indicates that such an enterprise was far from what God desired. Stephen quotes with regard to Solomon's temple (and, by implication, with regard to Herod's temple) the oracle of a later prophet than Nathan which deprecated the building of Zerubbabel's temple (7:49–50):

> Heaven is my throne
>   and the earth is my footstool;
> what is the house you would build for me,
>   and what is the place of my rest?
> All these things my hand has made,
>   and so all these things are mine.

These words (from Isaiah 66:1–2) are quoted to confirm that 'the Most High does not dwell in temples made with hands' – whether the temple built in his honour in Jerusalem (which is in view here) or the temples housing the many divinities worshipped throughout the pagan world, to which Paul refers at Athens when he assures the court of the Areopagus that the Creator 'does not dwell in shrines made with hands' (Acts 17:24). The same truth, indeed, was appreciated by the higher paganism, as when Euripides asks, 'What house fashioned by builders could enclose the divine form within enfolding walls?'[22]

It could be said in Solomon's defence that, in the Deuteronomistic account of the dedication of his temple, he himself gave expression to this truth: 'But will God indeed dwell on the earth? Behold, heaven and the highest heaven cannot contain thee; how much less this house which I have built!' (1 Kgs.8:27). The highest heaven was God's true dwelling-place, but he was pleased to locate his 'name' on earth in the house built for him by Solomon in Jerusalem. When his tent-shrine moved from place to place, any one of those places would not be looked upon as more holy than another; but when his 'name' was believed to reside in a fixed structure, the particular spot where that structure stood tended to be vested with peculiar sanctity. God, it was felt, was bound to defend the dwelling-place of his 'name' – both the holy house and the city in which it stood – from sacrilege and destruction. The deliverance experienced from Sennacherib's army in Hezekiah's day reinforced the conviction that Jerusalem and the temple were inviolable because Yahweh dwelt there. Over a century later, in face of the Babylonian menace, the Jerusalemites were still saying, 'Yahweh's temple, Yahweh's temple, Yahweh's temple', and they took it ill when Jeremiah warned them that, because of their sins, the house which was called by Yahweh's name would be given over by him to destruction as complete as that which formerly overtook Shiloh (Jer.7:1–15). That Yahweh could abandon his dwelling-place was unthinkable – to suggest it was blasphemous. Similarly Jesus' alleged undertaking to destroy the temple was cast in his teeth as he hung on the cross (Mark 15:29–30). And now the charge against Stephen, of saying that 'this Jesus of Nazareth will destroy this place' (i.e. the temple), was construed as blasphemy against God (Acts 6:11,13–14).

The Peroration

The peroration consists of an outburst of invective not specifically related to the central argument of the apologia. Stephen's hearers are charged in general terms with running true to the precedent set by their forefathers' record of killing the prophets: they, in their turn, have killed the one to whom the prophets pointed forward. This topic appears also in the gospel tradition. Jesus is safe away from Jerusalem, no matter how many plots may be laid against him in Galilee or elsewhere. Jerusalem is traditionally the prophet-killing city; it would never do for a prophet to be killed anywhere else (Luke 13:31–35). Previous generations of Jerusalemites have killed the prophets; the present generation tries to make amends by erecting monuments in their honour, but it is about to fill up the measure of its predecessors, bringing their actions to a climax by its treatment of Jesus himself (Matt.23:29–32).

The idea that the current generation of Israel has consummated the rebellion of previous generations features at an early date in the church's controversy with the Jews, not only among Gentile Christians but among Jewish Christians, not least among the Hellenists. This is the less surprising when we reflect how a puritan minority in Israel, like the Qumran community, could take the same line in denouncing the apostasy of the nation as a whole. The critique of the nation in the Song of Moses (Deut.32) is applied as pointedly in the Qumran literature[23] as it is by Paul in Romans 9–11 (except that Paul is more optimistic in his hope for the restoration of 'all Israel' than the Qumran sectaries are).

Luke's Perspective

Luke's perspective on the temple, as has already been said, differed from that which he ascribed to Stephen. For the greater part of Luke-Acts the temple is a holy place; it is, pre-eminently, a house of prayer. In Stephen's eyes the temple never possessed true sanctity; in Luke's eyes it did, but before the end of his narrative it loses the sacred status it had enjoyed for long. That was when Paul, during his last visit to Jerusalem, was dragged by his assailants out of the sacred precincts – 'and immediately the gates were shut' (Acts 21:30). The symbolic significance of this shutting of the gates was well caught by the Bampton Lecturer for 1864. On Paul's expulsion he said:

> 'Believing all things which are written in the Law and in the Prophets', and 'having committed nothing against the people or customs of [his] fathers', he and his creed are forced from their proper home. On it as well as him the Temple doors are shut.[24]

As Luke saw it, the exclusion of God's messenger and message from the house formerly called by his name sealed its doom; it was now ripe for the destruction which befell it not many years later. Henceforth, the only true temple of God on earth was the new sanctuary 'not made with hands'.

Jesus Christ in the Old Testament

To quote William Neil once more: 'It has been well said that, although the name of Christ is never mentioned, Stephen is all the while "preaching Jesus". He is demonstrating that everything in Israel's past history and experience pointed forward to God's culminating act in his plan for the redemption of the world in sending the Christ.'[25]

Some twenty years ago Professor A. T. Hanson enriched our study of both Testaments with his work entitled *Jesus Christ in the Old Testament*.[26] The expression 'Old Testament' would have been unfamiliar to Stephen, but if it had been explained to him he would have eagerly agreed that this title was what his argument was all about. It is fitting that these observations on Stephen's argument should be offered as a small tribute to Professor Hanson, coupled with the hope that he will continue for many years to enrich us with further insights in biblical interpretation.

Notes

1. *Corpus Inscriptionum Iudaicarum* 1404; cf. A. Deissmann, *Light from the Ancient East* (2nd ed., London, 1927) pp. 439–41; M. Hengel, *Between Jesus and Paul* (London, 1983) pp. 17–18, 148.
2. Cf. C. F. D. Moule, 'Once more, who were the Hellenists?' *ExpT* 70 (1958–9) 100–2; M. Hengel, *Between Jesus and Paul*, p. 11.
3. This episode is absent from Luke's account of the trial of Jesus; the theme is one of those which he reserves for his second volume (Acts 6:11–14).
4. Cf. Mark 13:2; John 2:19.
5. So they are called by W. M. Ramsay, *St Paul the Traveller and the Roman Citizen* (14th ed., London, 1920) p. 375.
6. Cf. A Spiro, 'Stephen's Samaritan Background', in J. Munck, *The Acts of the Apostles*, Anchor Bible (Garden City, N.Y., 1967) pp. 285–300; C. S. Mann, ' "Hellenists" and "Hebrews" in Acts VI 1', ibid., pp. 301–4; M. H. Scharlemann, *Stephen: a singular saint* (*Analecta Biblica* 34, Rome, 1968); C. H. H. Scobie, 'The Origins and Development of Samaritan Christianity', *NTS* 19 (1972–3) 390–414.
7. Cf. Amos 5:21–24; Isa.1:10–17; Jer.7:21–26.
8. W. Neil, *The Acts of the Apostles*, New Century Bible (London, 1973) p. 116.
9. Ibid.
10. James Ussher's chronology harmonises the situation by making Terah 130 when Abraham was born; Gen.11:26 is interpreted to mean that Terah was

70 when his oldest son (not Abraham) was born. Abraham could thus wait until Terah's death before leaving Harran for Canaan.

11. Cf. P. E. Kahle, *The Cairo Geniza* (London, 1947) pp.147–8.
12. S. Sandmel, 'Philo's Place in Judaism', *HUCA* 25 (1954) 237.
13. E.g. in Acts 7:14 Jacob's family, when it went down to Egypt, amounted to 'seventy-five souls' (as in Gen.46:27; Exod.1:5 LXX); contrast the MT total of seventy (Gen.46:27; Exod.1:5; Deut.10:22).
14. Cf. Josephus, *Ant*.2.229–231, 238–253; Philo, *Vit. Moys*. 2.20–24.
15. The Latin version of the Assumption refers to *Moyses . . . qui multa passus est in Aegypto et in mari rubro et in eremo annis quadraginta* (3:11).
16. Cf. 1 Cor.5:7b; 10:1–11.
17. Cf. Heb.3:7–4:11; Jude 5 (reading '*Jesus*, who saved . . .').
18. Justin, *Dial*.75.1–2.
19. The plural (εἰς διαταγὰς ἀγγέλων) may be generalising, if 'the angel that appeared to him in the bush' (7:30,35) is primarily in view here.
20. Cf. Gal.3:19; Heb.2:2.
21. LXX, following the Hebrew text, reads ἐπέκεινα Δαμασκοῦ. The change to ἐπέκεινα Βαβυλῶνος in Acts 7:43 adapts the oracle to the circumstances of the Babylonian exile.
22. Euripides, fragment 968.
23. Cf. the application of Deut.32:33 in the Damascus Rule 8.9.
24. T. D. Bernard, *The Progress of Doctrine in the New Testament* (5th ed., London, 1900) p. 121.
25. Neil, *Acts*, p. 116.
26. (London, 1965).

4

Paul Shipwrecked[1]

C. K. Barrett

Chapter 27 is a passage which the student of Acts is apt to pass over quickly. Both to the historian and to the theologian Paul at sea is a less interesting figure than Paul in the synagogue or Paul on Mars' Hill. Even the late Robert Maddox has practically nothing to say about it in his excellent book.[2] It has perhaps been too easily dismissed. There are some things an author must say if he is to deal with his subject at all. There are others that he introduces not because he has to do so but because he wishes to do so. These surely are among the parts of his work that will show up his interests and presuppositions most clearly. An author who set out to tell the story of the first three decades of the church's life could hardly fail to mention its expansion from Jerusalem to Rome, but it was not necessary that he should mark the passage with references to Sidon, Cyprus, Cilicia, Pamphylia, Myra, Lycia, Cnidos, Crete, Salmone, Fair Havens, Lasaea, Phoenix, Clauda, Syrtis, Adria, Malta, Syracuse, Regium, Puteoli, Appii Forum and the Three Taverns. These stations, and the accompanying narrative, are in no way essential. That means they are in the text because Luke found them interesting and wished them to be there. Again, a historian of the first three decades could hardly avoid writing of Paul, but it was not necessary that the story of Paul's journey should be told at six times greater length than the report of his Areopagus speech, that we should hear his landsman's advice to captain and crew, the number of his fellow travellers, the changes he was required to make *en route*, the rainy weather he encountered in Malta and so on. These things are in Acts because Luke enjoyed writing about them; and he enjoyed writing about them because he was the sort of man who enjoyed writing about that sort of thing.

A study of Acts 27[3] may therefore illustrate some of those themes of Acts that are most characteristic of its author and significant for his work. I shall deal with three.

1

In the first place there arises the question where the story came from. It is told, as are some other narratives in Acts, in the first person plural: We were to sail to Italy (27:1); Aristarchus was with us (27:2); we put in at Sidon (27:3); and so on, up to the end – we learned that the island was called Malta (28:1). The question of the sources of Acts is thus raised in a special form. It is well known that different views are held with regard to these 'We-passages': that they represent the author's own recollections, taken perhaps from a personal diary; that the author drew them from such a record kept by another person, who was an eye-witness; that they are an expansion of a Pauline itinerary, which originally contained little more than place-names; that they are pure fiction, cast in this form in order to add verisimilitude to the narrative and claim authority for it. There are difficulties in all these views and it is not easy to decide between them. Chapter 27 may throw some light upon them.

One of the most interesting recent studies of the 'We-passages' in general and of chapter 27 in particular has been made by V. K. Robbins,[4] who argues that the use of the first person plural was simply a characteristic of first-century accounts of voyages; it is a feature of style from which conclusions ought not to be drawn regarding the source of the information given. He writes (pp. 10–11; cf. p. 225): '(a) the genre of the sea voyage narrative within Greek literature was first person plural narration; (b) the standards of historiography brought in a necessity for third person narration, but, in spite of this, first person plural narration emerges in accounts of battles and voyages'. It is this emergence of the first person plural in association with, or in alternation with, a third person, singular or plural, that forms a particularly striking parallel with Acts, and leads Dr Robbins to conclude, 'The evidence within contemporary Mediterranean literature suggests that the author of Luke-Acts used "we" narration as a stylistic device within the sea voyages' (p. 13; cf. p. 229).

Particularly striking – if Dr Robbins' evidence will support his case. I shall consider only what seem to be among the strongest and most important examples. Many of those cited are undoubtedly passages in which the author was (or at least wishes to suggest that he was) taking part in the journey he describes. I can see no significance in such passages, even when the plural alternates with the singular. Thus Dr Robbins quotes *Odyssey* 9.39–41:[5] 'From Ilios the wind bore me and brought me to the Cicones, to Ismarus. There I sacked the city and slew the men.' A little later, however, we read (9.62–3): 'From there we sailed on, grieved at heart, glad to have escaped death, though we had lost our dear comrades.' I do not draw, with Dr Robbins, the conclusion that 'first person *plural* narration becomes a formulaic means for launching the ship, sailing for a number of days, and beaching the ship at the end of the voyage' (p. 3; p. 217). It is simply that in any vehicle larger than a bicycle there may well be a number of passengers who become, for a time, a community. 'I left Durham on the 14.55, and we reached London on time.' So *we* did. Moreover, to take up Dr Robbins' illustration, Odysseus was not only a member but the leader of a group, and some alternation is natural. In the intervening score of lines he has differentiated himself sharply from his men, who have been behaving very foolishly; now he has got them together and 'we', united once more, take the boat to sea.

Other examples, even some that are initially impressive, lose their force on examination. Thus Dr Robbins refers (p. 10; p. 225) to Julius Caesar, and claims that he 'allowed first person plural comments within a third person narrative style . . . in at least one voyage account the author allows first person plural to intrude.' He then cites *Gallic War* 5.11 and concludes that 'an autobiographical feature is allowed within historiography, especially in battles and a voyage. Is it too much to suggest that this becomes a characteristic typology for historiography in the first century BC and AD, and that the writer of Luke-Acts construes his narrative in relation to this typology?' (ibid.). Examination of the passage cited does nothing to justify this conclusion. In the first place, the passage does not describe a voyage. In the second, though the opening words quoted by Dr Robbins come from 5.11, the 'we' is in 5.13, though this is not indicated. In fact, thirdly, the 'we' does not occur in narrative at all. 5.11 is narrative; Dr Robbins translates, 'When the ships had been beached and the camp thoroughly well entrenched, Caesar left the same forces as before to guard the ships . . .' Narrative: and we note that the beaching of the ships (*subductis navibus*) is *not* expressed in the first person plural. 5.13 contains geographical and meteorological observations. Caesar mentions Mona,[6] and says that there are also other islands. It is of these (*de quibus insulis*), not of Mona only,[7] that some have written that 'at the winter solstice night lasts for thirty days. Of this we found nothing by our inquiries, except that by careful measurements, made by the water clock (*ex aqua*), we saw that the nights were shorter than on the continent'. Caesar's customary third person of narrative would have been out of place here.

Dr Robbins goes on to cite *The Voyage of Hanno the Carthaginian*, a document of uncertain date, probably translated into Greek from Punic, so that, incidentally, if it is a literal translation any stylistic observations made on the basis of it will apply rather to Punic than to Greek. Dr Robbins rightly observes that the document begins with narration in the third person singular and shifts into the first person plural. In fact, the whole document apart from a very short opening paragraph is in the first person. It is represented as Hanno's account, which he set up in the holy place of Kronos.[8] The opening paragraph then proceeds with the official Carthaginian decision: 'The Carthaginians decided[9] that Hanno should sail beyond the Pillars of Hercules and found cities of the Liby-Phoenicians. And he sailed with sixty fifty-oared ships and a multitude of men and women, in number thirty thousand, and food and other supplies.' After this Hanno tells in natural terms the story of what 'we did'. Thus we have first the Carthaginian resolution, then Hanno's narrative.

Dr Robbins finds a further example in the Antiochene Acts of the Martyrdom of Ignatius, 'where third person narration shifts unannounced to first person plural in relation to a sea voyage' (p. 12).[10] 'Third person narration is established as the style for recounting the events which occur . . . However, when a sea voyage begins the narration shifts, without explanation, to first person plural' (p. 12; cf. p. 227). If the whole story is read it appears at once that this is not correct. The first person does not begin where the voyage does. '*He* went down from Antioch to Seleucia, and from thence *he* set sail (κατελθὼν . . . εἴχετο τοῦ πλοός). And having put in at the city of the Smyrnaeans after much stress of weather, *he* disembarked . . . *he* set sail from Smyrna . . . *he* put in at Troas . . . *he* took ship and sailed across the Hadriatic sea . . . '[11] It is after this that the first person is introduced, not because the author is giving a summary of the voyage but for a reason which it is not difficult to see. The ship is approaching Puteoli; Ignatius wishes to land there in order to follow as closely as possible in the steps of Paul, but unfavourable weather prevents this. Later the weather improved. 'Thus in one single day and night, meeting with favourable winds, we ourselves were carried forward against our will, mourning over the separation which must soon come between ourselves and this righteous man [Ignatius]; while he had his wish fulfilled, for he was eager to depart from the world quickly, that he might hasten to join the Lord whom he loved' (§5). That is, *we* (Ignatius's companions) would have welcomed delay in Puteoli, for it would have postponed our loss of our master; *he* (Ignatius) rejoiced in the quicker journey, because it brought nearer the day of martyrdom for which he longed. There is no sea voyage formula here.

Dr Robbins' interesting exploration of ancient seafaring narratives is to be taken seriously and should be continued, but I do not think that his conclusions can be accepted, even in their latest form. In fact, the occurrence of the first person plural in such narratives means, in almost every case, that the writer was claiming to be present – and that not only on the sea. Just as the 'we' of Acts is not confined to the water so neither is it in, for example, the voyage of Hanno. Of course, any of the authors concerned may be lying – he would like to be thought to have been present though in truth he was not. And he may perhaps quote someone else's first person narrative, though I do not find that this happened. There is therefore, if we are judging by analogy, a fair measure of probability in what may seem an old-fashioned, and was to me an unexpected, conclusion, namely, that the narrative of Acts 27 was written by one who actually made the voyage. It is true that difficulties remain in this view. E. Haenchen,[12] for example, points out that Paul is treated as a person of consequence who has the opportunity of giving advice about the conduct of the voyage, whereas in truth he was a prisoner on the way to trial. Three things, however, may be said about this. First, in the stress of a storm any man who keeps his head may be listened to. Secondly, Festus and Agrippa had (according to Acts) decided that Paul was innocent, indeed that there was virtually no case for him to answer. They were well disposed towards him, and may have given appropriate instructions to the centurion. Thirdly, we see here precisely the way in which a story could develop: Paul's muttered forebodings to Luke become public pronouncements. Whether the person who wrote the eye-witness account of the voyage was the author of Acts as a whole is another question, which I am not at present discussing.

2

'Paul's muttered forebodings to Luke': these words provide a transition to the second topic, for they may sound like the rationalizing of a narrative that has a very different atmosphere. Paul, prisoner as he is, is a figure who grows throughout the story till he becomes undoubtedly the dominant character, and one recalls the popular, perhaps now the accepted view, that in Acts Luke depicts the apostles as belonging to the category of θεῖοι ἄνδρες, divine men. A very distinguished New Testament scholar, H. Koester, writes:[13]

> The same theology of the divine man is even more blatantly present in the Lucan Acts of the Apostles. What the apostles do in their mighty works corresponds exactly to the things Jesus did *in his lifetime* (contrast Paul, who sees *Jesus' death* documented in his own apostolic life!). Thus, the apostle has become the successor of his master, is endowed with the same divine power, and is guided by the same divine spirit. Even Paul himself, as Acts sees him, has now become a primary example of the missionary who is a "divine man" – the same Paul who wrote 2 Corinthians against such an understanding of the apostolic ministry. The elements which are constitutive for the image of the missionary in Luke's Acts of the Apostles correspond exactly to those found among Paul's opponents in 2 Corinthians: powerful preaching, spiritual exegesis of Scripture, performance of miracles, visionary experiences.

This assertion has been so often uncritically accepted that it is necessary to observe bluntly that it contains statements that are unproved or plainly mistaken. I shall not linger over the fact that its representation of the Pauline epistles is so one-sided as to be seriously misleading. It is true that Paul speaks of carrying about in his body the dying of Jesus (2 Cor.4:10); it is also true that in the same verse he explains his purpose in doing so: that (ἵνα) the life of Jesus too may be manifested in our body. Paul speaks of miracles he has performed (Rom.15:19; 2 Cor.12:12; cf. Gal.3:5), and of visions he has received (1

Cor.9:1; 15:8; 2 Cor. 12:1; Gal.1:16). If 'spiritual exegesis of Scripture' refers to a non-literal, non-historical kind of interpretation, it is to be found in chapter after chapter of the undoubtedly genuine letters. There is an outstanding example in 2 Corinthians 3. Paul depreciates his powers as a preacher, but they seem to have been effective as a converting instrument. What we may – and Dr Koester should – say about Paul is that he possessed and used these gifts (as he might himself have said) *as if he had them not* – ὡς μή; and this is a very different proposition, different both theologically and phenomenologically. That Dr Koester's view of the Corinthian 'invaders', in which he follows D. Georgi,[14] is mistaken I have sought to show in a number of publications; this is, for the present, less important.

The question before us at present is whether Dr Koester has given a correct picture of the apostles in Acts. I have to confess that I once came fairly near to giving such an account myself. I did not go quite so far,[15] and the more I have studied Acts the less inclined I am to accept the popular θεῖος ἀνήρ picture of the Acts apostles. The divine man is characterised, caricatured perhaps, by Celsus.

> There are many . . . who prophesy . . . It is an ordinary and common custom for each one to say: I am God (or a son of God, or a divine Spirit). And I have come. Already the world is being destroyed. And you, O men, are to perish because of your iniquities. But I wish to save you. And you shall see me returning again with heavenly power. Blessed is he who has worshipped me now![16]

Here speaks the divine man; and this is precisely how the apostles in Acts do not speak. Indeed, they go out of their way to contradict anything of the kind. 'Men of Israel, why do you marvel at this, or why do you gaze at us as though by our own power or piety we had made him walk?' (Acts 3:12). 'Peter raised (Cornelius) up, saying, Get up; I too am a man' (10:26). 'When they heard it, the apostles Barnabas and Paul tore their clothes and sprang into the crowd, shouting out, Men, why are you doing these things? We too are men of like passions with yourselves, bringing you the good news that you should turn from these vanities to the living God' (14:14–15). It is true that in Acts the main actors, Peter and Paul, come out of the story unharmed (though not unhurt); but this does not mean that the story consists exclusively of miraculous escapes and happy endings. Peter and John are imprisoned (5:18), the apostles are beaten

(5:40), Stephen is killed (7:60). Paul is attacked and escapes from Damascus in a basket (9:25). James is executed and Peter imprisoned (12:2, 3). Paul and Barnabas are persecuted (13:50). At Iconium there is a move to stone Paul and Barnabas (14:5). At Lystra Paul is stoned and left for dead (14:19). At Philippi Paul and Silas are stripped, beaten, and imprisoned (16:22–23). It is idle to continue the list. It would be wrong to overlook the fact that the apostles do perform wonders and usually emerge safely from their sufferings. Luke emphasises that they are not divine because it is necessary to do so. But he insists, through their mouths, that the resemblance is superficial and misleading. They are witnesses to one other than themselves, who alone is Lord. Their knowledge is limited (1:7); their effectiveness is in the name of Christ, not in their own.

At this point we may return to Acts 27; 28. Here there are, as there are elsewhere in Acts, features that might be taken to suggest that Paul is a supernatural person. (a) He shows supernatural knowledge of what is to happen. His forecast in 27:10 is indeed not necessarily to be thought of as other than a meteorological prediction. The Fast (that is, the Day of Atonement) was past, and it was acknowledged that after this date sailing was a risky business and might well lead to the loss of ship and life. But 27:21–26 is genuine prediction: there will be no loss of life but only of the ship. (b) He gives advice which contributes to the well-being of the whole company. At 27:31 he tells the centurion and his men that the sailors must not be allowed to leave the ship; at 27:34 he urges all to take food. Compare also 27:10, where Paul implicitly advises the centurion and the whole company to stay at Fair Havens for the winter. (c) At 27:23 he reports that he has had a vision and audition of an angel. (d) At 28:3–5 Paul is bitten by a snake but suffers no harm. (e) At 28:8, 9 he cures the father of Publius, and many other islanders, of their sicknesses. (f) Most striking of all, at 28:6 the islanders, disabused of the notion that Paul is fleeing from justice, decide that he is a god, ἔλεγον αὐτὸν εἶναι θεόν. From all these indications it might seem reasonable to infer that Luke intended to represent Paul as a divine man, but, as elsewhere, there are other considerations which mean that we arrive at the result: you might think that that was what he was; but he was not.

It will have been observed that the two predictions contradict each other. According to the first, there will be loss of the ship and of life; according to the second, there will be loss of the ship but not of life. Luke does not draw attention to this discrepancy, but he can hardly have been unaware of it and may well have thought that the first prediction represented (as I have suggested) Paul's human opinion, the second what was communicated to him by the angel. He did not possess supernatural knowledge in his own right. To suggest (27:33) that men who have gone without food for a fortnight would find that something to eat would do them good is common sense. To give warning (27:31) that the ship and its passengers would be in trouble if deserted by the ship's crew also seems good sense, though there are commentators who think that the sailors knew very well what they were doing and that Paul's advice was foolish. Miracles are not uncommon in the New Testament; Paul himself believed that he performed them but certainly did not for that reason think himself divine. Most important of all, however, are two simple observations. (a) When Paul reports the angelic message he speaks of the God 'whose I am and whom I serve'; that is, he affirms plainly that so far from being himself a god he is a servant and worshipper of one who truly is God. There is no hint that he is θεῖος; rather the contrary. (b) Those who think him to be a god are οἱ βάρβαροι (28:2, 4). A Greek could hardly pour greater scorn on their opinion. They were ignorant savages and knew no better. It is to be noted that there are no conversions on Malta. The inhabitants were very impressed, loaded the travellers with honours, and supplied what they needed, but their response was not the response of Christians. For Luke, to think of Paul as God was to misconceive both the man and his message. Greeks and Romans were by no means always convinced and converted but they did not make such a crass mistake as the barbarian Maltese and the Lycaonian inhabitants of Lystra (14:11–18), or, if they did, were speedily convinced of their error (10:25–26).

Thus the story of the voyage and shipwreck throws unexpected light on a major question regarding Acts and confirms the conclusion, based on Acts as a whole, that a widely held view is completely mistaken.

3

We have already noted the fact that in the course of the voyage, after a fortnight's fighting with the storm during which the crew had eaten nothing, Paul encouraged them to take food; this, he said, would make for their σωτηρία, a usefully ambiguous word which could refer to general well-being or to salvation in a Christian sense. He proceeded to set them an example, initiating a meal in which all shared. The language in which this action is described is very striking. It may be set out (from Acts 27:35–36), with certain parallels, as follows:

λαβὼν ἄρτον: cf.λαβὼν ἄρτον, Luke 22:19; λαβὼν δὲ τοὺς πέντε ἄρτους, Luke 9:16.

εὐχαρίστησεν τῷ θεῷ: cf. εὐχαριστήσας ... εὐχαριστήσας, Luke 22:17, 19; εὐλόγησεν, Luke 9:16.

κλάσας: cf. ἔκλασεν, Luke 22:19; κατέκλασεν, Luke 9:16.

ἤρξατο ἐσθίειν: cf. ἐπιθυμίᾳ ἐπεθύμησα τοῦτο τὸ πάσχα φαγεῖν, Luke 22:15.

ἐπιδιδοὺς καὶ ἡμῖν (Western Text): cf. διαμερίσατε εἰς ἑαυτούς, Luke 22:17; ἔδωκεν αὐτοῖς, Luke 22:19; ἐδίδου τοῖς μαθηταῖς, Luke 9:16.

προσελάβοντο τροφῆς: cf. ἔφαγον καὶ ἐχορτάσθησαν πάντες, Luke 9:17.

It seems unthinkable that Luke should have forgotten that he had written at significant points in his gospel the words that he uses here, and very improbable that the words were not used, and were not known by him to be used, by the church of which he was a member at its regular meeting for supper. We should recall also his references in Acts to the breaking of bread: 2:42, 46; 20:7, 11.

In the light of these parallels what are we to say of the meal over which Paul presided on the ship? As far as language goes it is more 'eucharistic' than any other passage in Acts; here only does the word εὐχαριστέω occur, and here only is the leading figure said to take (λαμβάνω) the loaf before breaking it. The action is a necessary one, but the coincidence in language with that of the Last Supper can hardly be accidental. At the same time, however, the whole context demands not a purely symbolic but a real meal, eaten to overcome the physical hunger of men who have for days been too busy and pre-occupied to eat. Paul himself began to eat, and the others took food (προσελάβοντο τροφῆς; cf. μετελάμβανον τροφῆς, 2:46). The whole company of 276 persons (27:37) did not eat from the loaf Paul took and broke; they were drawing on the ship's stores. The enumeration just mentioned includes sailors, soldiers, and Paul's party: ἤμεθα δὲ αἱ πᾶσαι ψυχαί. No distinction is made, except in the use of the third person plural in verses 36, 38. The Christians did not withdraw to hold a special, still less a secret, rite of their own: ἐνώπιον πάντων (27:35) is clear, though possibly mentioned as an unusual feature.

These facts are usually, and quite understandably, taken to constitute a problem; but it will be worthwhile to examine the presuppositions that make them a problem. We have few facts about the very early Christian eucharist, and the lack of facts must not be compensated by assumptions based on the practice of later times. Thus, for example, it is very often assumed that the eucharist was sharply distinguished from other Christian gatherings and that those who had not been initiated into the Christian faith were carefully excluded, the proceedings being kept secret from all outsiders. This practice indeed obtained at a later time. The Catechetical and Mystagogical lectures of Cyril of Jerusalem, for example, make this very clear.[17] Only those who have successfully completed the catechumenate are admitted, and they are given the requisite information only at the last moment. This was the practice in the fourth century. Was it normal practice in the first? It is certainly true that as we move back into the second century there was less secrecy, if we may judge from the readiness of Justin to include in a published work[18] a fair amount of detail about the Christian meal and the food 'which we call eucharist'. In many commentaries on 1 Cor.14:23 (ἐὰν ... εἰσέλθωσιν δὲ ἰδιῶται ἢ ἄπιστοι) it is tacitly assumed that the 'coming together' (συνέλθῃ ἡ ἐκκλησία ὅλη ἐπὶ τὸ αὐτό) referred to cannot be that of 1 Cor.11:17–34, the gathering for the κυριακὸν δεῖπνον, although the language is the same: 11:17 ... συνέρχεσθε ... 18 ... συνερχομένων ὑμῶν ἐν ἐκκλησίᾳ ... 20 συνερχομένων οὖν ὑμῶν ἐπὶ τὸ αὐτό ... 33 ... συνερχόμενοι εἰς τὸ φαγεῖν ... 34 ... ἵνα μὴ εἰς κρίμα συνέρχησθε ... There is no reason in the text for distinguishing two kinds of gathering, one for prophesying and other kinds of speech, which outsiders might attend, the other for the sacred meal, from which they were excluded. The presence of outsiders at the meal would be the more natural if, as is very probable, it was not purely symbolical but one which satisfied the physical hunger of the participants.

Overlapping with this is a second assumption, that the sacred meal, the eucharist, that which we call (though the New Testament does not) the sacramental meal, was clearly distinguished from all other meals. Every Jewish meal was a religious occasion; Paul's εὐχαριστέω (in Acts, and in 1 Cor.11:24) and his εὐλογία, εὐλογέω (1 Cor.10:16) correspond to the Jewish *berakah* which preceded meals, and as words they will not have served to distinguish one meal from another. If the story (also Lucan) of the encounter of two disciples with Jesus at Emmaus (Luke 24:28–32) may be taken as representative of what sacred meals meant to Luke and the Lucan church, we may fairly say that Christians could never be sure when a meal might turn out to have a eucharistic, sacramental character. Liturgical formulas could not guarantee that it would do so, nor would the absence of such formulas prevent it. Christ would manifest his presence if and when he chose; he controlled what was to happen, and was not to be manipulated. A group of Christians sitting together at the end of the day over their bread and wine might find their weariness transformed by a presence they could not account for; but on other evenings there was nothing to do but push back the chairs and go to bed.

Having questioned some assumptions, and speculated a little on its religious environment, we may return to our text and make a few simple observations. The first is that Luke describes the meal on the ship in unmistakably eucharistic terms; neither he nor his Christian readers can have failed to notice the allusions. Yet these terms and allusions are all such as are rooted in ordinary Jewish practice; Paul might well have seemed to be simply a Jew saying grace before his meal. A second observation is that the reference to bread is not accompanied by the use of wine. It may suffice to remark simply that the fetching, pouring out, and drinking of wine in hurricane conditions would be incredible and ludicrous; but one recalls also that though Acts contains other references to the breaking of bread it never mentions the use of wine. This, however, is not the place to pursue H. Lietzmann's theory[19] of two primitive eucharists, one with and one without wine, or any more complicated alternative. Perhaps we may say that the proceedings were somewhat irregular; but even in much later times emergencies have led to a good deal of variation in sacramental practice. Thirdly, there is no attempt to maintain any kind of secrecy; Paul spoke and acted ἐνώπιον πάντων (27:35). To say this, however, is not to say that everyone present understood his words and actions in the same way. The Christians present no doubt saw the full meaning of what was going on, and to them the food they took not only broke a dangerous fast but proclaimed the presence of the crucified Lord. Some noting this may have been led into their fellowship. To others, the food revived their bodily strength – that, and nothing more.

I have written the last paragraph as if we had before us a plain factual account of something that really happened. The first part of this paper may suggest that that is indeed true – that we have a first-hand eye-witness account of the events of the voyage. But it may not be so. The story may be Luke's fiction. In either case we should be justified in ascribing to Luke and his church a primitive kind of receptionism in their understanding of the Supper. By this I mean not a Pelagian interpretation of the Supper, which ascribes all initiative and effectiveness to the human participant, whose faith, in effect, creates any value the event may have, but the recognition that since the divine initiative seeks the response of faith, the same initiative on the same occasion, whether expressed in word or in action, will have different effects on different witnesses and participants. It would express this in too rigid a way if we were to say that Paul's Christian companions celebrated a eucharist while the ship's company by filling their stomachs restored their failing physical energy. Paul too ate a meal; and it may be that some of the crew found that what was going on was a 'converting ordinance'. What we may affirm is that the meal on the doomed ship points to a Lucan understanding of the Lord's Supper which shows an often neglected glimpse of early Christian life and thought.

Notes

1. It is perhaps appropriate that an earlier form of this paper was once read to the Hull Theological Society. The only sadness that marked that occasion was that Anthony was not present; he had already left Hull. But I can now look forward to the trenchant comments that he would have made orally.
2. *The Purpose of Luke-Acts* (Edinburgh, 1982).
3. I include also 28:1–10.
4. First in a Society of Biblical Literature Seminar paper, 'By Land and by Sea: a Study in Acts 13–28' and 'The We-Passages in Acts and Ancient Sea Voyages' in *Biblical Research* (1975). These were combined and somewhat expanded in 'By Land and by Sea: The We-Passages and Ancient Sea Voyages', in *Perspectives on Luke-Acts*, ed. by C. H. Talbert, Macon, Georgia, and Edinburgh, 1978. This last has been reprinted in a privately circulated volume of Dr Robbins' papers; his generosity in giving me a copy almost makes me ashamed to disagree with him in public. I give two page references, to the second and third publications respectively.
5. I use Dr Robbins' translation.
6. For Caesar, the Isle of Man, as Dr Robbins rightly renders.
7. As Dr Robbins' abbreviated translation suggests.

8. ὃν καὶ ἀνέθηκεν ἐν τῷ τοῦ Κρόνου τεμένει.
9. ἔδοξε Καρχηδονίοις, official language.
10. On p. 226 of the latest version the last words are 'as the author gives a summary of the voyage'. This, however, does not quite succeed in putting things to rights; see below.
11. There is much more in §§3 and 5. Dr Robbins and I both use J. B. Lightfoot's translation.
12. *Die Apostelgeschichte* (Kritisch-exegetischer Kommentar über das Neue Testament, Göttingen, 1977) p. 678.
13. J. M. Robinson and H. Koester, *Trajectories through Early Christianity* (Philadelphia, 1971) p. 191.
14. *Die Gegner des Paulus im 2. Korintherbrief*, Wissenschaftliche Monographien zum Alten und Neuen Testament 11 (Neukirchen-Vluyn, 1964).
15. *Luke the Historian in Recent Study* (London, 1961) pp. 12–15, 58.
16. Origen, *Contra Celsum* 7.9.
17. Cf. *Apostolic Constitutions* 8.12: 'Let none of the catechumens, none of the hearers, none of the unbelievers, none of the heterodox, stay here.'
18. 1 *Apology* 61.
19. *Messe und Herrenmahl* (Arbeiten zur Kirchengeschichte 8, Bonn, 1926) especially pp. 249–63.

5

The Offender and the Offence: A Problem of Detection in 2 Corinthians[1]

Margaret E. Thrall

In 2 Cor. 2: 5–11 Paul refers obscurely to some anonymous offender who has caused pain both to the apostle himself and to the whole Christian community in Corinth. Some penalty has been imposed, and it seems that the offender has been moved to penitence. In consequence, Paul urges that he should be forgiven, and assured of the congregation's love for him. In the preceding verses there is mention also of an earlier apostolic letter to Corinth which was clearly concerned with the same incident, since its composition had been an occasion of considerable distress. To this matter Paul returns in 7: 5–13, where he describes how the letter had been received. Titus, its bearer, has been able to assure him that it has evoked a thoroughly satisfactory reaction. It had certainly caused grief to the Corinthians, but this had led to penitence, to zealous support for Paul, and to eagerness to prove their own fundamental innocence. He can now tell them, therefore, that he wrote it, not on account either of the wrongdoer or of the person injured, but so that his readers might come to realise the extent of their own zeal on his behalf. If we put together the evidence in these two chapters, we get the following sequence of events:

(1) the commission of the offence;
(2) Paul's letter about it;
(3) the Corinthians' favourable reaction, and their imposition of a penalty on the offender;
(4) Titus's return to Paul with the good news about the reception of the letter;
(5) Paul's response in 2 Cor. 2: 5–11 and 7: 5–13.

After all this, however, we are still left entirely in the dark about the nature of the offence and the identity of its perpetrator. Traditionally he was identified with the man who committed incest, whose punishment Paul calls for in 1 Cor. 5. We shall discuss this briefly, then look at some more recent theories, and finally propose a hypothetical reconstruction of the situation, which will attempt to do justice to all the items of evidence which can be gleaned from Paul's obscure and tantalising allusions to it.

The Traditional Interpretation

The all but unanimous exegetical tradition of the ancient church is represented by Chrysostom, who clearly identifies the offender with the man guilty of the πορνεία to which Paul refers in 1 Cor. 5:1–5.[2] It is true that this exegesis was opposed by Tertullian. But his was scarcely an impartial view, since he was contesting the Catholic Church's claim to have the power to reconcile penitent fornicators, and was determined to deprive the Catholics of what might appear to be scriptural support for their position, i.e. Paul's lifting of the sentence of excommunication he had originally imposed on the incestuous man.[3] Furthermore, P. E. Hughes may be correct in claiming that Tertullian's counter-arguments serve to underline the fact that the traditional interpretation was well established in the church little more than a century after the apostolic age. Hughes himself would count this as one of the arguments in its favour.[4] The other main argument consists in the verbal parallels between 1 Cor. 5:1–5 and 2 Cor. 2: 5–11. In both cases the man in question is referred to as τις (1 Cor. 5:1; 2 Cor. 2:5), and as ὁ τοιοῦτος (1 Cor. 5:5; 2 Cor. 2:6–7), and in both contexts there is mention of Satan (1 Cor. 5:5; 2 Cor. 2:11).[5]

It can hardly be said, however, that the traditional view is compelling. The early tradition may well have derived simply from the internal evidence of the letters themselves, with their allusions in the first canonical epistle to an individual offender who was to receive some specific punishment, and in the second to an offender who had been punished. Furthermore, the traditional interpretation requires that the Painful Letter mentioned in 2 Cor. 2:3–4 be identified with our present 1 Corinthians, and the opinion of the majority of commentators is that 1

Corinthians as a whole does not fit Paul's own description of his state of mind when he wrote the Painful Letter.[6] The verbal parallels do not require the identification of the two offenders either. As regards the use of τις, the reasons for it may be different in the two cases. In the first instance, it is by no means improbable that Paul himself did not know the man's name. It is hearsay evidence that he is relying on for his information, and it may not have been too precise. Moreover, since his own stay in Corinth on the occasion of the founding of the church there, other converts will have joined the congregation, who will have been unknown to him personally. In the second instance, where, as we hope to show, it is highly likely that he did know the culprit's identity, he may have used the anonymous form of address out of consideration for him, since he is now penitent.[7] Precisely the same reasons could be given for the use of τοιοῦτος in the two passages. In any case, Paul's use of ὁ τοιοῦτος (and its plural) is too varied to allow any conclusion to be drawn as to the identity of the offenders. In 1 Cor. 5:11 it refers to any Christian who is leading an immoral life; in 2 Cor. 10:11 it is used of one of Paul's opponents, but in 2 Cor. 12:2, 5 of himself; in Gal. 6:1 it refers to a Christian who has hypothetically committed a sin. The plural is used in a bad sense in Rom. 16:18 and 2 Cor. 11:13, but in a good sense in 1 Cor. 16:16, 18 and Phil. 2:29; it occurs in a neutral sense in 1 Cor. 7:28 and 15:48. The same can be said, with even greater justification, of the use of the indefinite τις. Reference to Satan does not necessarily tie the two passages together either. The thought of Satan seems to be present in Paul's mind in a general sort of way throughout the Corinthian correspondence: see (in addition to the two passages under consideration) 1 Cor. 7:5; 2 Cor. 11:14; 12:7; also 2 Cor. 4:4 (ὁ θεὸς τοῦ αἰῶνος τούτου); 2 Cor. 6:15 (Beliar); and 2 Cor. 11:3 (ὁ ὄφις). Furthermore, in writing about a second individual offender, he may have been reminded of the first, whom he had handed over temporarily to the control of Satan. In this second case he is desperately anxious that there should be no further gain for Satan through further loss to the church. This brings us to the main positive reason for rejecting the traditional view, i.e. the impossibility of equating the two penalties imposed. As Bruce points out, the handing over of the incestuous man to Satan 'suggests something more drastic and permanent than temporary suspension from certain privileges of church membership' – the penalty envisaged in 2 Cor. 2:6–7.[8]

Modern Theories

A basic presupposition of the two main types of theory to be discussed is
that the offence was something which affected Paul himself directly and
personally, either because he himself suffered it when present in Corinth
or because it was perpetrated against someone who represented him. In 2
Cor. 2:5 he says, εἰ δέ τις λελύπηκεν, οὐκ ἐμὲ λελύπηκεν. It is argued
that this makes sense only if a superficial view of the situation would
suggest that it was, in fact, Paul who had been subjected to injury.[9]
Hughes, it is true, would disagree, claiming that the statement must be
taken literally, and pointing to verse 10, where it is the Corinthians who
are allowed the initiative in forgiving the offender.[10] But in the second
clause of this verse Paul refers to his own forgiveness and refers to it in
the perfect tense, κεχάρισμαι, which indicates that he himself has
already taken the initiative. What is more, the highly personal tone of the
preceding reference to the Painful Letter (2:3–4) strongly confirms his
personal involvement. Consequently, we seem to be justified in accepting this basic presupposition. It must be allowed, however, that the
allusion to the injured person in 7:12 does give a rather different
impression. Paul says that he did not write his letter on account of the
man who committed the wrong, nor on account of the man who suffered
it: οὐχ ἕνεκεν τοῦ ἀδικήσαντος οὐδὲ ἕνεκεν τοῦ ἀδικηθέντος. This
third person reference to the ἀδικηθείς needs to be accounted for in any
satisfactory solution of the exegetical problem.

The two main forms of solution can be distinguished according to the
different answers given to the question of the identity of the person
against whom the injury was actually perpetrated; some exegetes
suppose him to be Paul's representative, others Paul himself in person.

Allo may be taken as typical of the former group. He would recon-
struct the situation in the following way.[11] After Paul's return to Ephesus
at the conclusion of his interim visit to Corinth, there took place in the
Corinthian church a serious act of injustice or some grave outrage. The
culprit met with complicity or excessive indulgence on the part of the
congregation at large, and their attitude cast doubt on their obedience to
Paul himself. He felt himself to be affected, at least indirectly. This was
because the direct victim of the outrage was someone who had close
personal ties with him and in some way represented his authority. Allo
does not think, however, that this person was either Timothy or Titus.

The offender was one of the newcomers to Corinth. He had grasped some opportunity of setting himself against those members of the church who wished to act in accordance with Paul's instructions, and had opposed in particular some member who had appealed to the apostle's authority.

At first sight this reconstruction may appear plausible, but it does, nevertheless, present certain difficulties. The identification of the ἀδικ-ηθείς with a member of the Corinthian church causes problems. Why does Paul not urge this individual to forgive the offender, as well as urging the congregation to do so? Alternatively, if he knew that the ἀδικηθείς had already forgiven the ἀδικήσας, why does he not say so? The only mention of individual forgiveness is Paul's own. Furthermore, to have regarded himself as directly affected by some insult offered to one of his Corinthian supporters might have been tantamount to encouraging the existence of that very Paul–party which he so strongly disapproves of in 1 Corinthians. It would be equally unsatisfactory to modify the theory somewhat, and to suppose that the ἀδικηθείς was either Timothy or Titus, i.e. one of the only two named persons whom we know to have been sent to Corinth as Paul's delegates. The former is co-signatory of 2 Corinthians, and the latter is mentioned several times within the epistle. Had either been involved in the incident, it would surely have been made clear that he had himself forgiven the offender.[12] But who else is there whom the apostle would have regarded as representing himself to such an extent that he would have been directly and personally affected by an injury inflicted on this other person? It may well be that it is correct to identify the ἀδικηθείς of 7:12 as someone other than Paul. All the same, in terms of the kind of theory just outlined it is difficult to explain satisfactorily who he might have been. The identification of the offender, moreover, with one of the newcomers to Corinth likewise causes problems. These, however, are common to one version of the second main solution, about to be discussed.

According to this second theory, it was actually Paul himself who was insulted to his face, during his interim visit to Corinth. J. Weiss supposes that the offender was leader of a coalition group of Cephas-supporters and libertines, united on the ground of common antagonism to Paul. Nothing had been done, it would appear, to effect the expulsion of the man who had committed incest. When the apostle arrived in Corinth and demanded that action should be taken, the offender 'flung violent insults in his face without anyone uttering a word of protest.'[13] It is obvious that opinions would vary as regards the precise nature of the opposition, but several commentators would agree with Weiss on the main point, i.e. that the offender had insulted Paul face to face in some outrageous way, and that the apostle had been humiliated, and had not, at the time, found himself able to deal with the situation.[14] Allo, on the other hand, rejects this form of solution precisely because it does entail the hypothesis of Paul's humiliation and inability to assert his authority. The apostle, he claims, was not the sort of person to put himself at a safe distance before attempting to repel an outrage affecting his apostolic status, not daring to complain except by letter, after he had left Corinth.[15] For Allo, Paul must always have been in control, and would never have suffered such a defeat as Weiss's theory implies. This is pure supposition, however. Had there been no apparent justification for the kind of charges reflected in 2 Cor. 10:9–11, why would the Corinthians so readily have given credence to them?

Several supporters of the theory that the injury was some insult offered to Paul would agree with Weiss that the offender was a Corinthian.[16] But Barrett argues that he was a visitor to Corinth, for two reasons. First, according to 2 Cor. 7:11 the Corinthians had proved their innocence in the matter. They had defended and vindicated themselves to Titus, and their protestations had been accepted both by Titus and by Paul himself. Secondly, they had punished the offender, which would hardly have been proper, had they shared his guilt. All the same, they did themselves have something to repent of (7:9). Barrett argues that the only way of integrating this evidence is to suppose that whilst the offender was closely associated with the Corinthian congregation he was not himself a member of it. He had challenged Paul's apostolic authority, claiming superior rights on his own account, and had thus insulted him and done him personal injury. Since he was not a Corinthian, the Corinthians themselves were in a sense innocent. Nevertheless, they had not rallied to Paul's support, so that on this count they had cause for penitence.[17] It is not at all clear, however, whether these suggestions solve all the problems. If the Corinthians' guilt lay in their not having come to Paul's support at the time when he was attacked, it is difficult to see how they could later have vindicated themselves as having been *in every respect* innocent (2 Cor. 7:11). According to this theory it was the apostle himself, present in person, who was insulted: he would have had firsthand knowledge of how they had behaved. There are objections also to the hypothesis that the offender was a visitor to Corinth. Would Paul have been as concerned as he appears to be in 2 Cor. 2:7–8 for the welfare of someone who was not a member of his own Corinthian community? Would a visitor have been subject to the discipline of the Corinthian church? Kümmel is clear that he would not, and that the wrongdoer was therefore a member of the Corinthian congregation.[18] Furthermore, if we try to determine who the visitor might have been, other difficulties arise. If he was simply a chance comer, why would he have behaved in the outrageous way postulated, and why and how would he have gained such an influence over the congregation that they would have permitted such behaviour? Did he, then, belong to an advance contingent of the opponents who make their appearance in the last four chapters of 2 Corinthians? If he did, it might be easier to see how he had established an ascendancy over the congregation, but very difficult to understand how he could have later submitted to a penalty they imposed on him, and even more difficult to believe that he would have displayed genuine remorse for his conduct. This simply does not square with the picture of these opponents in 2 Cor. 11:20.

Another Solution

Since all the theories we have considered have certain drawbacks, it is not superfluous to suggest yet another hypothetical reconstruction of events. As a preliminary, we shall note a common feature of a number of theories already advanced which has almost come to be accepted as essential to any reconstruction, but which is not, in fact, necessary at all, and which will not form part of the solution to be suggested here. We shall then look at the criteria which any theory would need to satisfy. Lastly, we shall propose a new theory and try to show how it meets the criteria.

The common feature in question is the supposition that the offence itself was some outrageous public insult, offered either to Paul or to one of his delegates or supporters. As Zahn points out, however, this is pure speculation, and is not positively supported by the language Paul actually uses. Certainly it is true that the idea of injured reputation could be included under the general heading of ἀδικεῖν. But there is no instance anywhere in biblical Greek where the verb or any of its cognates could be shown to mean insult, libel, or slander. The meaning is the general one of illegal action or illegal injury. Zahn quotes Aristotle:

> ἔστω δὴ τὸ ἀδικεῖν τὸ βλάπτειν ἑκόντα παρὰ τὸν νόμον (*Rhetoric* 1.10).[19]

If Paul had wished to speak of abuse or insult, either by word or by deed, he would have used λοιδορεῖν or ὑβρίζειν.[20] Kümmel, in agreement with Zahn, adds that the apostle would scarcely have interpreted a personal insult as a disturbance affecting the whole church, nor would he have left a promising mission-field in Troas to find out from Titus what they had done about it.[21] Thus the 'insult' theory is pure hypothesis, and, according to Kümmel, not very plausible either. This, perhaps, is debatable. Furthermore, it is true that in 1 Cor. 6:9–10 the λοίδοροι are included in the general category of the ἄδικοι who will not inherit the kingdom of God. All the same, Zahn's main point still remains valid and needs to be stressed. Paul's actual language provides no positive evidence for the 'insult' theory. Consequently, there is nothing to prevent our proposing some alternative identification of the nature of the offence.

Any alternative theory would need to account for the following items of evidence which emerge from a careful reading of the text.[22]

(1) The offence was a single definite act. This is indicated by the aorist participles in 7:12.
(2) It was something to which the verb ἀδικεῖν could properly be applied.
(3) It was a single individual who was responsible. Note the singulars in 2:5–8, 10 and 7:12.
(4) This person was subject to the discipline of the Corinthian church (2:6), and thus, in all probability, a Corinthian himself.
(5) Paul considered it an act which affected him personally (2:5, 10).
(6) In some sense, however, it had affected the whole community as well (2:5).
(7) The offence was something in which the church had appeared originally to be implicated, but also something that they were later able to prove themselves innocent of (7:11).
(8) Nevertheless, their own conduct had been such as to move them to

penitence when they received Paul's letter (7:9–10). The incident must have been of such a kind, therefore, as to involve them in some sort of guilt.

(9) The offence was of a very serious nature. It had caused Paul to write the Painful Letter, to postpone a further visit to Corinth, and then to abandon a promising opportunity of missionary work in Troas, in his anxiety to know from Titus what the response to his letter had been.

What, then, could the offence have been? The reconstruction we shall propose has something in common with a suggestion made originally by Krenkel and then taken up by Windisch.[23] Although the two theories are not identical, some points from this earlier reconstruction of events may usefully be noted. The suggestion is that the culprit had committed some legal offence of the kind referred to in 1 Cor. 6:11, and that this was connived at by the congregation. Perhaps it was a matter of injury to property. It may be that the injured party turned to Paul for redress and that the apostle's attempts to deal with the situation were harshly repudiated. Windisch draws attention to the use of ἀδικεῖν with reference to the violation of a person's legal rights in business and money transactions in Philem. 18 (εἰ δέ τι ἠδίκησέν σε ἢ ὀφείλει, τοῦτο ἐμοὶ ἐλλόγα) and Matt. 20:13 (the vineyard owner says to the labourer who expects more pay, ἑταῖρε, οὐκ ἀδικῶ σε); see also Lev. 6:2–5 (LXX 5:20–26), where the verb is used in a context which deals with matters such as robbery and deceitful dealing in respect of deposits or securities. Philo similarly uses it with reference to the pilfering of a deposit by a third party:

ἄτοπον γὰρ ἢ τὸν μηδὲν ἠδικηκότα ζημιοῦν ἢ τὸν συνδράμοντα εἰς φίλου πίστιν ὑφ᾽ ἑτέρων ἀδικηθέντα βλάβης αἴτιον ἐκείνῳ γενέσθαι. (*De Spec. Leg.* 4.34).[24]

Lastly, it occurs in 1 Cor. 6:7–8, used of the various injustices which were the subject of the litigation Paul disapproves of. Their nature is not specified, but in view of the fact that he urges the appointment of arbiters from amongst the congregation it seems very likely that it is business disputes, concerned with money or property, that he has in mind, rather than injury to reputation by means of insult or slander. This would be confirmed by the question in verse 8, διὰ τί οὐχὶ μᾶλλον ἀποστερεῖσθε; thus, this passage in 1 Corinthians may fit in very well with the passages Windisch draws attention to, which contain ἀδικεῖν with reference to financial matters.

In several respects this general suggestion about the nature of the offence is plausible and persuasive. But there is one thing which it does not explain. It does not explain how and why Paul himself could have seen himself as so directly affected by the *offender* that he needs both to repudiate the suggestion that his personal interest is of importance (2 Cor. 2:5) and also, paradoxically, to refer to his own forgiveness of the offender (2:10). Certainly, in terms of this theory, he would have been distressed by the attitude of the congregation to his attempts to deal with the situation. But in 2:5–10 this is not his concern: all the emphasis here lies on the guilt and forgiveness of the individual. Consequently, this reconstruction of events would need some modification.

The modification proposed here runs as follows. After Paul had arrived in Corinth on the occasion of his interim visit, one of the members of the Corinthian church handed over to him his own contribution to the collection the apostle was organising amongst his gentile churches for the benefit of the poor of the Jerusalem church. Up to this point he will have kept his savings at home, in accordance with the instruction in 1 Cor. 16:2. Perhaps he was now leaving Corinth for a while on business, and so had to entrust the money to someone else for safe keeping. He would have handed it over to Paul, initially, both because he may have wished him to be able to attest the amount contributed and also because he saw it as the apostle's business to appoint some local treasurer for the fund from among the members of the church. We may then suppose that Paul was robbed of this money, in circumstances which strongly suggested that some particular member of the congregation was responsible. The man denied the charge, however. It was the apostle's word against his, and the church as a whole was uncertain whom to believe. Because they did not immediately accept Paul's view of the matter, he began to suspect that some of them (perhaps in substantial numbers) might themselves have had something to do with the theft, at any rate as accomplices after the fact. Since he was unable to persuade them to take the necessary action he left Corinth, and returned to Ephesus. It is possible that he had originally intended to use his stay in Corinth to further, or even complete, his plans for the collection. Since the kind of incident we have postulated would have made it impossible for him to do this, there may have been little point in prolonging the visit, altogether apart from any personal humiliation he may have experienced. On his return to Ephesus he wrote the letter which caused such a revulsion of feeling amongst the Corinthians. They were moved to investigate more closely, and their investigation brought about the offender's confession and punishment.

Whilst this reconstruction is pure hypothesis, it does appear to satisfy the criteria listed earlier. The offence was a single specific act (1), committed by an individual (3), who was a member of the Corinthian church (4), and the verb ἀδικεῖν was obviously appropriate to it (2), as the evidence provided by Windisch shows (the reference in Philo to the pilfering of a deposit is of particular interest). The matter concerned Paul directly and personally because it was he from whom the money had been stolen (5). We may note, however, that this interpretation of events would easily allow us to identify the ἀδικηθείς of 7:12 with someone *other* than Paul, i.e. with the Corinthian who had originally deposited the money with him. In the kind of situation we are postulating, the actual ownership of the money would be a little ambiguous. In one sense it could be thought of as Paul's, in his capacity as organiser of the collection. In another sense, however, if the collection was not yet properly in train in Corinth, it could be seen as money on deposit, and as belonging still to the person who had deposited it. In ch. 2, Paul could be thinking in the former way, but in the latter fashion in ch. 7. In ch. 2 he speaks in the first person of his own forgiveness of the offender, whilst in ch. 7 he refers in the third person to some other injured party. And if he does not speak of the ἀδικηθείς as having directly forgiven the culprit, this could be because the man in question had left Corinth for a prolonged period of time, and so knew nothing of what had happened there after his departure. In some sense the community as a whole had also been injured (6), since the stolen money had been intended as part of the congregational contribution to the collection. Paul, however, had supposed some of them to have been positively implicated in the theft. But Titus, having heard the offender's confession and explanation, was able to assure him that this was not so (7). The congregation's guilt, of which they had repented, had lain in their doubting Paul's version of what had happened (8). The seriousness of the offence (9) would lie in its further repercussions. If not dealt with satisfactorily, it might well completely disrupt the plans for the collection in Corinth. Moreover, the implicit charge, as Paul would have felt it to be, that he was not telling the truth when he originally confronted the church with the situation would have appeared to be a serious challenge to his authority.

If the nature of the offence was such as has been suggested here, it might perhaps seem strange that it is not mentioned in chs 8–9, which are specifically concerned with the collection.[25] But if these chapters are part of the same letter as chs 1–7 one would not expect any further reference to something that has already received adequate attention in the preceding paragraphs. Alternatively, if they are to be separated from chs 1–7 (and perhaps from each other), ch. 8 would seem to be later than the first seven chapters, and Paul would not wish to refer again to a painful incident in the past that was now over and done with. If ch. 9 is also later, the same argument would apply, whilst, if it belonged to some earlier communication, it might have preceded the commission of the offence altogether. More positively it might be argued that Paul was, in fact, influenced, in the writing of ch. 8, by his recollection of it (whether the incident lay in the immediate or in the more remote past). This would help to account for his obvious concern to make his arrangements for the collection as foolproof as possible, so that no one who was involved in them could be accused of any kind of financial misconduct. Those Corinthians who had initially disbelieved his charge against the offender might also have insinuated that he was himself not altogether blameless in the matter. We might also have a more plausible explanation of the reference in 8:6 to the fact that Titus has already made a beginning in his work concerning the collection in Corinth. Other explanations of the nature of the offence fail at this point. For if it was some incident unconnected with the collection which had evoked the letter Titus took to Corinth, it is difficult to see that he would have been charged with getting the collection going at the same (unpropitious) time as he had to administer the apostle's stern rebuke in respect of the offence. But if the offence itself had something to do with the collection, and if the Corinthians seemed genuinely eager to make amends, he might well have thought it an exceedingly appropriate opportunity to revive their participation in the project.

Notes

1. This essay is a revised and expanded version of a paper read to the Hull Theological Society on 12 March 1982, at a meeting at which Professor Anthony Hanson was present. I count it as a privilege to be able to offer it now as a contribution to the Festschrift in his honour.
2. *Hom. in 1 Cor.* 15:1 (*MPG* 61.121); *Hom. in 2 Cor.* 4:3 (*MPG* 61.421).
3. Tertullian, *De Pudicitia* 13–16.
4. P. E. Hughes, *Paul's Second Epistle to the Corinthians* (Grand Rapids, 1962) pp. 62–3.
5. See, e.g., T. Zahn, *Introduction to the New Testament*, vol. 1 (Edinburgh, 1909) p. 348; Hughes, op. cit., p. 64 n.6.
6. See, e.g., A. Plummer, *A Critical and Exegetical Commentary on the Second Epistle of St. Paul to the Corinthians* (Edinburgh, 1915) p. 50; H. Windisch, *Der zweite Korintherbrief* (Göttingen, 1924) p. 82; F. F. Bruce, *1 and 2 Corinthians* (London, 1971) p. 184; C. K. Barrett, *A Commentary on the Second Epistle to the Corinthians* (London, 1973) p. 209.
7. Cf. P. Bachmann, *Der zweite Brief des Paulus an die Korinther*, 4th ed. (Leipzig, 1922) p. 133.
8. *1 and 2 Corinthians*, p. 185; cf. E.-B. Allo, *Saint Paul: seconde epître aux Corinthians*, 2nd ed. (Paris, 1956) p. 57.
9. H. Lietzmann, *An die Korinther I–II*, 4th ed. rev. by W. G. Kümmel (Tübingen, 1949) p. 105; Bachmann, op. cit., p. 112; Allo, op. cit., p. 56; Barrett, op. cit., p. 89.
10. Hughes, op. cit., pp. 64, 70.
11. Allo, op. cit., pp. 55–6, 62.
12. Cf. Windisch, op. cit., p. 238.
13. J. Weiss, *Earliest Christianity*, vol. 1 (New York, 1959) pp. 342–3; quotation on p. 343.
14. See, e.g., Plummer, op. cit., pp. xvi, xviii, 55, 225; Bruce, op. cit., p. 164; Barrett, op. cit., pp. 89, 213; R. Bultmann, *Der zweite Brief an die Korinther*, ed. E. Dinkler (Göttingen, 1976) p. 51.
15. Allo, op. cit., p. 61.
16. Plummer, Bruce and Bultmann (see the references in n. 14).
17. C. K. Barrett, "Ο'ΑΔΙΚΗΣΑΣ (2 Cor. 7:12)', *Verborum Veritas: Festschrift für Gustav Stählin*, ed. O. Böcher and K. Haacker (Wuppertal, 1970) pp. 149–57.
18. W. G. Kümmel, *Introduction to the New Testament* (London, 1966) p. 208.
19. 'Let injustice, then, be defined as voluntarily causing injury contrary to the law' (Loeb translation).
20. Zahn, op. cit., vol. 1, p. 349.
21. Lietzmann-Kümmel, op. cit., p. 198.
22. Cf. Allo, op. cit., pp. 55–6.
23. M. Krenkel, *Beiträge zur Aufhellung der Geschichte und der Briefe des Apostels Paulus* (Braunschweig, 1890) pp. 305–6; and Windisch, op. cit., pp. 11, 238–9.

24. 'Otherwise an innocent party would be mulcted and the person who ran to avail himself of the good faith of a friend would on account of the wrong he has suffered from others cause injury to that friend, and either of these is preposterous' (Loeb translation).
25. This point was made by the Revd George John at a meeting of the Bangor Theological Society.

6

Fashions in Exegesis: Ephesians 1:3

Ernest Best

This is not an attempt either to present an exegesis of Eph.1:3 or to trace the history of its exegesis. It is rather an attempt to see what particular issues occupied the attention of exegetes at particular times and if possible to account for some of these preoccupations. In order to carry this through and at the same time to limit the material I shall consider only the commentators and leave aside the more specialised material in monographs and articles in learned journals. New ideas tend first to appear in the latter and then work their way into commentaries, though it can often take quite an appreciable time for this to take place. Limitations of space forbid reference to every commentator. Many simply repeat what their predecessors have written with only minor linguistic variation. I shall therefore treat only those commentators who display new trends or stress old ones in a new way.

In English, Eph. 1:3 runs as follows:

> Blessed is the God and Father of our Lord Jesus Christ who has blessed us with every (all) spiritual blessing in the heavenlies in Christ.

It is only the beginning of a long sentence which runs through to verse 14. This raises the question of the relation of v.3 to what follows. Within the verse itself there are certain issues which must be discussed. There is no copula ('is') in the original; what should be inserted? What is the significance of the 'and' between 'God' and 'Father'? Why do we have a past tense in 'has blessed' (which translates the Greek aorist participle)? To whom does 'us' refer? Is 'every (all)' inclusive? What is a 'spiritual' blessing? What are 'the heavenlies'? What noun should be understood with this adjective? Is 'in Christ' to be taken locally, corporately, mystically, instrumentally? Other problems will appear as we proceed. The manner in which I have set out at least some of these questions follows the methods of modern scholarship. That in itself is an instance of 'fashion in exegesis'.

The first known commentator on Ephesians is Origen. Only fragments of his commentary survive[1]. Fortunately a reasonably long discussion of our verse is extant, though we cannot be sure we still possess all that Origen wrote.

He says that some have taken the reference to spiritual blessings as an attempt to distinguish Christian blessings from those of Leviticus and Deuteronomy which are physical. He accuses the 'heterodox' of doing this but does not identify them more exactly. Since he goes on to indicate that this permitted them to separate God from such a view (i.e. God is not interested in the blessings of Leviticus and Deuteronomy) it is probable that he has in mind those who reject the Old Testament, the Marcionites. This is confirmed when he argues that even under the Law there were spiritual blessings quoting Rom. 7:14 and points out that the prophets did not obtain material blessings such as those instanced in Deut. 28 (their barns were not filled). He also used Heb. 11:37–38 to prove his point.

He then discusses 'the heavenlies' and quotes Phil. 3:20 with its reference to citizenship in heaven and Matt. 6:19–21 about those who lay up treasures in heaven. These texts are used repeatedly by the Fathers in discussing this phrase. Origen points out that we have a past tense in 'has blessed' and not the future we would expect. He therefore suggests that 'in the heavenlies' should be understood as 'what is perceptible to the mind and beyond the senses'. He concludes that it is for our easier understanding of the passage that there is reference both to 'spiritual' and 'the heavenlies'.

A large part of the comment of Origen has then been dictated to him by an existing controversy, the Marcionite view of God and of the Old Testament, and therefore emerges at least in part from the situation of the church of his time. This is a clear example of what this paper hopes to disclose in exegesis. We note also that finding difficulty with the second clause, particularly with the past tense of the participle, he translates it into a meaning which he believes people can understand. Whereas the reference to Marcion disappears from later commentaries the attempt to find a suitable understanding of the second clause does not.

Jerome[2] knew Origen's commentary, acknowledges his debt to it[3] and in many instances simply rewrites it. It is possible that where he appears to add material to what our fragments of Origen tell us he is simply repeating portions of Origen which no longer survive. The additions which concern our text seem to be accounted for more easily in other ways. He drops the reference to the 'heterodox'; they no longer bothered him or the church of his period. Like Origen he recognises that the Old Testament prophets did not enjoy material blessings and that therefore the blessings of that Testament cannot be restricted to those which are physical. In his discussion of the heavenly blessings he introduces several more passages from the New Testament, viz. John 15:19; 1 Cor.15:49; Rom.8:9. He draws attention to one element of importance over and above the discussion of Origen. God is both the God and Father of our Lord Jesus Christ, i.e. the genitive is attached both to God and to Father. He was not necessarily the first to introduce this issue for we encounter it in other contemporary commentators. It arises almost certainly from the christological controversies of the period. If Christ is God can God be said to be his God? Jerome answers (others offer different answers) that God is God of the manward side of Christ and Father of the one who was Word of God from the beginning with God. Interestingly Jerome offers no grammatical arguments to sustain his view that the genitive is attached to both nouns. Long after the christological controversy has died down we find scholars in the modern period discussing this point in great detail but on grammatical grounds. There is then in Jerome and contemporary commentators an awareness of an exegetical problem, an awareness caused by contemporary theological concerns. It is not however possible to make a direct correlation of christological and grammatical views. Within the school of Antioch Theodore of Mopsuestia[4] and Theodoret of Cyrus[5] opt for the splitting of the reference to both God and Father and take the reference to God to be a reference to God as our God and that to Father to be one to him as Father of Christ; Chrysostom[6] however takes the phrase as one with God as God of the incarnate Jesus and Father of God the Word.

Theodore is interesting in other respects. He regards v.3 as a thanksgiving like the generally recognised thanksgivings of Phil.1:2; Col.1:3; 1 Thess.1:3; 2 Thess.1:3.He does not comment on the renewal (?) of the thanksgiving at 1:15–16. We shall see discussion of this emerging much later. Theodore explains 'blessed' as meaning that God is worthy to be praised. That he gives an explanation is curious for this is the normal meaning of the Greek root. What is not normal is its later use in the verse to indicate gifts by God.[7] The latter is a meaning derived from the Septuagint. Theodore joins together the two halves of the verse: God is worthy to be blessed because he has blessed us. This point which he is apparently the first to make recurs in many later commentators. He also discusses 'in Christ' and gives it an instrumental sense. More importantly he discusses the spiritual gifts in the heavenlies and isolates them as resurrection, immortality, the capability of not sinning, and the continual possession of good gifts. He thus places them in the future, concluding this from the reference to the heavenlies. But at this point he also brings in v.4 in order to indicate something of the way God has blessed us. He thus begins a trend which identifies the blessings with blessings mentioned in vv. 3–14. By means of 1 Cor.15:42–44 he relates 'spiritual' to the spiritual body which we have in the heaven. With him the possible difference between the blessings of the two testaments disappears, though this is by no means true of other Fathers. Chrysostom, for instance, denies that the Jewish blessings were spiritual and identifies the spiritual blessing as those of freedom, immortality, adoption, etc., picking up some of the themes of the succeeding verses. John 16:33 excludes any carnal blessings from their number. Without discussion Chrysostom and Theodoret do not give 'heavenlies' a local significance but refer to gifts, i.e. the noun to go with 'heavenlies' is not τόποι but πράγματα. Chrysostom now completely free from having to deal with Marcionites contrasts the blessings of v.3 with those of the Jews and employs Heb.3:5–6 to prove their superiority since Christ is superior to Moses. He also introduces a new identification of the blessings which he deduces from other parts of scripture as Christ's presence (John 14:23), as being built on the rock (Matt.7:24–25) and as being confessed before God by Christ (Matt.10:32–33). In addition he draws in the beatitudes (Matt.5:3 ff).

There is another strain in the Fathers which concentrates on exhortation rather than on exegesis and seems to have little to do with theological controversy. This stream is first found in Marius Victorinus Afer.[8] He moves from the phrase 'the Father of our Lord Jesus Christ' to the sonship of Christians. The reference to spiritual blessings in the heavenlies is used to remove any idea that believers are necessarily blessed in this world; Peter and Paul were not. Spiritual blessings belong to the future. Although the persecution of Peter and Paul is introduced there is no suggestion that spiritual blessings are regarded as compensation for the sufferings of persecution. With the exception of Origen all the other Fathers write from a period when persecution was no longer a threat. Marius in fact lies nearer the persecution period than any of them, except Origen, and perhaps his introduction of Peter and Paul is the reflection of an earlier exegesis, no longer extant, in which spiritual blessings in heaven were contrasted with persecution.

We must now move on more quickly looking only at a few commentators until we reach the modern period. Thomas Aquinas[9] notes the difficulty presented by the past tense 'has blessed' and explains it as Paul's certainty that God will bless in the future. He gives no justification for such a use of the aorist. He shows no awareness of the frequent distinction in the Fathers between Jewish and Christian blessings and indeed uses Ps.127:4 in his description of the blessings. His explanation of them is worked out in terms of efficient, material and final causes and so is governed by his general philosophical approach and terminology, an interpretation into the language of his own period and its type of understanding. Finally we should note that he is aware of the theological issue which lies in the 'and' of 'God and Father' and explains it.

While commentators of the Middle Ages are usually aware of what the Fathers have written Calvin[10] is the first of those we are examining who explicitly refers to them by name when he says he does not object to Chrysostom's contrast between the blessings of Moses and those of Christ. He notes that the adjective 'heavenlies' could be followed either by a word denoting place or gift and refuses to rule firmly in favour of one or the other. He includes a brief word study of 'bless' noting that it is used in four different ways in scripture: of men blessing God, of God blessing men, of men blessing one another in prayer, and of priestly blessings. He is aware that words can carry more than one meaning and that the context must determine between meanings. There is no theological discussion of 'God and Father'. This is true also of the commentary of H. Zanchius.[11] It is more surprising in his case since he did not restrict himself in any way as regards space. His is the longest commentary (some 750 pages) until Markus Barth. It is also surprising since he follows each portion of his exegesis with a set of theoretical conclusions (*loci theologici*). This has no section on Christology but a long one on soterio-

logy, presumably because while Protestants and Catholics agreed on the
former they did not on the latter. So far as I am aware he is the first who
points out that 2 Cor.1:3 begins in the same way as Eph.1:3 and that
similar phrases commencing with 'blessed is' are to be found in the Old
Testament and that we find this form in the New Testament in Luke 1:68.

J. A. Bengel[12] (1687–1752), as we might expect, begins to notice new
aspects and wastes no words in his comments. The double use of 'bless' is
an *antanaclasis*, a term which commentators have used ever since to
display their learning! He notes the similarity of Eph.1:3 with 1 Pet.1:3
and points out that 1 Peter was also sent to Ephesus. He views vv.3–14 as
a summary of the epistle, a view which re-emerges in the twentieth
century as if something new. He notes the recurrence of the word
'heavenlies' at other points in the letter but does not expand on this; he
takes it to denote the glorious abode of the heavenly ones. He makes an
explicit mention of a Trinitarian reference in the verse, the Holy Spirit
entering through 'spiritual'.

G. C. A. Harless[13] may not have been the first genuinely modern
commentator but he stands very near the beginning of the line. Since he
treats the passage in great detail it is important to indicate the points he
raises though not necessarily the conclusions he reaches. Of his commentary Charles Hodge[14] wrote 'This is the most elaborate commentary on
this epistle which has yet been published. It is orthodox and devout, but
is wearisome from its diffuseness and lack of force' (Hodge was fortunate
that he did not have to read some of Harless's successors!). With Harless
there is an entirely different approach from anything we have previously
encountered. Not only does he refer to earlier commentators, especially
the Fathers, but he makes explicit use of grammars and lexica.

Much of his long note of seven pages is taken up with detail. He
observes that the letter begins like all Paul's letters with thanksgiving,
though he does not comment on the particular form in this letter or on
the renewal of the thanksgiving at 1:15–16. In grammatical matters he
discusses the missing copula with 'blessed . . .', the order of the words in
this phrase, the distinction between the verbal adjective εὐλογητός and
the participle εὐλογημένος He notes that 'the God and Father of our
Lord Jesus Christ' is a common New Testament formula but says that if
God and Father were one phrase we should expect a τε καί. Interestingly
he does not draw any christological conclusion from his discussion. He is
the first to show himself aware of a variant reading, the omission of ἐν

before Χριστῷ, but does not accept it. Pointing out the aorist participle he relates it to the once-for-all sending of Christ. He seems to be aware of the unusual double meaning of 'bless' in Greek and says it comes from the Septuagint but he does not make any further attempt to account for it. 'Us' is not used of Paul alone but of all believers; any distinction that its meaning may hold first appears in v.11. He rejects any idea that 'spiritual' is used to distinguish the present gifts of God from those of the Old Testament; the word designates the blessings as the work of the Holy Spirit. He devotes considerable space to 'the heavenlies' which, noting parallels, he argues refer to heaven but not to a 'super-heaven' above the ordinary heaven nor to heaven as the place where God is when he blesses. The blessings we receive are those of a higher world for God has given us in Christ every spiritual blessing which is in heaven.

Harless set the terms of the discussion for the next century. Different commentators assess details differently and discuss details Harless over-looked but with Harless the historical-critical method has now taken over and determines the course of the discussion. Succeeding writers are normally briefer and their selection of the points they discuss indicates their interests but even those who set out to write 'practical' or exhorta-tory commentaries cannot escape discussion of some of the detail; and if they do not explicitly discuss it they have read it and have made decisions which are incorporated in their writing. However it ought not to be assumed that the historical-critical method has taken full control; even those who use it most thoroughly still employ non-critical arguments to settle critical points. Thus J. Eadie[15] defends the linking of the genitive 'of our Lord Jesus Christ' to God on theological grounds as well as grammatical. J. Macpherson[16] includes a long discussion of the ortho-doxy of the phrase taken as a unit.

The issue which commentators find most difficult is the understanding of 'spiritual blessing in the heavenlies (the great majority now take this locally) in Christ'. Thus Macpherson[17] writes:

The atmosphere in which we live and breathe becomes heavenly . . . For us this heaven is at first a state – simply the reflection of our heavenliness of soul; at last, it will be realised as a place, where condition and locality perfectly correspond. Meanwhile, we have days of heaven upon earth, in proportion as our conversation, our way of life is in heaven.

The best known explanation is probably that of J. B. Lightfoot for it is regularly quoted by others: 'the heaven which lies within and about the true Christian.'[18] J. A. Robinson[19] is deserving of a little more attention since he both writes on this point at greater length than most and gives an exposition as well as exegesis of the passage. He begins by distinguishing the blessing of the Old Testament as primarily 'a material prosperity' from that of the New Covenant which 'is in another region: the region not of the body, but of the spirit' and argues that the reference in 'spiritual' is not to the Holy Spirit but to the human. The 'heavenlies' are a 'region of ideas, rather than locality' (p. 20), '. . . the sphere of spiritual activities: that immaterial region, the "unseen universe", which lies behind the world of sense' (p. 21). The phrase 'in Christ' 'belongs to the same supra-sensual region of ideas to which the two preceding phrases testify' (p. 24). It should be noted that Robinson unlike many earlier commentators examines each phrase in some detail before coming to his conclusions. He and similar commentators realise the need to make some sense out of this difficult passage. They do this by reducing the terms to earthly concepts. It is a kind of demythologisation but made in a platonic rather than a gnostic or existentialist framework.

It is worthy of note that four major commentaries appeared in eight years at the turn of the century: E. Haupt, 1897; T. K. Abbott, 1897; J. A. Robinson, 1903; P. Ewald, 1905. No other commentary approaches these in understanding or learning until the first edition of H. Schlier (1957). We must however mention one, J. C. F. Murray.[20] Though not a major commentary it treated in some detail issues which were to become prominent as time went by. He has a relatively lengthy note on εὐλογέω in dependence on F. J. A. Hort's 1 Peter;[21] he notes that the word's double meaning comes via the Septuagint from the Hebrew *brk*. Observing the frequent appearance of the phrase 'in Christ' in Ephesians he has a long note about it in his introduction (pp. lxii–lxxvi), making extensive use of the work of A. Deissmann[22] on the phrase; although Deissmann's work was published in 1892 it is surprising how long it took for its ideas to find a place in commentaries. Since Murray believed Paul wrote Ephesians he does not discuss possible differences of meaning from the genuine Paulines.

With H. Schlier[23] we begin a new batch of major commentaries (J. Gnilka, 1971; M. Barth, 1974; R. Schnackenburg, 1982) which have benefitted from new avenues of discussion in the general study of the

New Testament and as a result are no longer content to repeat old themes but attempt to look anew at the verse. We give the major attention to Schlier, not because it provides the correct answers but because it first opened up the new areas. The first edition appeared in 1957; I have used the seventh of 1971.

We now find greater attention being paid to the form of the benediction than formerly. It is traced back to the Old Testament through inter-testamental Judaism. The tendency to examine 'forms' began with the gospels but spread into other areas after World War II. The benediction form is now seen as clearly distinct from the thanksgiving and commentators begin to note that Ephesians possesses both. But while v.3a is a benediction form the whole of vv.3–14, or at least vv.3–10, are recognised as a 'eulogy form'. This form is found also in 2 Cor. 1:3 ff., and 1 Pet.1:3 ff. as well as widely in contemporary Jewish literature. Closely associated with this is a discussion of the actual structure of vv.3–14. So far as I can trace, M. Dibelius[24] was the first to introduce this but it had been under consideration for some years in the academic journals, apparently stemming from an article by M. T. Innitzer in 1904.[25]

Is Eph.1:3–14 a hymn? If so, was the hymn written by the author of Ephesians or did he use an existing entity? If it is not a hymn does it have any kind of structure and how is it to be categorised? We may discern here not only the influence of form-criticism but also and more importantly the revival of interest in the twentieth century in liturgy. If liturgies appear reasonably early in the history of the church can we trace them back into the New Testament itself? Coincident with this and affecting it has been the attempt to discover pre-written elements in the New Testament. While this may have originated in the desire to reach some primitive kerygma it quickly took over as a subject in itself. Consequently almost all contemporary commentaries have a section on these issues. An examination of them would suggest that opinion has gradually swung against any idea of a pre-existing hymn incorporated in Ephesians chapter 1 towards the use by the author of liturgical language. Schlier's actual phrase is often quoted by others: in the eulogy we deal 'mit einem einheitlichen, ad hoc geschaffenen, hymnus*artigen* Abschnitt in rhythmischer Kunstprosa' (p. 41). Evidence drawn from Qumran has reinforced this conclusion. Here we may note how new discoveries of material have also helped in the solution of old problems. The papyri found at the close of last century threw much light on language and grammar while Qumran and Nag Hammadi have helped rather in respect of concepts.

The examination of other letters of the Pauline corpus suggested that their introductory section set out the pattern for what was later to be discussed in the body of the letter. Thus attempts have been made to relate 1:3–14 to the succeeding main section of the letter. In the case of Ephesians this seems to have begun with an article by C. Maurer,[26] or at least he was the first to study the idea seriously and work it out in detail.[27]

Looking at more individual points we find that there is still diversity of opinion as to the reference of the aorist in the participle translated as 'has blessed'. While a connection with baptism had often been conjectured N. A. Dahl[28] appears to have been the first to attempt to connect the letter as a whole to the sacrament. This connection, and also one to the eucharist, is now more generally made. It has probably been spurred on by the revived interest in all denominations in worship coupled with ecumenical discussion of the sacraments.

The question of authorship has not been of great importance in the exegesis of our verse with the exception of the discussion of the phrase 'in Christ'. We noted earlier Murray's long treatment of this theme. Discussions of the phrase itself now usually exclude the material from Ephesians on the ground that it is non-Pauline. So beginning with J. A. Allan[29] commentators tend to look at the use of the phrase in the epistle apart from its use by Paul generally. It cannot be said that this has led to any general agreement on what it means in this verse.

The more recent discussion of 'spiritual' has seen agreement that it must be related in some way to the Holy Spirit but with the revived interest in charismatic gifts in the sixties of this century commentators have been more careful to say that its use in v.3 cannot be restricted to such gifts. So far as I can see, this denial comes to the fore first in M. Simajoki.[30] It again shows how outside pressures affect exegesis.

The most difficult phrase in the verse has always been 'the heavenlies'. Earlier commentators had been content to introduce verses from other parts of the New Testament which included the word 'heaven' or to examine the way in which the particular form of the word was used in Ephesians. Schlier however was able to make use of the rich field of material unearthed by the *religionsgeschichtliche Schule*. Dibelius had already availed himself of it as had Schlier in earlier work. The latter now utilised it in his commentary in conjunction with an existentialist approach to create a new interpretation. 'Heaven' is that which gives transcendance to life, gives man a width and depth of existence and allows him to stand outside himself. Since the 'powers' exist in heaven this means that there is more than one possibility of existence for man and he is continually challenged to choose between them. Each heaven, that of Christ and that of the powers, claims him. It cannot be said that this existentialist approach has won over a majority of commentators but it has affected much writing. 'The world-picture' of Paul (Schlier takes Ephesians to be Pauline) which he deduces has also of course been controverted.

With regard to the phrase itself one other approach should also be mentioned. A. T. Lincoln[31] is in the process of producing a commentary on Ephesians and we may assume that this will contain the views he has promulgated elsewhere.[32] Unlike Schlier he has gone to Jewish rather than to Hellenistic material and explained the phrase in terms of the two ages. 'Paul conceives of the two ages as coexistent, and in this period of overlap the believer is regarded as involved in two spheres of existence simultaneously' (p. 48). We see here in this limited area traces of the wider conflict between two different general approaches to the New Testament, one dominated by the attempt to elucidate difficulties from the Hellenistic field (Schlier) and the other from the Jewish (Lincoln).

I hope the preceding survey, short as it has been, has justified the title of this paper. We have seen how questions arising in areas exterior to our verse have affected its interpretation – the non-Ephesian factors which affect the interpretation of Ephesians. Commentaries which treat the same issue differently or treat different issues are written because scholars are invited by the circumstances in which they stand to pose different questions to the text. Consequently new aspects have been uncovered and at the same time new answers given to previously recognised problems. Techniques and methods developed for the study of other parts of the New Testament have been extended to apply to our text, and of course to all texts. For what we have attempted to show in respect of Eph. 1:3 could be equally demonstrated in respect of a thousand other verses. There is then no such thing as a neutral exegesis. The questions we pose to any text have been created for us in the first instance by those who have previously studied that text. We either agree with them or are forced to examine further and justify our disagreement. But our environment, and I use this term in its widest sense, leads us also to ask new questions and to see the material in new ways. This can happen as new philosophies come to the fore or as new interests, e.g. in worship and liturgy, are raised by others for us, or as new methods of examining the text, e.g. form-criticism, are transferred from one part of the New Testament to other parts.

The main difficulty in the verse has always been the reference to the 'heavenlies'. At first many commentators simply ignored the past tense of the participle 'blessed' and thought of future blessings in heaven. Others who took seriously the past tense have been forced to interpret it within various frameworks of Platonism, gnosticism, existentialism, Jewish two-age ideas. Platonic and existentialist interpretations have been attempts to put the term into words which readers could understand(?). It cannot be said that they have been successful but then such interpretations quickly pass out of date and require to be carried through again for each generation. Perhaps commentators should not attempt them but be content merely to explain first century ideas in terms of other first century ideas (i.e. the two ages) within a first century background. But do those who restrict themselves in this way really get to the heart of the matter? Here we come to the centre of the hermeneutical discussion and must desist.

Notes

1. For an edited text see J. A. F. Gregg, 'The Commentary of Origen upon the Epistle to the Ephesians', *JTS* (old series) 3 (1902) 233–44, 398–420, 554–76.
2. *In Epistolam ad Ephesios* (*MPL* 26.467–590).
3. Cf. Gregg, loc. cit., p. 233.
4. See H. B. Swete, *Theodore of Mopsuestia on the Minor Epistles of S. Paul*, vol. 1 (Cambridge, 1880) pp. 112–96.
5. *Interpretatio Epistolae ad Ephesios* (*MPG* 82.505–57).
6. *Ad Ephesios* in *Interpretatio Omnium Epistolarum Paulinarum*, vol. 4 (Oxford, 1852) pp. 104–365 (*MPG* 62.9–176).
7. Note the almost total absence of this meaning in classical lexica. See also H. W. Beyer, *Theologisches Wörterbuch zum Neuen Testament*, vol. 2 (Stuttgart, 1935) p. 752; W. Schenk, *Der Segen im Neuen Testament* (Berlin, 1967) pp. 36 ff.
8. *In Epistolam Pauli ad Ephesios* (*MPL* 8.1235–94).
9. *Opera omnia* ed. S. E. Fretté and P. Maré, vol. 21 (Paris, 1876) pp. 260–343. ET by Matthew L. Lamb (Albany, N.Y., 1966).
10. *Corpus Reformatorum* 79 (1895) *Calvini opera* vol.51, pp. 141–240; ET by

T. H. L. Parker, *The Epistles of Paul to the Galatians, Ephesians, Philippians and Colossians* (Edinburgh, 1965) pp. 121–224.

11. *Commentarius in Epistolam Sancti Pauli ad Ephesios* (ed. A. H. de Hartog, Amsterdam, 1888; 1st ed. 1594).

12. *Gnomon Novi Testamenti* (editio tertia recusa adjuvante Johanne Steudel, Tübingen, 1850).

13. G. C. A. Harless, *Commentar über den Brief an die Epheser* (Erlangen, 1834).

14. Charles Hodge, *A Commentary on the Epistle to the Ephesians* (Grand Rapids, 1980; 1st ed. 1856).

15. *A Commentary on the Greek Text of the Epistle of Paul to the Ephesians* (London and Glasgow, 1854).

16. *Commentary on St. Paul's Epistle to the Ephesians* (Edinburgh, 1892).

17. Ibid., p. 120.

18. *Notes on Epistles of St. Paul* (London, 1904) p. 312.

19. J. A. Robinson, *St. Paul's Epistle to the Ephesians* (London, 1903).

20. *Ephesians* (Cambridge Greek Testament, Cambridge, 1914).

21. *The First Epistle of St. Peter, I,i–ii.17* (London, 1898).

22. *Die neutestamentliche Formel 'In Christo Jesu'* (Marburg, 1892).

23. *Der Brief an die Epheser* (Düsseldorf, 1957).

24. *An die Kolosser, Epheser, an Philemon* (Tübingen, 1st ed. 1913; 3rd ed. 1953).

25. 'Der Hymnus in Eph 1,3–14,' *Zeitschrift für Theologie und Kirche* 28 (1904) 612 ff.

26. 'Der Hymnus von Epheser I als Schlüssel zum ganzen Briefe', *EvT* 11 (1951) 151–72.

27. Cf. Bengel, supra.

28. N. A. Dahl *et alii, Kurze Auslegung des Epheserbriefes* (Göttingen, 1965) p. 11.

29. 'The "In Christ" Formula in Ephesians', *NTS* 5 (1958/9) 54–62.

30. Dahl, op. cit. p. 104.

31. In the series Word Biblical Commentary.

32. 'A Re-Examination of "the heavenlies" in Ephesians', *NTS* 19 (1972/3) 468–83.

Firmness in Faith:
Hebrews 11:1 and Isaiah 28:16

Otto Betz

The Problem of Faith in the Epistle to the Hebrews

In his recent work *The Living Utterances of God*, Anthony T. Hanson rightly remarks on the eleventh chapter of the Epistle to the Hebrews: 'If one examined that eleventh chapter in detail, one would learn much about our author's understanding of scripture' (p. 111). Stimulated by this statement I am going to consider that famous chapter on faith, and in particular the definition with which it begins: 'Now faith is the assurance of things hoped for, the conviction of things not seen' (Heb.11:1; RSV). This will involve an examination of that translation in order to see whether it renders the difficult terms ὑπόστασις and ἔλεγχος correctly,[1] a discussion of the possible background to this beautiful definition, and a search for the way in which it is confirmed by the 'cloud of witnesses' (12:1) who are 'well attested by their faith' (11:39).

In his monograph on faith in Hebrews, E. Graesser reports that many exegetes emphasise the Hellenistic character of both the form and content of Heb.11:1.[2] He himself seems to agree with their judgment, which he confirms by the following argument: the very fact that the author of Hebrews in this important statement about the nature of faith has used a term such as ὑπόστασις with its many shades of meaning is quite awkward. In Graesser's view the use of this word shows both that salvific Christian faith is subordinated to the arguments of speculating reason and that its author belongs to the thought-world of the Greek. That is why faith in Hebrews is different from faith as understood by Paul. It is no longer saving faith in Christ's atoning sacrifice, but is directed to the sphere of things hoped for (11:1; p. 77). In Hebrews there is no affirmation analogous to that of Jesus: 'Your faith has saved you' (p. 78). Rather, faith is the necessary link between promise and fulfilment, a bridge between the perishable world in which we live and the unshakeable realm of heavenly reality; faith is the equipment necessary for the wandering people of God (ibid.). Graesser holds that in Hebrews faith has become an abstract attitude without any personal relation to God or to Christ. To me, this would mean that the author of Hebrews has abandoned both the nature of faith in the Old Testament and its personal character as evoked by the historical Jesus and as understood by Paul and John.

In fact, I doubt whether faith in Hebrews has really become so hellenized. Following the methodology of A. T. Hanson, I want to raise the question whether the definition of faith in Heb.11:1, introducing such a long and impressive series of Old Testament witnesses of faith, might not in itself correspond to a Jewish concept by bringing a prophetic passage into a new, precise and definition-like form. We must admit that the terms 'faith' (*'ĕmûnāh*) and 'believe' (*he'ĕmîn*) do not often appear in the Old Testament; faith does not have there the importance characteristic of its use by New Testament authors. Although the latter use only a few of the sayings about faith in the Torah and in the prophetic books, those few became highly influential for them and their understanding of faith: Gen.15:6; Isa.7:9; 28:16; 53:1, and Hab.2:4. These five sayings are the ones best suited to describe the saving faith which leads to righteousness (Gen.15:6 in Rom.4; Gal.3), the saving power of God by faith in the gospel of Christ (Isa.53:1 in 1 Cor.15:1–4; Phil.2:5–11; Rom.1:16–17; 4:25; 10:16), the gift of (eternal) life (Hab.2:4 in Rom.1:17; Gal.3:11; Heb.10:35–37; John 5:24–25), and the maintaining of steadfastness in the trials at the end of the world (Isa.7:9 in 1 Cor. 13:7,13) and Isa.28:16. Of these five sayings, that in Isa.28:16 is the one on which I am going to concentrate here. It speaks about a precious foundation stone laid by God himself, and was 'a favourite text with early Christians', 'very popular with the New Testament.'[3] It is quoted in Rom.9:33;10:11; Eph.2:20; 1 Pet.2:6, it is often linked with other 'stone'-passages such as Isa.8:14; Ps.118:22, and it is usually applied to Jesus Christ as the cornerstone or foundation of the church.

The Meaning of Isa.28:16

The precious stone and firm foundation promised by God in Isa.28:16 is opposed to the establishment made by the rulers of Jerusalem. They have boasted of having made a covenant with Sheol, the realm of death. Therefore they believe they are going to live in security: the overwhelming power and destructive force of chaos will not come upon them; constructions made of lies and falsehood will offer them refuge and shelter (Isa.28:14–15). But God declares that this covenant with death will not stand, and that the flood of chaos will pass through (28:18). God will rise and himself do the strange deed of judgment (28:21). The prophet, who is permitted to listen to the heavenly council (see Isa.6:7–8), has 'heard a decree of destruction' from God upon the whole land (28:22). The only reliable refuge can be found in the building which will be raised by God himself: 'Therefore thus says the Lord God, Behold, I am laying in Zion for a foundation a stone, a tested stone, a precious cornerstone, of a sure foundation (*mûsād mûssād*): "He who believes will not be in haste" '[4] (28:16; RSV).

There is no agreement among scholars on the meaning of this oracle. Does it refer to a real building, such as the Solomonic temple in Jerusalem, being the true refuge for the believers (A. Bentzen)?[5] Is it the new Zion which will replace the old temple with its official, meaningless cult (H. Gese)?[6] Must the oracle be understood figuratively, the building being a picture for the true religion of Israel in which faith, justice, and order are fundamental (J. Lindblom)?[7] Or does the prophet point to the new congregation of believers, whose foundation will be laid on Mt Zion (S. Mowinckel,[8] A. Weiser[9] and others)? But the character of faith is clear: the believer will not be in haste, will not flee, but will remain firm; this is meant by the root *ʾāman–heʾĕmîn* = to be firm, to believe: there is thus a correspondence with the object of faith in Isa.28:16, the strong foundation of God.

The Translation and Interpretation of Isa.28:16 in Early Judaism

The Targum of the Prophets abandons the terminology of building (stone, foundation) and understands the oracle figuratively. The prophet speaks of a mighty king whom God will install on Mt Zion, strengthen and fortify: undoubtedly, the Messiah is meant.[10] Faith is the attitude of the righteous ones (*ṣaddîqayyāʾ*), who become the subject of the second half of Isa.28:16: they 'believe in these words; when distress will come, they will not be shaken' (*yizdaʿzěʿûn*).[11] I think that Hab.2:4b, which offers a similar succinct statement about the power of faith, has influenced the Targumic rendering of Isa.28:16 and strengthened its eschatological outlook: 'The righteous will live by his faith', which means that his faith will save him, will lead him to eternal life.

The Septuagint sees God laying a chosen, precious cornerstone (λίθον ἀκρογωνιαῖον) upon the foundations (εἰς τὰ θεμέλια). The often repeated root *yāsad* is rendered by a plural (θεμέλια). But it is the cornerstone in which one has to believe in order not to be put to shame (καταισχυνθῇ) in the Last Judgment. As in the Targum Hab.2:4b had influenced the rendering of the similar verse Isa.28:16, so in the Septuagint Isa.28:16 has enriched the statement in Isa.8:14. For there the phrase: 'And if you believe in it' has no basis in the Hebrew text, but must have been inspired by Isa. 28:16. The tendency to link prophetic passages about faith, which we find in the New Testament (see 1 Pet.2:5–8; Matt.21:42; Acts 4:11), has its antecedent in those early versions of the Hebrew Bible.

The eschatological orientation of these two versions is obvious. To believe means to be steadfast, firmly grounded on God's promise, and to stand as a righteous one in God's judgment.

Isa.28:16 played an important role in the self-understanding of the Qumran Community. We find strong allusions to it in the *Hodayot* (1QH) and in the *Serek Ha-Yahad* (1QS), the so-called 'Manual of Discipline'. The Qumran exegetes have retained the building terminology, but it is made to refer to the congregation set up by God. He has laid its foundation and constructs it with stones chosen by him. As in the Septuagint, the terms mentioned twice in the Isaiah text have been rendered in the plural: God lays the foundations (*yěsôdôt* from *mûsād mûssād*) and is building with chosen stones (*ʾăbanîm* from *ʾeben ʾeben*; see 1QH 6:26). The building and its stability are decisive. 'He who believes' is not mentioned at all, but included as a living stone in the building of God. His steadfastness has become a quality of this building.

1. In the *Hodayot* the community is praised as a refuge of salvation over against the 'gates of Sheol' and the power of death, which threatens man's life just as the roaring sea threatens that of a sailor in a small boat

(1QH 6:24). The city of salvation is a fortress with a high wall, a city of God on earth: 'For you lay a foundation on a rock (*sôd ʿal selaʿ*) and a pillar (*kapîs*) . . . so that they will not be shaken and all that enter it will not tremble' (6:26–27). As in Isa.28:16, we have here the contrast between the power of death and the fortress of God. It is even heightened by the eschatological colouring of the whole scene, into which Isaiah's oracle is integrated. The strength of the foundation (*sôd = yĕsôd*) is emphasised by the fact that it is laid on a rock – the term *selaʿ* is added in line 26 – and has a strong wall (line 26, the lacuna must be filled out by the word *ḥômāh*). God does not merely lay the foundation but is erecting a whole fortress, a fortified city. He uses chosen stones (line 26), which means that the members of the Qumran Community are elected from the mass of perdition. The promise of Isaiah's oracle is fulfilled in the present, in the existence of the community of salvation. But the process of God's building goes on (*ʾattāh tāśîm*, lines 25–26). The spiritual values of order and truth (line 26, see Isa.28:17) are used as the norm of God's construction, which is confirmed in a twofold way: its wall cannot be shaken (*titzaʿzaʿ*) and those entering it will not tremble (line 27). To believe means to follow God's call and to enter his community.

2. In the *Serek Ha Yahad* (1QS) the stability and the holiness of the Qumran Community is described by using Isa.28:16. As in 1QH 6:24 ff. the geographical connotation 'in Zion' is omitted. The community is compared with a temple because in its view the Jerusalem temple does not fulfil its proper task any more. It is 'a holy house for Israel and a foundation of the Holy of Holies for Aaron, witnesses of truth for judgment and chosen ones by God's will, in order to make atonement for the land and to pay back to the wicked their deeds' (1QS 8:5–6). But this holy house is, at the same time, a kind of fortress: 'This is the tested wall, the precious cornerstone; its fundaments shall not be shaken (*yizdaʿzĕʿû*) nor move (flee = *yāḥîšû*) from their place' (lines 7–8). Here again, 'he who believes' is not explicitly mentioned, and the firmness of the building, its foundations, and wall, is emphasised. But the building consists of the community and its members; they are God's living temple, performing worship in spirit and in truth (1QS 9:3), offering the atoning sacrifices of prayers of praise (9:4–5). Faith manifests itself in a life of holy and atoning service for God and his people; the community built by God is the eschatological *continuum* between the dark present and the bright future.

Isa.28:16 in the New Testament

Isa 28:16 is used especially by Paul, who quotes it in Rom.9:33 and 10:11. As in the Targum, a messianic interpretation is given to that oracle, and here again it is combined with other Old Testament passages, especially with Isa.8:14. For Christ is the stone laid by God in Zion; he has become to the Jews a stumbling stone and a rock (πέτρα) that makes them fall; 'but he who believes in him will not be put to shame' (Rom.9:33). The location 'Zion' is retained, because Christ's crucifixion and resurrection happened in Jerusalem; these are the events by which God has laid the foundation of the church.

In the New Testament the second part of Isa.28:16, the firmness of faith, became very important, especially for Paul. Both Christ's role and Christian faith were discovered in Isa.28:16 and considered to be the work of God. Faith is directed to Christ (see Col.2:5); it means to believe in his saving deeds and atoning sacrifice (Col.1:22–23).

1. This may explain why in the writings of Paul the oracle Isa.28:16 figures as a favourite prophetic prediction of the gospel. Like the author of Hebrews, Paul also teaches a lesson about the origin and nature of faith (Rom.10). He inserts the second half of Isa.28:16 as a proof-text into this lesson: 'no one who believes in him will be put to shame' (Rom.10:11). The Septuagint version, used here and in Rom.9:33, supports both faith in Christ (ἐπ' αὐτῷ) and the eschatological outlook: faith will protect against condemnation and 'being put to shame' in the Last Judgment. For Christ will acknowledge the believer before God and his holy angels (cf. Luke 12:8–9; Mark 8:38).

Isa.28:16 is alluded to in Paul's account of the Corinthian church in 1 Cor.3. Since he is its founder, he compares himself with a wise architect who has laid the foundation (θεμέλιον ἔθηκα), while another is building upon it (3:10). But actually 'no other foundation can anyone lay than that which is laid, which is Jesus Christ' (3:11). Since God is the ultimate subject who 'laid' the foundation, here again the christological interpretation of Isa.28:16 must be presupposed, Jesus being himself the foundation of the church established by God. But the apostles become co-workers of God. The goal of their mission can be described in terms of building on this foundation, and the criterion of their value and success will be the stability and endurance of their work, tested by the fire of the Last Judgment (3:13–14). The work has to 'remain' (the verb is μένω =

neʾĕman, 3:14). Its strength is made up by the faith (*ʾĕmûnāh*) of the church-members, the believers (*maʾămîn* (*-îm*) in Isa.28:16).

Very important are the passages Col.1:23 and 2:5b, where the firmness of faith is extolled in terms which are borrowed from Isa.28.16. By his death, Christ can present the members of the Church holy before God provided that they 'remain (the verb is ἐπιμένω =*neʾĕman*) in the faith, stable and steadfast (τεθεμελιωμένοι καί ἑδραῖοι: see *mûsād mûssād*), not shifting (see *lōʾ yāḥîš*) from the hope of the gospel' (Col.1:22–23), and in Col.2:5 there is praise for 'your order and the firmness of your faith in Christ' (ὑμῶν τὴν τάξιν καὶ τὸ στερέωμα τῆς εἰς Χριστὸν πίστεως ὑμῶν).

In Eph.2:20 the 'foundation' of Isa.28:16 is referred to in a different way: the church is 'built upon the foundation of the apostles and the prophets, Christ Jesus himself being the cornerstone.' Here the Old Testament prophets, such as Isaiah, must be meant, since they had announced the gospel of the Son of God (Rom.1:2).

In 1 Pet.2:4–8 we find Isa.28:16 quoted in the context of the doctrine on the origin and nature of the church: it is a spiritual house in which Christ is the precious stone laid by God on Mt Zion (2:4–6). He is also the stone rejected by the builders (Ps.118:22 in 2:7) and a stumbling stone for Israel (Isa.8:14 in 2:8). As in the Targum, disobedience to the word of proclamation is the real reason for stumbling and downfall (cf. 1 Pet.2:8).

2. *Isa.28:16 and the Faith of Peter (Matt.16:18; Luke 22:31–32)*.

It may be that the Pauline emphasis on Christ as the sole foundation of the church (1 Cor.3:11) contains an implicit criticism of the party of Cephas in Corinth (1 Cor.1:12) and its claim that Cephas was the 'rock' (*kêpāʾ*) of the church. This would point to an early origin of the famous saying of Jesus in Matt. 16:18, and I cannot see any reasonable objection to its authenticity. No one, except Jesus himself, had the authority to give a new significant name to one of his disciples. I also think that there is a reference to Isa.28:16 in this response to Peter's messianic confession, as is already evident from the context. For the rock (*kêpāʾ* = *selaʿ*) as the foundation of the church is to protect this building of the Messiah against the aggressive power of death (16:18). For this power the term 'gates of Hades (*šĕʾôl*)' is used here. Although it does not occur in Isa.28, it is in the Qumran passage IQH 6:24 (*šaʿărê māwet*) which is built upon Isa.28:15–18. So Peter is the foundation laid by God himself, protecting the church against the power of death. His confession is an act of faith, which makes him a spokesman of God's revelation (Matt.16:17). That this Isaiah oracle was familiar to Jesus may be concluded from the parable of the house 'founded on rock' (Matt.7:24–25), which remains unshaken in the tempest of the *eschaton*. In Luke the wording is even closer to its Old Testament model: 'He laid a foundation upon rock', which the flood could not 'shake' (6:48).

3. The fact that Matt.16:18 is only reported in the first gospel and is not to be found in Mark 8:29 or its parallel passages does not necessarily speak against its authenticity.[12] There is also a saying of Jesus to Peter mentioned by Luke alone, which like Matt.16:18 betrays the influence of Isa.28:16: 'Simon, Simon, behold, Satan demanded to have you, that he might sift you like wheat, but I have prayed for you that your faith may not fail; and when you have turned again, strengthen your brethren' (Luke 22:31–32). In this saying Jesus presupposes that Simon is *kêphā*ʾ, 'the rock', the foundation laid by God (Isa.28:16). For this rock is attacked by Satan, whose role of an accuser at the throne of God is intended here. He represents the aggressive power of destruction, similar to that of death and Sheol in Matt.16:18 and in Isa.28:15,18. Satan has asked God that he may test the strength of this rock ('sift him like wheat'), and shake him terribly, just as the foundation in Isa.28:16 will be shaken and tested by the power of chaos in the turmoil of the *eschaton* (see also 1QS 8:7–8; 1HQ 6:22–27). A further element of Isa.28:16 which reappears in Luke 22:32 is faith. Jesus has prayed as the intercessor for Peter and as the main adversary of Satan, that the faith of his disciple may not fail (μὴ ἐκλίπῃ). God's word of assurance, 'he who believes will not be in haste' (Isa.28:16b), is alluded to, and perhaps also the faith (ʾĕmûnāh) that must 'remain' (neʾĕman, see 1 Cor.13:13) in Isa.7:9. Peter's behaviour in Antioch, where he 'drew back' from eating with the gentiles, fearing the circumcision party of Jerusalem (Gal.2:12), is a perfect example of failing faith. When trusting in his own strength, this disciple was lost (Matt.14:31; 16:22–23; 26:69–75). Jesus has had to lay his hand upon *kêphā*, 'the rock', holding him during the attacks of Satan and Sheol. The Messiah himself becomes a kind of *maʾămîn*, 'making firm' (Hiphil of ʾāman), strengthening his disciple. Through him, Simon is able to take over the role of the *maʾămîn*, 'making firm' the faith of his brethren (Luke 22:32). Thus the promise of Isa.28:16b: 'he who believes will not be in haste' becomes true only because of the

work of Jesus, and the term *maʾămîn* is rendered in a causative way: to strengthen faith, to make the brethren firm.

The saying in Luke 22:31–32 confirms my view that Jesus used Isa.28:16 and that this oracle may be the 'foundation' of the sayings to Simon Peter in both Matt.16:18 and Luke 22:31–32. We have to turn to Matt.16:18 again. In an interesting article, P. Lampe[13] holds that the Greek πέτρος and the Aramaic *kêpāʾ* mean 'stone', Peter being merely a stone in the building of the church or one of the three 'pillars' (Gal.2:9). But one should not omit the traditio-historical analysis of a saying such as Matt.16:18 which is as important as philological inquiry. One has to realise that the Old Testament oracle Isa.28:16 is used in Matt.16:18. There the foundation (upon a rock) is decisive; that is why the Qumran-Hodayah 1QH 6, alluding to this oracle, says: God 'lays the foundation upon a rock' (*ʿal selaʿ* 1QH 6:25–26) and then builds a strong wall with tested stones (ibid.). The term *selaʿ* = 'rock' is introduced, despite the fact that Isa.28:16 mentions *ʾeben* = 'stone'. And in Isa.8:14 we have 'stone' and 'rock' as parallel terms; this passage is used in 1 Pet.2:8 which has both λίθος and πέτρα. Jesus wanted to build his church not on stone, but 'upon (ἐπί) a rock'. Like the prophet in Isa.28:16, he certainly had in mind the sacred rock on Mt Zion, the foundation of the Holy of Holies in the temple. The rabbis speculated about the 'foundation-stone' (*ʾeben šĕtiyyāh*) and its cosmic meaning.[14] I think that the term 'foundation-stone' and the ideas connected with it are derived from Isa.28:16 and are related to the sacred rock on Mt Zion, for the rabbis the starting-point and firm ground of the creation of the world.

Finally, the admonition of Jesus to his disciples in John 14:1 clearly reflects Isa.28:16: 'Let not your heart be troubled; believe in God, believe also in me.' Faith that 'will not be in haste' (Isa.28:16b) is not afraid of the impending pressures. In John 14:1 the object of faith (see ἐπ' αὐτῷ in the Septuagint version of Isa.28:16b) is both God and Jesus Christ, who has overcome the world and its tribulations (John 16:33).

Heb.11:1 and Isa.28:16

After this long journey through early Judaism, the gospels, and the letters of Paul we now may return to Hebrews 11. I intend to examine the definition of faith in 11:1 and its context, in order to find out whether they can be linked with Isa.28:16 and evaluated in its light.

We have first to consider the form of Heb.11:1. Although it gives the impression of a philosophical definition belonging to the thought-world of the Greeks, the famous sentence 'Now faith is the assurance of things hoped for, the conviction of things not seen' has the form of a Hebrew *parallelismus membrorum*, consisting of two nominal clauses. Such a nominal sentence of definition-like character is not alien to the Old Testament and is often used in Wisdom literature. For instance, there are the well-known famous statements 'the fear of the Lord is the beginning of knowledge but fools despise wisdom and instruction' (Prov.1:7) and 'the fear of the Lord is hatred of evil' (Prov.8:13).[15] These proverbial sentences describe the value of wisdom and piety, not that of faith. But the latter is praised in brief verbal clauses such as Isa.28:16: 'he who believes will not be in haste', and Hab.2:4 'the righteous shall live by his faith.' The character of a definition seems to be stronger in Heb.11:1 than in those Old Testament statements about wisdom, fear of the Lord, and faith. The latter are not mere definitions. They must also be understood as utterances of confession, praise, and exaltation; they are intended to extol their subject, to make it attractive for others.

This is true for Heb.11:1, too, as it is the continuation of the confession in 10:39 and the introduction and theme of a long and beautiful testimony to outstanding men of faith. The character of this 'definition' may be compared with the hymnic praise of love in 1 Cor.13: 'Love is patient and kind' (13:4) ... 'love never ends' (13:8) ... 'so faith, hope, love abide, these three; but love is the greatest of these' (13:13).[16]

I think that Isa.28:16 forms the background of Heb.11:1. Paul in 1 Cor.13:13 clearly alludes to Isa.7:9: 'If you do not believe, you will not abide', bringing the admonition of the prophet to a more general and abstract assertion of praise. So the author of Hebrews has compressed the verbal statement in Isa.28:16 into an admirable, brief and definition-like nominal sentence, describing and extolling the nature of faith. That the author of Hebrews could draw a general, definition-like consequence from a saying in the Old Testament is shown in 10:38–39, the verses which precede 11:1. From Hab.2:4a in the Septuagint, which discloses the nature of unbelief in terms of 'shrinking back' (ἐὰν ὑποστείληται 10:38), he derived a kind of confession (10:39) in which he uses the noun ὑποστολή as the opposite of ὑπόστασις; he also showed the eschatological consequence of both firm faith and failing faith. By a similar procedure Heb.11:1 came into existence. There the oracle Isa.28:16 was the basic text; even the nouns ὑπόστασις and ἔλεγχος were suggested by it. This I am going to explain in detail.

1. The term 'faith' (πίστις) in Heb.11:1 corresponds to the participle *ma᾽ămîn* ('he who believes', ὁ πιστεύων in the Septuagint version of Isa.28:16b); the desire to describe and to praise the character of faith has caused the change from the verb 'to believe' to the noun 'faith'. The object of faith in Isa.28:16a, i.e. the firm foundation laid by God, and the subjective attitude of the one who believes are in perfect agreement: to believe (*he᾽ĕmîn*), to have faith (*᾽ĕmûnāh*), means to be firm (*᾽āman*, *ne᾽ĕman*) and faithful (*ne᾽ĕman*), to ground oneself in the firmness of God and to believe in his faithfulness. This reciprocal working of faith is illustrated by Sarah, whose faith participated in the creative power of God: 'Through faith' she received the strength to bear a son despite her old age, 'because she held faithful the one who had made the promise' (Heb.11:11). Besides Isa.28:16 (see Heb.11:10) the author of Hebrews thought of Hab.2:4 (see Heb.11:38), which he understood in the following way: Sarah 'gives life (*tĕḥayyeh*) through her faith'.

2. The difficult noun ὑπόστασις expresses first the attitude of the one who believes according to Isa.28:16b: he will 'not be in haste' (*lō᾽ yāḥîš*). It is necessary to take into account the translations of this statement in the Septuagint and in the Targum, and in addition the passages in the Qumran texts and in the New Testament in which Isa.28:16b is freely used or alluded to: he who believes will 'not be ashamed' (Septuagint), not be 'shaken' or 'embarrassed' (Targum; Qumran; John 14:1; Col.1:23; 2:5); his faith 'will not fail' (Luke 22:32). He will stand steadfast in the troubles of the *eschaton*, he will not yield to the attacks of Satan and Hades, or 'shrink back' (Heb.10:38–39) – all this is indicated in the promise of '*lō᾽ yaḥiš*' and meant by ὑπόστασις. The nature of faith as expressed by the noun ὑπόστασις is Heb.11:1 is illustrated by the attitude of Abraham, who believed the promise of an inheritance (11:8) and of descendants through his own son (11:18); Abraham even trusted in the power of God to raise men from the dead (11:19) – all these being 'things not seen', but hoped for.

3. But ὑπόστασις in Heb.11:1 is also suggested by the first part of Isa.28:16. I think that the term 'founded foundation' (Isa.28:16a) has influenced the choice and meaning of the nouns ὑπόστασις and

ἔλεγχος in Heb.11:1. As a foundation laid by God is firm, so is faith that is founded by God and grounded in him.

Faith itself is (1) a foundation (ὑπόστασις), laid by God himself.[17] The term ὑπόστασις can have the meaning 'foundation' (of a building) in the Septuagint (Nahum 2:7; Ezek.43:11), and 'foundation, ground for existence, conviction, hope' is a translation suitable for almost all its occurrences there.[18] The usage of this word is in perfect agreement with that in the Epistle to the Hebrews, especially in 11:1. This is hardly surprising since the quotations in Hebrews usually reproduce the text of the Septuagint. Faith is a kind of base and platform, 'standing under' (ὑφισταμένη) and bearing the heavy load of the promise of God, the 'things hoped for and not seen.' The meaning of ὑπόστασις in Heb.11:1 is more literal and illustrative than philosophical and abstract; it must be related to the foundation, built by God according to Isa.28:16a. It therefore designates a substructure, *sub-stantia*, laid by God. Faith is the place and platform where the word of God can be deposited, carried and kept. ὑπόστασις as 'foundation' reveals the objective character of faith: it is given by God, it is his creation.

Faith is (2) the subjective attitude of one 'who believes' (Isa.28:16b). Without faith there would be no starting point[19] for the promises of God, no house for his wisdom on earth. In the term (ὑπόστασις) of Heb.11:1 the objective act of God 'laying a foundation' is combined with the subjective attitude of man, who believes in it.[20] This becomes evident from the context of Heb.11:1. The series of Old Testament heroes in chapter 11 discloses faith as the attitude of courage and firmness, by which men of old have accepted and held the word of God and grounded their lives upon it (πίστει = 'by faith'). Furthermore, the ὑπόστασις of faith in Heb.11:1 is the opposite of the ὑποστολή of unbelief in Heb.10:39, which means the attitude of 'shrinking back', of cowardice, faithlessness. Therefore, ὑπόστασις also means standing firmly upon the foundation laid by God, to receive the things hoped for, to be assured of them. Luther's translation *Zuversicht*[21] and 'assurance' in the RSV are better than *Wirklichkeit* or *Verwirklichung* (H. Koester; H. Braun). ὑπόστασις cannot be the 'reality' of things hoped for, because the Old Testament men of faith could not realise such a reality. This is shown by the remarks of Heb.11: 'These all died in faith, not having received what was promised, but having seen it and greeted it from afar, and having acknowledged that they were strangers and exiles on the earth' (11:13);

'and all these, though well attested by their faith, did not receive what was promised, since God had forseen something better for us' (11:39–40a). They had received and kept the word of promise, 'the things hoped for and not seen', despite the fact that they did not realise its fulfilment. They lived by the ὑπόστασις, a 'confidence' which they 'held firm to the end' (Heb.3:14). So the ὑπόστασις of faith in Heb.11:1 is the attitude of being firm and faithful to the foundation as in Heb.3:14. This Greek word must be linked with the Hebrew roots ʾāman and qûm, especially in the passive and intransitive forms neʾĕman = 'to remain steadfast' (Isa.7:9), in Aramaic ʾitqayyam (see the noun qĕyāmāʾ = 'endurance, existence'). To believe means 'not to be in haste' but to 'run with perseverance the race that is set before us' (Heb.12:1).

4. The parallel noun ἔλεγχος in Heb.11:1b appears to be strange also. Its Hebrew equivalent *tôkaḥat* = 'reproof, admonition, threat of punishment', must mean in Heb.11:1 the attitude of being admonished, 'convinced' by God, of being 'convicted' by the reality of things unseen. Ἔλεγχος occurs especially in the Book of Proverbs for the teaching of wisdom. In Prov.6:23 we find it in a nominal clause and definition-like statement: 'For the commandment is a lamp and the teaching a light, and the reproofs of discipline (*tôkḥôt mûsār* = ἔλεγχος καὶ παιδεία in the Septuagint) are the way of life.' Here ἔλεγχος is closely connected with παιδεία, the Septuagint rendering of the important Hebrew word *mûsār* = 'discipline, chastisement', which describes both the method and the result of teaching wisdom, which is good education in the fear of God. The author of Hebrews gives a whole lesson on how God educates: he disciplines and punishes those whom he loves (12:3–11). This passage includes the quotation of Prov.3:11–12, in which *mûsār* (παιδεία) and *tôkaḥat* (ἔλεγχος) stands together: 'My son, do not reject the discipline of the Lord (παιδείας κυρίου), nor lose courage through his reproof' (ὑπ' αὐτοῦ ἐλεγχόμενος; Heb. *bĕtôkaḥtô*). The choice of the word ἔλεγχος = 'reproof, admonition', which in Heb.11:1 has the meaning of 'conviction', may have been suggested by the fact that the term *mûsād* in Isa.28:16a could have been read as *mûsār* ('admonition, discipline, reproof') which is similar to *tôkaḥat* (ἔλεγχος).[22] The teaching on faith in Heb.11 is thus connected with a lesson on discipline in Heb.12. As faith, Christian discipline is oriented towards the final revelation of God; and a statement concerning its pain in the present and its reward in the future is made (12:11). This is followed by the admonition to strengthen

the weak knees (12:12, cf. Isa.35:3), which is mean to encourage the faith of the Christians.

5. I am therefore convinced that the terms ὑπόστασις and ἔλεγχος in Heb.11:1 were suggested by the strange and powerful repetition of the root *yāsad* in Isa.28:16a, where the words *mûsād mûssād* mean 'a founded foundations'. Like the Septuagint (which has θεμέλια), the author of Hebrews understood the repetition in a plural sense ('foundation') and related it to faith as an attitude achieved with the help of God. So ὑπόστασις is the fundamental assurance of things hoped for and ἔλεγχος means the fundamental conviction of things not seen. The 'divine passive', strongly emphasised in *mûsād mûssād* in Isa.28:16a, is effective in the terms ὑπόστασις and ἔλεγχος in Heb.11:1: faith involves being founded by God, in God, being assured by him and by the reality of things not seen.[23] Therefore, 'he who believes will not be in haste' (Isa.28:16b).

6. The best parallels to Heb.11:1 are the passages Col.1:23 and 2:5,7. In them, ample use of Isa.28:16 is made. I also think that the Hebrew terms *mûsād mûssād* and *lō᾽ yāḥiš* are rendered there in a way similar to Heb.11:1 in order to illustrate the firmness of faith. In Col.2:5 there is praise for 'your order and the firmness of your faith in Christ' (ὑμῶν τὴν τάξιν καὶ τὸ στερέωμα τῆς εἰς Χριστὸν πίστεως ὑμῶν); these two fundamentals of faith reflect the strength of God's foundation (*mûsād mûssād*) in Isa.28:16. This passage helps to explain the connection of Heb.11:1 with Isa.28:16, the translation 'foundation' for the noun ὑπόστασις there, and the objective, God-given character of faith (see Col.2:7). Its subjective nature is evident from Col.1:23. There the Colossians are reconciled through Christ's death if they 'remain in faith, stable and steadfast and not shifting from the hope of the gospel.' As in Heb.11:1, faith is here linked with hope and its firmness: εἴ γε ἐπεμένετε (= *ne᾽ĕman*) τῇ πίστει (*᾽ĕmûnāh*) ... μὴ μετακινούμενοι (cf. *lō᾽ yāḥiš*. Isa.28:16) ἀπὸ τῆς ἐλπίδος τοῦ εὐαγγελίου, while the words τεθεμελιωμένοι καὶ ἑδραῖοι are the equivalents of *mûsād mûssād*, reminding us that faith is the firm attitude of the Christians because it is the foundation laid by God.

7. The objects of faith as defined by the terms ὑπόστασις and ἔλεγχος in Heb.11:1 are 'things hoped for' and 'things not seen', which are then illustrated by the examples of Old Testament faith given in the rest of the chapter. God created the world 'out of things which do not appear'

(11:3); Noah was warned by God concerning 'events as yet unseen' (11:7); Abraham and Sarah had faith that was contrary to all expectations (11:8–19), and the faith of Isaac, Jacob and Moses was directed toward the future (11:20, 21, 26). The things hoped for and unseen in this chapter are thus not only events in the history of salvation but also realities of the heavenly world. The main object of faith in Heb.11:1 becomes clear later on: it is the city of God, the heavenly Jerusalem, i.e., the construction built by him. We must remember that faith in Isa.28:16 has an object, too, but only in the Septuagint. There we read ὁ πιστεύων ἐπ᾽ αὐτῷ ('he who believes in him (it)'). Since God is the speaker in Isa.28:16, faith must be directed toward the work promised by him. According to the Septuagint, this is the chosen and precious stone to be laid on the foundation of Mt Zion. The author of Hebrews knew this Septuagint text, as we can see from 11:10. There he speaks of the 'city which has foundations, whose builder and maker is God.' This shows that for him the oracle in Isa.28:16 foretells the 'city of the living God, the heavenly Jerusalem' (12:22), which 'is to come' (13:14). It cannot be seen, but the Christians seek it; it is the lasting place of rest for the wandering people of God (13:14). Faith has always been oriented toward this city, even that of the fathers of Israel.

The Context of Heb.11:1

Our argument that the definition of faith in Heb.11:1 is not influenced by any Greek ideas but is rather strongly reminiscent of the Old Testament and a free rendering of Isa.28:16 can be supported by the context of Heb.11:1, especially by 11:10 and other passages speaking of the city of God, and by 10:34–39, which is based upon Hab.2:4 and prepares the way for 11:1.

1. According to Heb.11:8–10, Abraham, together with Isaac and Jacob, was an example of those who live by the promise that they will receive an inheritance, without seeing its fulfilment: 'By faith he sojourned in the land of promise ... living in tents with Isaac and Jacob' (11:9), 'for he looked forward to the city which has foundations (θεμελίους), whose builder and maker is God' (11:10). The Old Testament does not tell us explicitly anything about such an expectation of Abraham. But the author of Hebrews takes it for granted that the city of God was the real

object of his faith.[24] For Abraham neither the land of Canaan nor the land which God was going to show him could have been the promised inheritance (Gen.12:1). Rather this was the city built by God 'which has foundations' (11:10), and is thus the true counterpart of the tents in which Abraham lived with Isaac and Jacob as a sojourner in the land (11:9). Abraham must have known an oracle similar to Isa.28:16 or seen the city of God in a vision.[25] Its foundations are emphasised as in the Septuagint and in Qumran (1QS 8:7). God is declared to be its 'builder and maker' (11:10) which means that the term *ʾeben* = 'stone', mentioned twice in Isa.28:16, suggested the act of building (*bānāh*), as in 1QH 6:24–25. In that Hodayah and in Heb.11:10, God sets up a whole city. Abraham's faith is that of the Christians who 'seek the city which is to come' (13:14). The Old Testament witnesses had not received what had been promised to them (11:39), but saw it and greeted it from afar (11:13). The Christians have come to it (12:22) through the death of Christ, the mediator of a new covenant (12:24). That is why the readers of Hebrews could tolerate the plundering of their property, since they knew that they themselves 'had a better possession and an abiding one' (10:34). But the Old Testament heroes of faith, too, shall receive it and become perfect together with the Christians (11:40). Therefore they, too, must have longed for this place of fulfilment and perfection.

Thus Heb.11:10 can serve as an illustration and as confirmation for my contention that Isa.28:16 stands behind the 'definition' of faith in Heb.11:1. Moreover, the author of Hebrews related this oracle about the foundation of God on Mt Zion to the heavenly Jerusalem, which was the promised place of rest for the wandering people of God. Faith that is directed toward this heavenly city is also founded by God and gets its stability and strength by being attached to[26] and hoping for this everlasting city.[27] It is because he is a citizen of the new Zion that 'he who believes' (Isa.28:16) does not flee. The New Testament idea of a heavenly Jerusalem may be originated from or been supported by this oracle in Isa.28:16.

2. The definition of faith in Heb.11:1 is preceded in Heb.10:37–38 by a free and abbreviated quotation of Hab.2:3–4, followed by a brief confession (10:39):

For yet a little while, and the coming one shall come and shall not tarry (Hab.2:3 in 10:37); but my[28] righteous one shall live by faith (Hab.2:4b in 10:38a). And if he shrinks back, my soul has no pleasure in him (Hab.2:4a in 10:38b). But we are not of those who shrink back and are destroyed, but of those who have faith and keep their souls.

With these words of the prophet Habakkuk, the author reminds his readers of the parousia of the Lord, the 'coming one', and strengthens their faith in the future perfection. Because he wants to emphasise the firmness of that faith, he changes the sequence of the two parts of Hab.2:4. The first part, twice omitted by Paul (Rom.1:17 and Gal.3:11), stands here as a climax at the end: if the believer 'shrinks back',[29] God has no pleasure in him. The translation of the Septuagint is used and commented on in 10:39: 'shrinking back', forsaking one's faith, will lead to destruction, to condemnation in the judgment of God. But those who remain faithful will 'keep their souls', i.e. they will have eternal life.[30] For the righteous will live by his faith (Hab.2:4b).

The whole passage Heb.10:34–39 is a good introduction to the praise of faith in chapter 11 and its definition in 11:1. It may serve as a further proof of my thesis that the concept of faith in Hebrews is built upon Old Testament prophecy, in which Hab.2:4 and Isa.28:16 play an important role. For we should remember that these two succinct statements on faith, which are often quoted in the New Testament, were already combined in the Targum of Isa.28:16 and in the Septuagint of Hab.2:4.[31] This seems to be the case in the Epistle to the Hebrews, too, especially in 11:11: through her faith in God, the faithful one (Isa.28:16), Sarah not only lived, but also gave life (Hab.2:4 = *tĕḥayyeh bĕʾ ĕmûnatah*). Since Hab.2:3–4 is quoted and explained in 10:37–39, Isa.28:16 may be found in the following verse 11:1, which means that it has become the foundation of the so-called definition of faith. And the strange verb ὑποστέλλω in the Septuagint version of Hab.2:4 and in Heb.10:38 means practically the same as the Hebrew *ḥûš* in Isa.28:16, 'to be in haste, to flee'; it is the opposite of ὑφίσταμαι, which in the Septuagint renders Hebrew *ʿāmad* = 'to stand, to survive' (1 Sam.30:10; Ps.129:3), and of the related noun ὑπόστασις. Thus Heb.10:39 is a statement parallel to 11:1, defining faith negatively by revealing the nature and consequences of its opposition, faithlessness.

Paul and Hebrews

To what extent is the concept of faith in Hebrews different from that in the letters of Paul?

In Hebrews there is a shift of emphasis with regard to the object of faith, from the Christ-event in the past to the work of God in the future, and from the open manifestation of the righteousness of God at the cross to the things not seen. Although the author knows the burning issue of justification by faith over against righteousness through works of the law, it has for him become part of the elementary doctrine of 'repentance from dead works' and of 'faith in God' (Heb.6:1). On the other hand, for Paul, too, faith in the present will be followed by sight in the future (2 Cor.5:7). Christians believe in the promise (Gal.3:22), and Abraham is the outstanding example of faith, whose blessing for the gentiles is realised through Christ (Rom.4; Gal.3:14). Moreover, Paul admonishes the Corinthians to 'stand firm' in their faith (1 Cor.16:13), and praises the abiding force of faith (1 Cor.13:13; see Col.1:23; 2:5,7). This means that he is fully aware of the root *ʾāman* = 'to be firm' in the biblical terms for faith. As we have seen, he quotes Isa.28:16 twice in Romans (9:33; 10:11), and he uses the noun ὑπόστασις and the verb καταισχύνομαι. The word ὑπόστασις occurs twice in a kind of stereotyped phrase (ἐν ταύτῃ τῇ ὑποστάσει καυχήσεως, 2 Cor.11:17, and similarly in 2 Cor. 9:4), in both cases being related to pride and boasting. In 2 Cor. 9:4 Paul is proud of the Corinthians and praises them, before they actually have the chance to confirm his 'confidence'. Then he asks the Corinthians to allow him to boast a little 'in this boastful confidence', before he then actually does so (2 Cor.11:16–17, see 22–29). Thus ὑπόστασις means the 'foundation' for boasting, the 'confident' assumption that it will be allowed and justified to some extent.

Besides this, Paul describes a failure of faith in a way similar to that of Heb.10:37–39. With regard to the conflict at Antioch he uses the verb ὑποστέλλω = 'to shrink back' for the behaviour of Peter, which was contrary to firmness and freedom of faith in Christ (Gal.2:12,16). It is possible that Paul here has Isa.28:16 and Hab.2:4 in mind. For over against the withdrawal of Peter, he emphasised righteousness by faith and life with Christ. He is perhaps also using Isa.28:16 in Gal.2:18: 'If I build up again those things which I tore down, then I prove myself a transgressor.' For Peter had tried to 'build up' righteousness through works of the law (2:16, 21); this is against the 'truth of the gospel' (2:14) which proclaims the death of Christ (2:20) as the gift of justification for those who believe (2:16–17). Besides this, Paul is drawing on Hab.2:4 when he combines faith with life: 'I live by faith in the Son of God' (Gal.2:20). For him, the life-giving, saving power of faith is attested by Hab.2:4.

I think that this also holds true for the much debated passages John 5:24–25, 11:25–26, 40 (see 1QpHab. 7:17–8:3): faith in Christ means new life in the present and leads to eternal life. Moreover, Hab.2:4 became actualised in the crucial word of Jesus: 'Your faith has saved you (made you well)' (Mark 5:34; 10:52; Luke 7:50; 17:19). For faith, created by Jesus and confirmed by him, helps to restore physical life and leads to eternal life; this is the way Jesus understood Hab.2:4 in the light of the Kingdom. We saw that the author of Hebrews quoted Hab.2:4. Could he have forgotten the life-giving, saving, power of faith as offered by Jesus and proclaimed in the gospel? That would have been strange, indeed.

Notes

1. The translations of these two terms show considerable differences, especially of ὑπόστασις: *substantia* (Vulgate), *Zuversicht*, (Luther, Erasmus, W. M. L. de Wette, F. F. Bruce, H. W. Montefiore and others), *Unterpfand* (O. Michel), *Feststehen* (E. Graesser, O. Kuss), *Wirklichkeit* (H. Koester), *Verwirklichung* (H. Braun). See the survey in H. Braun, *An die Hebraeer* (Handbuch für das Neue Testament, vol. 4, Tübingen, 1984) pp. 336–9.
2. E. Graesser, *Der Glaube im Hebraerbrief* (Marburg, 1965) pp. 102–3.
3. A. T. Hanson, *The Living Utterances of God* (1983) pp. 17, 98, see also 34, 98, 120, 141.
4. From *ḥûš* = 'to hurry'. The Hiphil *yāḥîš*, used here, means 'to flee', 'to make haste'. The Septuagint translates καταισχυνθῇ; did it read *yābôš*?
5. *Jesaja* vol. 1 (Kobenhaven, 1949), ad loc.
6. 'Der Messias', *Zur biblischen Theologie* (München, 1977) p. 134.
7. J. Lindblom, 'Der Eckstein in Jes.28,16', *Interpretations*, Festschrift S. Mowinckel (Oslo, 1955) pp. 123–32, esp. 130.
8. S. Mowinckel, *Profeten Jesaja* (Oslo, 1925) esp. p. 189.
9. A. Weiser, article πιστεύω etc., *TWNT* vol. 6, pp. 182-97, esp. p. 189.
10. So Rashi ad loc. Interesting is the Aramaic *mannî* = 'He (God) has established' the king; ὁρισθέντος Rom.1:4. The Targum of Isa.28:16 may have been used in Jubilees 17:17–18, where the faith and steadfastness of Abraham are praised in a kind of summary. See Jubilees 17:17: 'And the

Lord knew that Abraham was faithful in all his afflictions'; 17:18: 'And in everything wherein he had tried him, he was found faithful, and his soul was not impatient (cf. *lōʾ yāḥîš* in Isa.28:16), and he was not slow to act, for he was faithful and a lover of the Lord.'

11. See Heb.12:27–28: the Last Judgment will reveal 'what cannot be shaken '(τὰ μὴ σαλευόμενα), i.e. 'the unshakable kingdom' (βασιλείαν ἀσάλευτον). As in Qumran (1QH 3:13 ff.), the Last Judgment will be an act of 'shaking' heaven and earth (Heb.12:26).

12. It is interesting to note that because of *formgeschichtliche* considerations R. Bultmann holds that Matthew offers the answer to Peter's confession which was omitted by Mark (*Die Geschichte der synoptischen Tradition*, Göttingen, 1957, p. 277).

13. P. Lampe, 'Das Spiel mit dem Petrusnamen Matth 16:18', *NTS* 25 (1978/9) 227–45. See R. Pesch *Simon-Petrus* (Stuttgart, 1980) pp. 102–3. R. Bultmann is correct in assuming a Semitic background for Matt.16:17–19 (op.cit., p. 277).

14. Mishna Yoma 5:6; Babyl. Talmud Yoma 44b; Midrash Tanchuma §444, 15–18.

15. See also Prov.10:29–31, Eccles.1:11; 7:11; 9:16.

16. See Heb.13:1: 'Let brotherly love continue' (μενέτω).

17. See Heb.6:1: 'A foundation . . . of faith' is laid by human teaching. But the author of Hebrews sees God as a kind of architect and builder of things seen and unseen, especially at the beginning and at the end of the world: 'thou didst found the earth in the beginning' (Heb.1:10, see Ps.102:25) and he is 'the builder and maker' of the heavenly city with its 'foundations' (Heb.11:10). These foundations will be revealed at the end, when the removal of the visible earth and heaven takes place; then 'the kingdom that cannot be shaken' will 'remain' (Heb.12:27–28). Faith as the foundation of God is directed to this kingdom.

18. See Liddell and Scott, s.v. The article by H. Koester on ὑπόστασις is misleading (*TWNT* vol. 8, pp. 571–88, cf. esp. pp. 579–80). His rendering of ὑπόστασις as *Wirklichkeit* (reality) or *Plan* (plan), which he finds confirmed by many passages in the Septuagint, is dictated by his philosophical preference. In my understanding this term in the Septuagint means *sub-stantia* = 'that which is lying under'; in Nahum 2:7 and Ezek.43:11 it is the foundation of the temple, in other passages the 'ground of existence' (for *yĕqûm* in Deut.11:6; Job 22:20), the 'basic support of life' (Judg.6:4; Ezek.19:5), of strength (Ezek.26:11; cf. Ps.88:47; T. Reub.2:7). Interesting is Jer.23:22; εἰ ἔστησαν ἐν τῇ ὑποστάσει μου for: *wĕʾim – ʿāmdû bĕsôdî*. The Septuagint seems to have taken the Hebrew *sôd* as *yĕsôd* as in 1QH 6:26. Ὑπόστασις can also render the Hebrew *tiqwāh* (Ezek.19:5; Ruth 1:12), or *tôḥelet* (Ps.39:7) which means 'hope' as the attitude of man, which corresponds to the firmness of God's foundation.

19. M. Luther: '*Fides est creatrix divinitatis . . . in nobis*' (Weimar Edition, vol. 40, 1911, p. 360).

20. The same relation between the subject and the object of faith is implied by

the term *shĕmûʿāh* ('message') in Isa.53:1, which due to its Aramaic rendering *bĕsôrāh* ('good news') became the Old Testament model for the important Christian noun εὐαγγέλιον (see Rom.10:16; 1 Cor.15:1–4). For *shĕmûʿāh* is the message that demands 'obedience of faith' (Rom.1:5); 'to hear' (*šāmaʿ*) implies the attitude of obeying (*šāmaʿ*).

21. E. J. Kissane says: 'Jahwe has provided a safe refuge which can withstand both storm and flood. Its foundation-stone is confidence in Jahwe, its wall the upright conduct of the people' (*The Book of Isaiah*, vol. 1–2, Dublin, 1941, on Isa.28:16, quoted by J. Lindblom, note 7 above, p. 124.).

22. In Isa.53:5 the noun *mûsār* ('chastisement') is translated by the Septuagint as παιδεία, by the Targum as *ʾitmĕsar* '(the Servant) was delivered'.

23. In Targum Isa.28:16 the terms *mûsād mûssād* are rendered freely and understood as the act of God's strengthening the messianic king. The Christian teacher 'lays the foundation ... of faith', i.e. the basic content of the doctrine of the church; God lays the foundation of faith as an attitude of man.

24. Philo tells us that Abraham thanked God for the things to come, because 'his soul was made firm ... by good hope', reckoning with the fact that the things not yet present were present (*De Migr. Abr.*43–44). Philo may have been thinking of Gen.12:1, for he emphasises the future tense (δείξω) of God's promise to 'show' Abraham a homeland (loc. cit.).

25. Perhaps for the author of Hebrews Abraham had a vision similar to that of John, the seer on the island of Patmos, who saw Jerusalem 'coming down out of heaven' (Rev.21:10) having foundations adorned with jewels (21:14, 19–20). The Epistle to the Hebrews does not explain when God showed the heavenly city to Abraham. Perhaps this happened in the night when God brought him outside the tent and told him to look toward heaven and to number the stars (Gen.15:5). For the promise which followed this event was answered by Abraham's faith (Gen.15:6). In Hebrews the 'things not seen' are heavenly things (τὰ ἐπουράνια, 9:23; see 3:1; 8:5). Therefore faith is always restless until it finds its rest in God and his city (Heb.11:8, 13–14, 34–40). The expression 'foundation ... of faith in God' (6:1) may also have been derived from Isa.28:16. The idea of the heavenly Zion and the city of God may have been mainly suggested by Isa.28:16. The opposite of a heavenly city is a place such as Jericho whose walls fell down 'by faith' (Heb.11:30). Faith that is given by God and strengthened by the visionary sight of his heavenly city can become a destructive force against gentile cities such as Jericho.

26. See the attitude of desiring the heavenly city (Heb.11:16) and of looking to Jesus, the pioneer and perfector of faith (12:2).

27. 'Mit der Vokabel haeʾaᵉmin ist stets die Vorstellung verknüpft, daß jemand durch seine Teilnahme an fremder Festigkeit selbst festen Halt für sein Leben hat' (L. Bach, *Der Glaube nach der Anschauung des Alten Testament*, 1900, p. 52), quoted in the article 'Glaube' by K. Haacker in *Theologische Realenzyklopädie*, vol.13 (1984), p. 279. Unfortunately, this illuminating study appeared too late to be used extensively in this article.

28. The author has the Septuagint in mind: 'The righteous one shall live by my faith(fulness)'. But instead he says: 'My righteous one shall live by faith', because he wants to stress man's attitude and firmness of faith.
29. The Hebrew text is difficult: 'Behold, his soul is puffed up; it is not upright in him', or 'behold, he whose soul is not upright in him shall fail'. The Targum is very free: 'Behold, the wicked say: "All these things do not exist".'
30. They have a strong heart (Heb.13:9b); they are not 'led away by diverse and strange teachings' (13:9a).
31. In the Targum of Isa.28:16 'the righteous' of Hab.2:4 is inserted (in the plural form); in the Septuagint version of Hab.2:4 the verb ὑποστέλλομαι = 'to shrink back' is influenced by the Hebrew *ḥûš*, *hēḥîš* = 'to be in haste', 'to flee' in Isa.28:16.

8

The Bones of Joseph: Hebrews 11:22

Max Wilcox

It is a great pleasure to dedicate this paper to Anthony Tyrrell Hanson, who has made so many valuable contributions to the study of the ways in which the New Testament writers use the Jewish Scriptures. He has been a great colleague, a real friend, and a most stimulating member of the Seminars which we have co-chaired over the years.

The Letter to the Hebrews identifies 'faith' (πίστις) as the 'title' or 'proof of entitlement' (ὑπόστασις)[1] to those things which constitute the 'hopes' of God's people (11:1), for through it the men of old received their accreditation (ἐμαρτυρήθησαν) (11:2).[2] Among the examples of such faith our author cites that of Joseph (11:22):

Πίστει Ιωσηφ τελευτῶν περὶ τῆς ἐξόδου τῶν υἱῶν Ισραηλ ἐμνημόνευσεν καὶ περὶ τῶν ὀστέων αὐτοῦ ἐνετείλατο.	By faith Joseph – when dying – made mention of the 'exodus' of the Sons of Israel and gave directions about his bones.

The reference is to Gen.50:24–26, a passage which is taken up later in the Pentateuch in Exod.13:19, and reflected in Josh.24:32. One may, however, be forgiven for wondering why this particular detail of the Joseph-story should have been so significant to the author of Hebrews that he should place it alongside examples of the faith of Abraham, Sarah, Isaac, Jacob and Moses. If our writer had mentioned only that Joseph looked to – perhaps even 'prophesied' – the departure of the Israelites from Egypt to settle in the Land which God had promised on oath to Abraham and his descendants, that might have seemed suitable, but why the apparently equal stress on the reference to his having given directions about his bones? Of course, one may say that all that is intended here is a statement that Joseph (a) foresaw, or rather, confidently believed, that God would fulfil his oath to Abraham, and (b) was indeed so certain of this that he even swore his brothers to take his bones with them to that promised Land.[3]

Yet at a number of points in Heb.11 the writer shows that he has rather wider considerations in view. Thus, in vv. 13–16 he tells us that Abraham, Sarah, Isaac and Jacob 'all died in conformity with (their) faith,[4] without having attained the promises, but having seen them from afar and welcomed them'; the homeland for which they yearned was in fact 'a better one', that is 'a heavenly one.' At the close of the chapter, in vv. 39–40, a similar motif appears: all these great men and women of Israel's past, although they were accredited through faith, did not attain the promise, since God had foreseen 'something better' for us, 'that apart from us they should not be perfected.' That 'something better' is Jesus, and the 'better homeland' the Heavenly Jerusalem with a New Covenant mediated by Jesus (as the new and greater Moses) (Heb.12:22,24). Our author thus interprets the hopes and deeds of his roll of heroes and heroines in terms of the Christ-event and the eschatological consummation: the promises made to the forefathers are seen as being 'realised' in the Christ-event.

Now Heb.11:22 is very terse and contains no direct quotation of, or verbal allusion to, Gen.50:24–26, although the reference is otherwise quite plain. The author seems to expect his readers to be familiar with the passage; moreover, the use to which he puts it, in common with the other examples which he cites, seems to assume the possibility of some kind of messianic interpretation for it. But if so, we may ask if any hint of such an interpretation occurs elsewhere in Jewish exegetical material relating to Gen.50:24–26 and/or the other two passages, Exod.13:19 and Josh.24:32.

The aim of this paper is to explore the treatment of these passages as found within known Jewish exegetical sources in the hope of casting light on the problem of the choice and significance of the Joseph's bones motif in Heb.11:22.

1

Apart from Heb.11:22 Joseph is mentioned in three places in the New Testament, namely, John 4:5, Acts 7:9-18, and Rev.7:8. The last of these is in a list of the tribes of Israel, and we do not need to discuss it here.

John 4:5 alludes to Josh.24:32 (and perhaps also to Gen.48:22) in the course of an incidental comment on the town (?) of Sychar, 'a town of Samaria . . . near the field which Jacob gave to Joseph his son.' Even if we leave aside the somewhat uncertain identity of Sychar (= Shechem, as the Biblical references suggest, or more probably nearby mediaeval Askar),[5] the basic allusions stand; on the other hand, they add little to the present discussion. The main point is that the place is in Samaria, either at, or at least near to, ancient Shechem. It thus fits in with the traditional site of Joseph's tomb.

The case is rather different with Acts 7:9–18 (in Stephen's speech), where Joseph is a key figure. Acts 7:15,16 mentions Jacob's death (Gen.49:33) and those of the other patriarchs. Further, Acts 7:16 states that 'they' – the patriarchs, whether including Jacob or not the syntax does not by itself make clear – were taken to Shechem and buried in the tomb which Abraham bought for a sum of silver 'from the Sons of Hamor in Shechem' (παρὰ τῶν υἱῶν Ἐμμὼρ ἐν Συχεμ). It has often been noted that this raises problems. (1) Jacob was buried in the cave of Mechpelah at Hebron, bought by Abraham from Ephron the Hittite (Gen.50:13),[6] whereas Joseph was buried, or rather, re-buried, at Shechem in the portion of the field which Jacob bought from the Sons of Hamor (Josh. 24:32). (2) Gen.50:26 records the death of Joseph, Exod.1:6 those of his brothers, himself (again) and 'all that generation', but the Old Testament does not tell us where Joseph's brothers were buried. (3) Acts 7:16 seems to hold that all twelve were buried at Shechem. Josephus, however, states that the eleven, along with Jacob, were buried at Hebron;[7] but in the case of Joseph, he does not name the place specifically:[8]

τὰ δὲ Ἰωσήπου ὀστᾶ ὕστερον, ὅτε μετανέστησαν ἐκ τῆς Αἰγύπτου οἱ Ἑβραῖοι, εἰς τὴν Χαναναίαν ἐκόμισαν· οὕτως γὰρ αὐτοὺς ὁ Ἰώσηπος ἐξώρκισε.	But later, when the Hebrews migrated up out of Egypt, they carried the bones of Joseph into Canaan; for thus had Joseph sworn them to do.

Josephus seems to be supported here by Testaments of the Twelve Patriarchs, although at T. Jos.20:6 one manuscript (c) does state that 'on the exodus of the Sons of Israel from Egypt they brought with them the bones of Joseph and buried him *in Hebron with his fathers.*'[9] Now although Acts 7:15,16 has mixed up the two otherwise distinct burial places (Hebron and Shechem), it seems – as R. H. Charles and others have pointed out – to echo a similar tradition, at least regarding the eleven brothers of Joseph.[10] (4) Again, Acts 7:16 in using the phrase παρὰ τῶν υἱῶν Ἐμμώρ in its allusion to Josh.24:32, does not follow the Septuagint as we have it, but the Hebrew (or perhaps a Greek version akin to the Hebrew), for the Septuagint reads παρὰ τῶν Ἀμορραίων τῶν κατοικούντων ἐν Σικίμοις.[11] Thus, however we may evaluate the tradition in Acts 7:15,16 its affinities seem to lie not directly with the Septuagint, nor even wholly with the Hebrew, but rather with Jewish exegetical discussions bearing on the problem of the burial of the patriarchs. Now in view of the striking links which exist between the thought of Hebrews and that of parts at least of Stephen's speech (Acts 7:2a–53), the reference in Heb.11:22 to Joseph's bones may well reflect some similar basic Jewish exegetical tradition.

2

A first clue is afforded by a passage in T. Sym.8:3,4.[12]

(3) τὰ γὰρ ὀστᾶ Ιωσηφ ἐφύλαττον οἱ Αἰγύπτιοι ἐν τοῖς ταμιείοις (or: μνήμασιν)[13] τῶν βασιλείων (or: βασιλέων).[14]

(3) For the Egyptians kept the bones of Joseph in the repositories (v.l., tombs) of the kingdoms (v.l., kings) [of Egypt].

(4) ἔλεγον γὰρ αὐτοῖς οἱ ἐπαοιδοὶ ὅτι ἐν ἐξόδῳ ὀστῶν Ιωσηφ ἔσται ἐν πάσῃ γῇ Αἰγύπτῳ σκότος καὶ γνόφος, καὶ πληγὴ μεγάλη σφόδρα τοῖς Αἰγυπτίοις, ὥστε μετὰ λύχνου μὴ ἐπιγινώσκειν ἕκαστος (!) τὸν ἀδελφὸν αὐτοῦ.

(4) For the sorcerers told them that on the departure of Joseph's bones there would be darkness and thick cloud in all the land of Egypt, and a very great plague upon the Egyptians, so that even with a lamp a person would not recognize his brother.

The second element of the passage (8:4) looks like an attempt to explain the action attributed to 'the Egyptians' in the first (8:3), although it does nevertheless remind us of the Jewish tradition, preserved in the Babylonian Talmud, that the Egyptians buried Joseph in the Nile to bless its waters.[15] More about this later, but meantime we may note that 8:3 is strikingly akin to one of the traditions of the original fate of Joseph's bones as recorded in a number of Rabbinic sources, e,g., Mekhilta Beshall. 1:1 (78:16), t. Sota 4:7, b. Sota 13b, Tanḥuma Beshall. 2 and Eqev. 6, and Exod. R. 20:17 (on Exod.13:19). We may set out the relevant passages as follows:

Mekh. Beshall. 1:1[16]
R. Nathan says: Joseph was buried in the Capitol (*or*: casket)[17] of Egypt, to teach you that 'with the measure that a man measures, they measure to him'.

t. Sota 4:7
Some say: He was buried in the tombs[20] of the kings [of Egypt].

Exod.R. 20:17
And some say: He was buried in the midst of the palace (*or* Praetorium),[21] in the manner that the kings were buried.

b. Sota 13b
R. Nathan says: He was buried in the crypt (*or*: vault)[18] of the kings [of Egypt].

Tanḥ Beshall. 2
R. Nathan says: He was buried in the grave[19] of the kings [of Egypt], as it is said, 'And they embalmed him' (Gen.50:26).

Tanḥ. Eqev. 6
(Moses went and stood among the coffins).

It is fascinating how even the variant readings of the MSS at T. Sym. 8:3, ἐν τοῖς ταμιείοις and ἐν τοῖς μνήμασι, match a similar type of textual uncertainty in the Rabbinic material. This may be mere chance, but it may well be due to preservation of at least two distinct forms of the story in the Rabbinic sources. T. Sym. 8:3 in any case seems to support the view that the Rabbinic sources here possess quite ancient tradition, scarcely as late as R. Nathan, a point strengthened by the absence of his name from some of the material. The ultimate basis of both forms is presumably a discussion of Gen.50:26 which, in the Hebrew Bible, tells only that when Joseph died, 'they embalmed him and put him in an ark (MT: *ʾrwn* cf. LXX σόϱῳ, 'coffin') in Egypt.' Both forms of the tradition then seek to interpret Gen.50:26 by taking the subject of 'embalmed' as 'the Egyptians', as in fact the Tanḥuma explicitly states.

In the Rabbinic sources cited, however, the wider context is considering Exod.13:19, Gen.50:24–26 and Josh.24:32. The immediate occasion of the reference to the Egyptian burial-place of Joseph is the problem of how Moses managed to locate the bones of Joseph. This was possible, we hear, because Serah, the daughter of Joseph's brother Asher, had survived from that generation, knew the facts, and told Moses.[22] The detail of the Serah-tradition here varies somewhat from source to source, but the main point is common to all. Again, in all of them it is followed by the alternative story of the burial of Joseph, namely, that the Egyptians put him in a (metal) box and sank him (? it) in the Nile. Both versions of the burial story thus share the same exegetical view that in Gen. 50:26 the words 'and they embalmed him' refer to the Egyptians. We shall return to this in a moment, but first must look at the background of the Serah-motif.

At first sight the Serah-story looks like a convenient tale to explain how Moses knew the whereabouts of Joseph's bones, but in fact it belongs to a larger complex of traditional material about Serah. Indeed, in several streams of Rabbinic tradition she is honoured as a model of piety, the person who brought Jacob the news that Joseph was alive, and as one who was rewarded for that by being carried off alive to paradise by six myriads of angels.[23] Thus *Pirqê de Rab Eliezer* (PRE) 48:82–86 tells us that what it terms 'the Mystery of the Redemption' (*swd hgʾwlh*) of the People of Israel was passed down from Abraham to Isaac, from Isaac to Jacob and thence to Joseph, who in turn passed it on to his brothers. One of these, Asher, passed it to his daughter, Serah, who lived to a great age, surviving until the time of Moses. Now when Moses and Aaron came performing signs before the Elders of Israel, the latter sought her advice. At first she was dismissive, but when they told her that Moses had said to them, 'God has surely visited you' (Exod.3:16), she exclaimed, 'He is the man who is about to redeem (= free) Israel from Egypt, for thus did I hear from my father, "*p* and *p*".' as it is written, 'I have surely visited you' (Exod.3:16). At once the people believed God and Moses, as it is written, 'And the people believed and heard that God had visited the Sons of Israel' (Exod.4:31). The 'sign', '*p* and *p*', refers to the formula

'God shall surely visit you' (*pqd ypqd ʾtkm*) from Gen.50:24,25 and Exod.13:19.[24]

It thus appears that the formula 'God shall surely visit you' (a) enshrines 'the Mystery of the Redemption', (b) forms the exegetical link between Gen.50:24,25 and Exod.13:19, and (c) in this stream of tradition is depicted as the key to the identity of the coming Redeemer – hence of Moses. Similar motifs, albeit without reference to Serah, also appear in Tanḥ. Shemot 24, and in Gen. R. 97:6, where *pqdty* is one of the three signs of the identity of the Redeemer, signs which Jacob passed on to Joseph.[25] A further reflection of it is found in Targum Pseudo-Jonathan (Tg. Ps.-J.) Gen.50:25, where Joseph says that the People of Israel will be enslaved in Egypt until the coming of 'two redeemers' who will say to them the words, 'Surely the Lord has remembered you.'[26]

To return to PRE 48:82–86, it is interesting to note the striking parallel between the words with which Serah here acclaims Moses as the Redeemer and those in Luke 24:21 which Cleopas uses to describe how the disciples viewed Jesus prior to the crucifixion:

Serah (of Moses)[27]	Cleopas (of Jesus)
He is the man who is about to redeem/free Israel from Egypt.	he is the one who is about to redeem/free Israel.
hwʾ hʾyš šʿtyd lgʾwlh ʾt-yśrʾl mmṣrym.	αὐτός ἐστιν ὁ μέλλων λυτροῦσθαι τὸν Ἰσραηλ.

The similarities are the more impressive when we observe that (a) ὁ μέλλων corresponds very closely to *šʿtyd*, (b) the use of λυτροῦσθαι here is akin to that of *gʾl* (and the noun *gʾwlh*) in certain of the Bar Kokhba documents and also on the coins of that Revolt,[28] and perhaps most important of all, (c) in both PRE 48 and Luke 24 the formula is intended also to fit the Messiah. It would be tempting to see here some indication of an element of traditional material, underlying both.

Be that as it may, PRE 48:82–86 sees the kernel of the Joseph's bones statements in Gen.50:24–26 and Exod.13:19, the formula *pqd pqdty*, as 'the Mystery of the Redemption', known to the forefathers, passed down to Joseph and realised in Moses (as the First Redeemer). It is still to be realised in the Second Redeemer, the Messiah. It is the clue to the identity of the Redeemer when he comes.[29]

Thus the references to Serah in our sources for the Joseph's bones traditions are not just convenient explanations of an otherwise insoluble problem but enshrine a pervasive element of Jewish exegesis of Gen.50:24–26 and Exod.13:19, based ultimately on the verbal tally between *pqd ypqd ʾlhym ʾtkm* (Gen.50:25,26; Exod.13:19) and *pqd pqdty ʾtkm* (Exod.3:16,17; cf. 4:31).

Now we noted earlier that our Rabbinic sources present us with two quite distinct traditions of Joseph's (Egyptian) burial, although the complex containing them is introduced by Serah's words to Moses and thus the Nile-story comes first throughout. However, it is one thing for Moses to learn the whereabouts of Joseph's bones and quite another for him to identify the coffin and gain possession of it and its precious contents. However, although the two burial stories differ radically, there are striking links between the respective accounts of how Moses gained possession of the coffin and its contents. We now look at these accounts in detail, beginning with the Nile-story, which not only comes first in our sources but also is reflected in Tg. Ps.-J. at Gen.50:26 and Exod.13:19.

(1) The Nile-story

Mekh. Beshall. 1:1	b. Sota 13a
He (= Moses) came and stood by the Nile.	Moses went and stood on the bank of the Nile.
He took a pebble (*ṣrwr*)[30] and throw it into the middle of it and cried out and said:	
Joseph! Joseph![31] The oath is about to be fulfilled which the Holy One, Blessed be He, swore to Abraham our father, that he would redeem (*gwʾl*) his sons. Give glory to the Lord the God of Israel and do not delay your redemption, for on your account we are waiting; but if not, we are quit of your oath.	He said to him: Joseph! Joseph! The time is at hand about which the Holy One, Blessed be He, swore, 'I shall redeem (*gwʾl*) you', and about which you swore Israel. If you show yourself, fine; if not, we are quit of your oath.
At once Joseph's coffin floated up and Moses took it.	At once Joseph's coffin floated up and Moses took it.

Both texts counter doubts about this by referring to the story of Elisha and the floating axe-head (2 Kgs.6:5–6). If Elisha the disciple of Elijah could make the iron float, *qal vaḥomer*, how much the more could Moses, Elijah's teacher, do so? The second tradition then follows. Once again, how is Moses to identify Joseph's coffin amidst all the others in the royal vaults?

(2) The Royal Vault story

Mekh. Beshall. 1:1[32]	b. Sota 13a
Moses went and stood among the coffins.	Moses went and stood by the royal vault.
He cried out and said:	He said to him:
Joseph! Joseph! The oath is about to be fulfilled which the Lord (*hmqwm*) swore to Abraham our father, etc.	Joseph! The time is at hand about which the Holy One, Blessed be He, swore, 'I shall redeem you', and about which you swore Israel. If you show yourself, fine; but if not, we are quit of your oath.
Joseph's coffin shook and Moses took it.	At that moment Joseph's coffin shook and Moses took it.

There seem to be two main bonds between these two stories: (a) Joseph's bones were put in a (metal)[33] box by the Egyptians (cf. Gen.50:26), and (b) Moses, addressing the coffin and its contents, uses in both cases an all but identical formula which recalls God's oath to Abraham (Gen.22:16–18) and Joseph's oath regarding his bones (Gen.50:25,26; cf. Exod.13:19). Yet Joseph's oath in Gen.50:25 concerns not only the disposal of his bones but also the fulfilment of God's oath to Abraham, to Isaac and to Jacob. Thus we read in Gen.50:24–25,

> (24) 'God will surely visit you (*ʾlhym pqd ypqd ʾtkm*) and he will bring you up from this land to the land which he swore to Abraham, to Isaac and to Jacob'. (25) And Joseph swore the Sons of Israel, saying, 'God will surely visit you (*pqd ypqd ʾlhym ʾtkm*) and you shall bring up my bones from here.'

Thus it is the same element, the formula 'God will surely visit you', which is central to both the Serah-sequence and the coffin-acquisition traditions. But if Joseph's oath is given in substance in Heb.11:22, the immediate occasion of God's oath to Abraham – the Binding of Isaac – is the subject of Heb.11:17–18. Indeed, Heb.11:17–22 really contains within itself the basic elements of Scripture which are also found in the coffin-acquisition formula cited above. This fact is the more interesting in that the allusion to Gen.22:1,2 in Heb.11:17 does not follow the Septuagint but agrees rather with the Masoretic text, or perhaps with Aquila and/or Symmachus.[34]

Our Rabbinic sources, however, present us with a further problem: what are the origins of the two traditions which we have discussed and why are they set down one after the other in our sources when they are so obviously mutually incompatible? Recourse of Tg. Ps.-J. may help us here. The Nile-story is reflected in its versions of Gen.50:26 and Exod.13:19, as appears if we cite them and mark deviations from the Masoretic text by italics:

> And Joseph died, being 110 years old, and they embalmed him *and adorned him*[35] and put him in a coffin *and sank him (it?)* in *the middle of the Nile of* Egypt (Gen.50:26).

This is then taken up in Exod.13:19 –

> And Moses *brought up*[36] *the coffin in which (were)* the bones of Joseph *from the Nile, and he used to carry (it)* with him, for he (Joseph) had sworn the Sons of Israel, saying, Surely *the Lord* will *remember*[37] you and you shall bring up my bones from here with you.

The motif of the 'bringing up' of Joseph's bones from the Nile seems to arise out of an interpretation of the Hebrew *whᶜlytm* which, like its Aramaic equivalent *wtsqwn*, can mean either 'and you shall bring up' (from one place to another) or 'and you shall cause to rise, come up.' But this word occurs in both Gen.50:25 and Exod.13:19 in all but identical sentences:

> Gen.50:25, and you shall bring up my bones from here.
> Exod.13:19, And you shall bring up my bones from here with you.

Thus, in Tg. Ps.-J., the verb has thus been interpreted as 'bring up (from the Nile)'. If so, the Nile-story would look like a haggadic exposition of this word in Gen.50:25, and as such has entered the text of Tg. Ps.-J. in Gen.50:25 and Exod.13:19 as its proper (that is, traditional) explanation. This might also explain why the same Targum replaces the Hebrew *wyqḥ* 'and he (Moses) took' in Exod.13:19 by *wᵓsq* 'and he brought up'. Although the Nile-story has not so far been found in any other Targum,

Tg. Onkelos and the Fragment Tg. (Paris BN ms. hébr. 110) do agree with Tg. Ps.-J. in reading *wᵓsq* 'and he brought up', in Exod.13:19, whereas Tg. Neofiti follows the Masoretic text here.[38] How are we to explain this? Have Tg. Onk. and Frag. Tg. preserved a tell-tale sign of an earlier (and fuller) form of the targumic traditions, from which the haggadic material has been largely removed? Or do they perhaps retain a more primitive stage of the tradition than does Tg. Ps.-J., where *wᵓsq* reflects interpretation of Exod.13:19a 'and he took the bones of Joseph with him' as performance by Moses (on Israel's behalf) of Joseph's oath as cited in Exod.13:19b, 'and you shall bring up my bones from here with you'? In the latter case, Tg. Ps.-J. would look like an embellishment of that earlier form.

However, if the targumic form of the tradition is derived from the other Rabbinic sources, why is the second story of the burial of Joseph's bones not represented in it somewhere? The form in Tg. Ps.-J. is indeed not only simpler than those in the other sources but also self-consistent and presents a definite haggadic exposition of Gen.50:25.

The second story – the burial in the royal vault – may, however, be traced to reflection on the meaning of the very next verse in Genesis, namely, 50:26, and in particular, of the words 'and they embalmed him' (*wyḥnṭw ᵓtw*). Who were the embalmers? In the light of Gen.50:24a, they may be identified as Joseph's brothers, and this, taken with the use of the word *ᵓtkm* 'with you' in Exod.13:19, may have given rise to the tradition that Joseph was buried with the other patriarchs.[39] But if the reference to the embalming is taken with Gen.50:2, where Joseph is said to have ordered the Egyptian physicians to embalm Jacob, it is not hard to see how the tradition may have arisen that Joseph also was buried at the hands of the Egyptians. It is interesting that both stories, the Nile-story and the royal vault story, assume an Egyptian burial of Joseph, and the antiquity of this element of tradition seems indicated by the evidence of T. Sym. 8:3. As for why the sources preserve these otherwise mutually incompatible stories of Joseph's burial, perhaps we may hazard the guess that they are really two distinct haggadic expositions, the one of Gen.50:25, the other of the very next verse, Gen.50:26. If so, we might have an explanation for their fixity of order in our sources – that is, they follow the order of the verses in Genesis upon which they comment, and in this sense form part of an older stream of verse by verse exposition of Gen.50:24–26.

The scripture passages dealing with the disposal of Joseph's bones have thus been subject to considerable, and indeed early, haggadic treatment. This is not the fate of every verse of scripture, but one key factor in these cases has been the role of the words 'God shall surely visit you.' There are, of course, other streams of tradition about Joseph, notable among which are those which dwell on his piety and purity.[40] For example, his purity is extolled in Tg. Ps. 81:6 and in Sir.49:15(17–18). In Ps.81:6, after the words 'He appointed it as a testimony concerning Joseph', the Targum has the following addition (not represented in MT or LXX): 'because he did not approach the wife of his master; in that day he went forth from prison and became ruler over all the land of Egypt.'[41] This recalls 2 Macc.2:53 which, in a passage praising the men of old, says: 'Joseph in the time of his distress kept the commandment and he became master of Egypt.'[42] In 4 Macc.2:2–5 'Joseph the prudent' (ὁ σώφρων Ιωσηφ) is praised for showing self-control and keeping the commandment not to covet his neighbour's wife nor anything that is his neighbour's.[43] Similar motifs occur in Testaments of the Twelve Patriarchs, in Stephen's speech (cf. Acts 7:10), and in Rabbinic sources. Thus, in Mekh. Beshall. 1:1 and b. Sota 13a, the two boxes ('arks'), the one containing Joseph's bones, the other the Tables of the Torah, accompany one another to the Promised Land. The lesson is drawn that the deceased man in the one box fulfilled all that was written on the contents of the other. The Mekhilta amplifies this to show in detail how Joseph kept each of the Commandments even before they were given, and the example of his resistance to the wiles of Potiphar's wife clearly finds a place here.[44] Sir.49:15(17,18) links the piety motif with that of the bones: 'Like Joseph was ever a man born! Even his body (Heb.: *gwytw*, but LXX: 'his bones', τὰ ὀστᾶ αὐτοῦ) was (were) visited!'[45] The Mishnah, Sifre to Numbers and the Tanḥuma all praise him: 'Whom do we have greater than Joseph, with whom no-one but Moses busied himself (in the care of his bones)?'[46]

The same thought recurs in the writings of Aphraat, but most interestingly linked with an exposition of Gen.50:24, set in a passage arguing that the patriarchs confidently expected the resurrection of the dead. The section even begins by referring to Heb.11:15,16. Thus Jacob wanted to be buried not in Egypt but with his ancestors, so that, when he was raised at the end, he would be raised with them and not in the company of wicked men whose destiny was Sheol.[47] Aphraat then turns to Joseph and refers to the latter's oath. Joseph's brothers acted according to his word and kept the oath one hundred and twenty-five years. and when the hosts of the Lord came forth from Egypt,

> Moses took up the bones of Joseph and went forth, and the bones of the pious man were precious to him, better by far than the gold and silver which the People of Israel took from Egypt when they took spoil from them (i.e., the Egyptians).[48]

He further tells us that the bones of Joseph were in the desert forty years, and when Moses died, he bequeathed them to Joshua. Here we have a close parallel to the tradition found in the Rabbinic sources, which similarly connect the Joseph's bones statements with (a) his piety, and (b) the hope in the resurrection of the dead and the life of the world/age to come.[49]

The bones of Joseph motif is thus seen to be an early, pervasive and central element in the portrait of the patriarch in Judaism. Joseph, by his piety and faithfulness to Torah even in advance of its being given formally, and by his steadfastness in his many (ten!) trials,[50] ranks next to Moses, who alone in Israel honoured the oath in respect of the patriarch's bones. But the scripture passages in question are linked by the formula, 'God shall surely visit you', which looks to the exodus and emancipation of Israel from Egypt. In later midrashim this formula becomes the mark of the Redeemer and shows that Joseph knew that God would fulfil his oath to Abraham. But the same pattern of Jewish exegesis links that event in turn with the ultimate redemption of Israel by the Messiah.

We may thus offer a possible reason why the author of Hebrews chose to refer to Joseph's words recalling God's oath to Abraham and giving instructions about his own bones. It fits at once with the picture found elsewhere in Jewish exegesis of the piety and faithfulness of Joseph, and of the view that the visitation of which he spoke referred not only to Moses and the exodus but also to the final liberation of Israel at the hand of the Second Redeemer. Or as Heb.11:39–40 puts it:

> All these – though they were attested through faith – did not attain the promise, since God had forseen something better for us, that apart from us they should not be made perfect.

Notes

1. Cf. J. H. Moulton and G. Milligan, *The Vocabulary of the Greek Testament* (London, 1930) 660a. The work will be cited as MM.
2. MM 889, especially 889b. Cf. G. Horsley and others, *New Documents Illustrating Early Christianity*, vol. 3 (1983) p. 15.
3. Thus, for example, T. H. Robinson, *The Epistle to the Hebrews* (Moffatt New Testament Commentary, London, 1933) p. 166, sees it as akin to the instance of Isaac's faith (Heb.11:20): for him God's promises regarding the future are as good as 'present facts'.
4. κατὰ πίστιν.
5. See M. Avi-Yonah, *Encyclopaedia of Archaeological Excavations in the Holy Land* (London, 1978) 4.1083.
6. Cf. also Gen.23:16–20 and 49:29–32.
7. *Ant.* 2.8.2 (199); so also Jub.46:9. The Israelites took up the bones of all the patriarchs except Joseph and buried them in Hebron. See also note 10 below.
8. *Ant.* 2.8.2 (200). Cf. also *Ant.* 2.15.1 (319).
9. Italics mine. The text is as follows: ἐν τῇ ἐξόδῳ τῶν υἱῶν Ἰσραηλ ἐξ Αἰγύπτου συνήγαγον τὰ ὀστᾶ Ἰωσηφ, καὶ ἔθαψαν αὐτὸν ἐν Χεβρων μετὰ τῶν πατέρων αὐτοῦ, κτλ. Cf. M. de Jonge, in co-operation with H. W. Hollander, H. J. de Jonge, and Th. Korteweg, *The Testaments of the Twelve Patriarchs* (Pseudepigrapha Veteris Testamenti Graece, vol. 1.2: Leiden, 1978) p. 166. The burials of the eleven brothers of Joseph are explicitly sited in Hebron in T. Rub. 7:2, T. Sym. 8:2, T. Levi 19:5, T. Jud. 26:4, T. Iss. 7:8, T. Zeb. 10:7, T. Dan 8:2, T. Naph. 9:1–3, T. Asher 8:1–2, T. Benj. 12:1–2.
10. R. H. Charles, *The Apocrypha and Pseudepigrapha of the Old Testament in English*, vol. 2 (Oxford, 1913) p. 77n. He sees Josephus, The Testaments of the Twelve Patriarchs, 'Stephen', and Jubilees as all preserving the same tradition here. The burial places of the patriarchs are not mentioned in the Old Testament.
11. See M. Wilcox, *The Semitisms of Acts* (Oxford, 1965) p. 31. Aquila and Symmachus read παρὰ τῶν υἱῶν Εμμωρ.
12. M. de Jonge, *Testaments*, p. 23. T. Sym. 8:2 tells that Symeon's body was put in a coffin of incorruptible wood by his sons to take his bones up to Hebron. They went there secretly during 'the war of the Egyptians' (also mentioned in Jub.46:6–9). The bones of Joseph, however, were retained by the Egyptians, as T. Sym. 8:3–4 states. Cf. Jub.46:9, and also Josephus, *Ant.* 2.8.2 (200), where there is, as it happens, no mention of the 'war'.
13. μνήμασι is read by MSS *chij*.
14. βασιλέων is read by MSS *deafchij*.
15. b. Sota 13b.
16. H. S. Horovitz and I. A. Rabin, *Mechilta d'Rabbi Ismael* (2nd ed. Breslau, 1930, repr. Jerusalem, 1970) p. 78, lines 16–17.
17. *qpyṭwlwn*, also attested in Syriac, meaning 'Capitolium'. Horovitz-Rabin

give in their text the alternative reading *[b]qypwswlyn*; J. Levy, *Neuhebräisches Wörterbuch über die Talmudim und Midraschim* (2nd ed. Berlin/Wien, 1924, repr. Darmstadt, 1963) traces this to Latin 'capsula', and would translate as 'box, casket', but suggests that it is here a corruption of *qwptwlyn*, from Greek κάπετος meaning 'grave', 'tomb' (Levy, 4.353a and 271b, respectively).

18. *(b)qbrnyt.*
19. *(b)qbwrt.*
20. *(b)qbry.*
21. *(btwk) hpltwryn*; Levy, *Wörterbuch*, 4.50b, gives it as 'palace', and hence, 'mausoleum' in the present context. It seems to derive from 'praetorium'. Cf. Tanh. Shemot 24, where Moses and Aaron are said to approach 'the Praetorium of Pharoah'.
22. So Mekh. Beshall. 1:1, b. Sota 13a, Tanh. Beshall. 2, t. Sota 4:7, PRE 48:83–84.
23. Targum Pseudo-Jonathan (cited as Tg. Ps.-J.), represented by BL Add. MS. 27031, at Gen.46:17, Num.26:46.
24. The text used is that of David Luria (Venice, 1837, repr. Jerusalem, 1970). The present form of the midrash is early mediaeval, but it appears to contain much ancient material. See the valuable introduction in G. Friedlander, *Pirke de Rabbi Eliezer* (London, 1916, repr. as 4th edition, New York, 1981) esp. pp. xiii-iv. See further note 29 below.
25. Tanh. Shemot 24 takes up Exod.4:28, 'And Moses and Aaron went and instructed all the elders of Israel', and depicts Moses's message as 'the Holy One, Blessed be He, said, "I have visited you".' This dictum is then identified as the sign which was passed down from the days of Abraham and Isaac, and which Jacob passed to Joseph, and he (Moses or Joseph?) said to them, 'Every redeemer who shall come and say to you, "I have surely redeemed (you)", is a genuine redeemer.' When Moses came and said, 'I have surely redeemed (you)', at once the people believed. Cf. also Gen.R. 97:6.
26. Note how the Targumim (and indeed the Peshitta) render the Hebrew verb *pqd* ('to visit') by *dkr* ('to remember'). Who are the two redeemers referred to here? Moses and Aaron? Or, perhaps rather, Moses and Messiah?
27. PRE 48:84.
28. As examples we may cite the Murabbaʿat documents: 22:1, 24B:2, 24D:2, 24E:1–2, 29:I:1, 29:II:1, 30:II:1, and for the coins refer to E. Schürer, *The History of the Jewish People in the Age of Jesus Christ* (New English Edition revised and edited by G. Vermes, F. Millar and M. Black, Edinburgh, 1973) vol. 1, pp. 605–6. Note that the phrase *lgʾlt ṣywn* occurs on some coins from the First Jewish Revolt also.
29. G. Friedlander, *Pirke*, p. 383 n. 8, interprets Wisd.18:6 to refer to the night ('of redemption') which 'was known *beforehand* to our fathers, that knowing surely on what oaths they trusted they might be cheered.' In PRE 48:81–82, which immediately precedes the Serah material, we have a tradition concerning the five special letters (or signs) delivered to Abraham – the five

Hebrew letters which have distinct final forms (k, m, n, p, ṣ): these trace the revelation of the mystery of the redemption from Abraham to Messiah, from 'Go get thee . . .' (Gen.12:1), through the sign of the Exodus, 'I have surely visited', to the final redemption in the future (Zech.6:12), referring to the 'Branch' who 'shall grow up . . . and build the temple of the Lord.' (Cf. Friedlander, *Pirke*, p. 384).

30. So in the Oxford MS. and the printed editions, but the Munich MS. has in place of ṣrwr, 'pebble', the text 'He took a gold plate and engraved upon it the Ineffable Name.' (The translations are mine).
31. The Munich MS. reads here: 'Joseph son of Jacob'!
32. Exod.R. 20:17 records both traditions of the burial of Joseph, but does not give separate accounts of the coffin-acquisition stories; it has only the words of Moses as in the Royal-vault story, which it presents in a form akin to, but briefer than, that in b. Sota and against Mekh.: 'the time is at hand of which you said, "God will surely visit you." At once Joseph's coffin wobbled, and Moses took it.'
33. That the box was a metal one is implied in the *qal vaḥomer* argument given in Mekh. Beshall. 1:1, but is stated explicitly in t. Sota 4:7, b. Sota 13a, and Tanh. Beshall. 2.
34. Thus, Heb.11:17 reads Αβρααμ . . . τὸν μονογενῆ προσέφερεν. The MT has ʾt-bnk ʾt-yḥydk; cf. Aquila τὸν μονογενῆ and Symmachus τὸν μόνον σου, against LXX τὸν ἀγαπητόν. Cf. also Gen.22:12, where the same difference occurs between LXX on the one side, and the Hebrew and Symmachus on the other.
35. wᶜṭrwn ytyh.
36. wʾsq, against MT wyqḥ, Tg. Neofiti wnsb; cf. Sy. The LXX reads καὶ ἔλαβεν.
37. See above, note 26. The same word appears in the Syriac writings of Aphraat and Ephraem Syrus.
38. The forms in MT and Tg. Neofiti are akin in meaning to that found in the Rabbinic sources (namely, nṭl, 'to take'); the other targumic sources thus not only differ from MT and Tg. Neofiti, but from the Rabbinic material here.
39. See above, note 9.
40. It is through his 'merit' (zkwt) and that of Jacob that Tanh. Tissa 30 (end) sees 'an eternal redemption' effected: 'by the merit of Jacob and by thy merit, as it is written, Thou hast redeemed thy people with might, O Sons of Jacob and Joseph, Selah' (Ps.77:16). Comparison with the Targum to Psalms, MSS Villa-Amil 5 and Paris ms. hébr. 110, 'Thou hast redeemed thy people with the might of thine arm, O sons whom Jacob begat and Joseph nourished, forever.' Note how 'Selah' is represented by lᶜlmyn ('forever'). The redemption envisaged thus seems to be an 'eternal' one.
41. dlʾ qryb lʾth rybwnyh bywmʾ npq mbyt ʾsyry wšlyṭ bkl ʾrᶜ dmṣrym.
42. Ιωσηφ ἐν καιρῷ στενοχωρίας ἐφύλαξεν ἐντολήν, καὶ ἐγένετο κύριος Αἰγύπτου.
43. ὁ σώφρων Ιωσηφ ἐπαινεῖται, ὅτι τῷ λογισμῷ διανοίᾳ περιεκράτησεν τῆς ἡδυπαθείας (2:2); the reference to lust and the relevant commandment comes in 2:5.

44. Thus Joseph did not murder Potiphar, nor commit adultery with the latter's wife, nor even covet her.
45. The Hebrew is taken from S. Schechter and C. Taylor, *The Wisdom of Ben Sira* (Cambridge, 1899) p. 19. For the word translated 'visited' (*npqdh*), the editors make the shrewd observation that we should compare Gen.50:25,26. The passage is absent from the Bar Kokhba fragments of Ben Sira. LXX reads: καὶ τὰ ὀστᾶ αὐτοῦ ἐπεσκέπτησαν.
46. m. Sota 1:9, Sifre Num. 106 (edition, p. 105), Tanh. Beshall. 2, etc.
47. Aphraat, *Demonstrationes*, 8.7-8 (On the Resurrection of the Dead). The edition is that of R. Graffin and I. Parisot, *Aphraatis Sapientis Persae Demonstrationes* (*Patrologia Syriaca* 1.1: Paris, 1894) 8:7 (col. 372 and 373).
48. *Dem.* 8:8 (col. 373). (My translation of the Syriac).
49. The reference to Joshua appears in 8.8 (col. 376). The same context – the preoccupation of Israel with the booty contrasted with Moses' concern for the bones of Joseph – appears in Ephraim Syrus, *Sancti Ephraim Syri in Genesim et in Exodum Commentarii*, (ed. R. M. Tonneau), *Corpus Scriptorum Christianorum Orientalism*, vols 152 and 153 (= Tom.71 and 72), Louvain, 1955, *Comm. in Exod.*, Sect. 13:1 (vol. 152/tom.71, p. 142). Cf. j. Sota 1:10; and Pesiqta Rabbathi 12 (49b), which states that Joseph confessed his faith in the Resurrection of the Dead (referring to his oath regarding his bones, Exod.13:19 being cited), whereas Esau denied it (cf. Gen.25:32, where Esau sees nothing beyond the grave).
50. m. Abot 5:4 tells us that Abraham was tested with ten trials, all of which he safely passed; so also, then, our texts refer to Joseph in the same way.

PART TWO: METHOD

9

Fundamentalism and Scholarship: The Case of Daniel

Lester L. Grabbe

There are many biblical fundamentalists, primarily Christian but also Jewish, who regard themselves as no less scholars because of their religious presuppositions. And there are scholars, not fundamentalists, who accept these claims at face value. The question is, Can one be a fundamentalist and still claim the label 'biblical scholar'?

The problem with biblical scholarship, as with many types of scholarship in the humanities, is that issues are frequently complex. It is therefore perfectly possible for one to raise valid objections to a consensus of scholarship such as, for example, the documentary hypothesis for the Pentateuch. Scholars a long way from being fundamentalist recognise that widely accepted conclusions in many areas by no means settle the question. Therefore, my purpose is to focus on one subject very close to the sensitivities of most fundamentalists, yet one in which the issues are much more clear-cut than with various literary theories: the Book of Daniel.

The subject of biblical fundamentalism has been dealt with in a comprehensive way by James Barr,[1] and it is not my purpose to retrace what he has already covered in breadth. However, this look at a specific topic of central concern to most fundamentalists might both illustrate some of the points he has made and bring other aspects of it to light. It should be noted that the term 'fundamentalist' in this article is used to designate a certain attitude and approach to the Bible, generally formalised as a belief that the biblical text is 'inerrant in the autographs'. Many of those who hold this view would not use the term 'fundamentalist' to refer to themselves but rather such terms as 'conservative' or 'evangelical' or both together. These are not always equivalent terms, however, since not every conservative-evangelical is a fundamentalist as I use the term here.[2]

To expose both my strength and my bias from the start, I am an ex-fundamentalist, an advantage or disadvantage which many writers on the subject have not had. I grew up in the American 'Bible belt' and attended what is often referred to as a 'Bible college' to the M.A. level. In addition to an unpublished thesis on the subject of biblical truth, I penned a number of articles in denominational magazines with a nation-wide circulation in defence of the objective accuracy of the Bible.[3] As far as I was concerned, scholarship was valid and necessary but true scholarship in no way conflicted with the truth of the Bible while, conversely, scholarship which did conflict was ultimately only 'science falsely so-called' (1 Tim.6:20, AV). Thus, it was as a convinced funda-mentalist that I commenced my doctoral study at a 'liberal' institution. When I began my studies I was aware of the dangers at such an institution and was determined not to be 'corrupted' by its influences. My conver-sion – or corruption, depending on one's point of view – from funda-mentalism was, despite my best efforts, done by scholarship. I was continually forced to face data relevant to my beliefs which also conflict-ed with them. Since I could not ignore this new information, which clearly needed to be taken into account, I had to accommodate it to my beliefs. Even though I could often do this without any apparent diffi-culty, it gradually dawned on me that my attempts to embrace both a fundamentalist approach to the Bible and the new intellectual experi-ences were often extremely contorted. Nevertheless, my eventual deci-sion to abandon fundamentalism was formulated over a considerable period of time and was not finally made until after I had obtained my Ph.D.

The essence of scholarship is objectivity, yet we all know that true objectivity is an impossible ideal. Subjectivity is inextricably built into the most scrupulously neutral investigation. But progress is made because the bias of one individual is countered by the scepticism of another. The prejudice of one generation is attacked by the next. The limitations of the individual are overcome by the process of many different persons hypothesising and criticising from various points of view. One of the ways in which scholarship attempts to overcome individual limitations is, as it were, for the researcher to put his cards on the table: to give references, acknowledge help, and recognise factors which may give a bias to the point of view being presented. This is done more conscientiously by some than by others but is accepted as a very desirable procedure by all. The aim of the scholarly method is to overcome the limitations of individual scholars, and it is by the application of this method that knowledge advances in an overall way, despite the lack of consensus on many points at any one time or the fact that favoured hypotheses are regularly abandoned.

But is it not true that many fundamentalists are recognised scholars and participate fully in the scholarly process? Yes, of course. On the other hand, their scholarship is almost invariably applied in areas in which there is no confrontation between it and their view of the Bible.[4] And – to come to my major point – when they deal with the Bible even in an apparently objective manner, this is only a cloak for the actual hidden agenda which is to defend the biblical data. My charge is a serious one but one which can be demonstrated from many examples. Time and again fundamentalists fail to be honest about their lack of objectivity but use the trappings of serious scholarly research as a cloak for what is really only an exercise in apologetics, since their basic conclusions were predetermined before a datum was examined.

I will draw on a variety of writings on Daniel which seem to me to represent a fundamentalist perspective.[5] Although by no means exhaustive, the list fairly represents a spectrum of recent writing on the subject, in most cases by individuals well respected among evangelicals in general or at least one of its particular communities (such as the Seventh Day Adventists). Most of the writers are scholars in a particular area – Egyptology, Assyriology, Gnosticism, Old Testament text – though not usually in Old Testament specifically. Some of the statements made are more extreme than others, sometimes because of the differing contexts (popular as opposed to a more scholarly context), and certainly there is no unanimity about the various arguments or their relative value. Nevertheless, despite some differences of expression or emphasis there is remarkable consistency in the basic data and argumentation used by the various authors. It is not my purpose to attempt to deal with the whole range of questions relating to Daniel but only with some of the main ones which have been adduced in the debate. Since the purpose is illustrative, it is not necessary to be comprehensive.

Predictive Prophecy

One of the charges often made by fundamentalists is that 'critical' scholars do not allow for genuine predictive prophecy:

> The German literary-critical movement seized avidly upon the supposition that the prophecy could contain no predictive element, and repudiated the Jewish and Christian tradition of a sixth century B.C. date . . . Objections to the historicity of Daniel were copied uncritically from book to book, and by the second decade of the twentieth century no scholar of general liberal background who wished to preserve his academic reputation either dared or desired to challenge the current critical trend.[6]

This represents a distortion on several counts. First, most people would allow that it is humanly possible to make correct predictions about the future within a limited scope. Predictions are made by economists, politicians, social scientists, meteorologists, and fortune-tellers. Some of them, of course, turn out to be right. I am not aware of a scholar of any persuasion who would consider it impossible for Deutero-Isaiah to foresee correctly Cyrus' conquest of Babylon, for Jeremiah to be right about the fall of Judah to the Babylonians, or for Nahum to prophesy in advance the fall of Nineveh. Secondly, even fundamentalists would object to the idea of detailed accurate prediction outside the biblical canon. For scholars to doubt that Daniel 11 was written before the events is not only to follow normal historical methodology used for all literature of the past but also simply to apply the common sense we all live by from day to day. Thirdly, if one wishes to find examples of 'uncritical copying' of arguments about Daniel, one only has to read the fundamentalist corpus on the subject, especially on the popular level. In many cases the writers are manifestly advancing arguments they themselves have not the intellectual equipment or training to maintain and are only borrowing from others. The lack of critical thinking is also pointed up by the habit which some have of quoting other fundamentalists to bolster their stance.

The fundamentalist approach asks scholarship to be inconsistent, to use criteria for the Bible which are different from those used with other literature. For example, Baldwin makes reference to the 'Dynastic Prophecy' in Babylonian literature[7] yet does not think it necessary to explain why she does not accept it as genuine prediction. But if we must allow for detailed prediction in Daniel, why not in Babylonian literature – or Egyptian prophecies or the Sibylline Oracles or the rest of the vast predictive literature outside the canon? Yamauchi seems to recognise the problem when he states:

> Now it is certain that there were cases in Egypt and Mesopotamia of prophecies after the event for the purpose of political propaganda. But whether any given ancient prophecy was made after the event must be proved by other criteria, and not initially assumed.[8]

This statement is rather disingenuous since Yamauchi obviously does not accept the genuineness of any other ancient *detailed* prophecy. In the end, it is not that fundamentalists wish scholars to take seriously claims of detailed foretelling but rather that they want the Bible – at least, *their* particular version of the Bible – to be allowed predictive prophecy *as a special case*. In other words, they want the normal canons of research to be suspended when it comes to the Bible.

Ironically, the existence of correct predictions with regard to Daniel is not unknown in scholarship. For example, Montgomery wrote in 1927 that the Daniel of Ezek. 14:14, 20 had to be not the figure of the book of Daniel, but 'an evidently traditional saint ... a figure of antique and cosmopolitan tradition, like the Noah-Utnapishtim of the Flood story.'[9] The discovery of the Ugaritic texts, which included the 'antique' figure of Dan'el, two years later was startling evidence of a correct prediction. (See also below regarding Nabonidus and Dan. 2–4.)

The concept of accurate detailed predictions actually brings up a theological problem which I have yet to see discussed in fundamentalist writings: the question of free choice. The idea of complete determinism is repugnant to most of us. Perhaps one can argue for an overall divine control of history and/or the universe while allowing individual freedom, but a detailed prophecy such as Daniel 11 would render free choice impossible. Only if the Ptolemies and Seleucids were mere puppets in the hand of God could such a prophecy be made. The religious views of some might see no problem with this, but most fundamentalists would face a conflict with their own theological presuppositions if they were to think through the implications of their statements about prophecy.

Selected Examples from Daniel

1. Daniel 1:1

In his publication of the Neo-Babylonian chronicles (Chronicles 2–6) D. J. Wiseman states with regard to a siege of Jerusalem in 605 BCE, 'The only possible evidence for a siege of Jerusalem in this year is Daniel i. 1, but the exegesis of this verse is difficult and uncertain.'[10] Dan.1:1–2 says that Nebuchadnezzar besieged Jerusalem in Jehoiakim's third year, captured it, and took the king and part of the temple vessels back to Shinar. There is nothing 'difficult or uncertain' about the passage; it just happens to be wrong. It is 'difficult and uncertain' only if one tries to maintain that it is historical, as is evident from the contorted explanations offered in defence of it.

Sometimes this defence takes the form of avoiding the issue by explaining how the first year of Nebuchadnezzar could be the third year of Jehoiakim instead of his fourth.[11] Another defence seems to be given in all seriousness; at least its absurdity does not seem to have struck those who advance it. Harrison remarks:

> It should be noted also that the reference in Daniel does not state that Jerusalem was captured in the third year of Jehoiakim (605 B.C.), but merely indicates that Nebuchadnezzar took with him to Babylonia certain Judaean hostages.[12]

Is Harrison jesting? When God delivers Jehoiakim into Nebuchadnezzar's hand during a siege of Jerusalem, are we to believe that Nebuchadnezzar still may not have taken the city? But Harrison seems to be in complete earnest, blinded to such points because of his intense desire to support the biblical account. Equally disingenuous is Yamauchi's statement: 'It should be noted that the biblical text in Daniel 1:1 does not explicitly state that Daniel and his companions were deported in the very first attack against Palestine.'[13] Evidently the author of Daniel has mentioned an attack against Jerusalem in the third year of Jehoiakim just to confuse the scholars who are not aware of such subtleties. These points all illustrate how fundamentalists evidently find it difficult to take passages at their most obvious face value when to do so would admit a historical difficulty. Needless to say, they would hardly tolerate such a strained explanation in any other context.

However, a few writers do face up to the real difficulties. Wiseman in a later, more popular writing did offer an explanation which his scholarly publication lacked. He refers to the fact that, according to 'Babylonian Chronicle' 5, ' "at that time Nebuchadrezzar conquered the whole of the Hatti-land" (i.e. Syria-Palestine).' But in a note he points out that 'Hatti' is a restoration which could just as easily be read as 'Hamath'; Grayson has in fact confirmed that the restoration should be 'Hamath' and that 'Hatti' is unlikely.[14] Ultimately, however, Wiseman admits that the silence of the Chronicle about any siege of Jerusalem is a problem and concludes:

> The argument against a specific Babylonian siege rests on silence just as must, at present, any defense of it.... The extant historical data does not allow any dogmatic assertion against the historical accuracy of this verse.[15]

Although some other writers appeal to one or two statements which they then interpret as circumstantial evidence for such an attack, they basically fall back on Wiseman's defence, viz., we just do not have enough information to be sure.[16]

Certainly, there are many periods for which we have little information and one should indeed reserve judgment. But there is hardly a period in Israel's history which is better attested than the last few years of Jerusalem, both from cuneiform sources and the Old Testament itself. And a siege of Jerusalem before 598 is practically unthinkable. Jer.52:27–30 lists three times of exile under Nebuchadnezzar, in the seventh, eighteenth, and twenty-third years. The writer could hardly have been uninterested in an exile in Nebuchadnezzar's first year. Similarly, elsewhere in Jeremiah there is considerable interest in what happens to the various kings, but no such siege as envisioned by Dan.1:1 is hinted at. Jer.27:19–22 speaks of the temple vessels which were taken by Nebuchadnezzar but mentions only the time of the captivity of Jehoiachin. In Jer.36 Baruch writes a scroll threatening Jehoiakim with punishment from the king of Babylon. Yet the king is alleged to have said *in his fifth year* (v. 9), 'How dare you write in it that the king of Babylon will come and destroy this land and cause man and beast to cease from it?' (Jer.36:29). Are we to believe that Jehoiakim said this *after* he had himself been besieged and captured, and part of the temple vessels carried away to Babylon only a year or two before? The statement that the 'extant historical data does not allow any dogmatic assertion against the historical accuracy of this verse' rings rather hollow when we look at the Old Testament sources closest to the alleged time of this siege.[17]

2. *Belshazzar (Dan.5)*

Fundamentalist writers usually make an issue of the fact that the existence of Belshazzar was once doubted, though most do not mention that this was before the heyday of the dreaded 'Higher Critical' movement of the nineteenth century. It is also common to quote Dougherty's statement that Dan.5 is the most accurate source of information this side of the cuneiform records though, again, the reservations of other Assyriologists about this statement are not usually mentioned.[18] Nevertheless, one of the issues which must still be faced is that Belshazzar is called 'king' when in fact he was never king. Several arguments are used to get around this. One is to point out that Belshazzar was entrusted with the 'kingship' (*šarrutu*) during the time that Nabonidus was away in Tema. Certainly, it is true that Belshazzar was regent during this time, or at least part of it. But it is also a fact that he is *never* called king in any of the extant texts, and to be regent is not to be king. Some writers confuse the issue by saying that being entrusted with the 'kingship' was the same as being king, which it obviously was not. Otherwise, Belshazzar would have been called 'king' (*šarru*) in some of the many texts which mention him during this time. Instead, we find that the inscriptions which mention Nabonidus and Belshazzar side by side always refer to him only as 'the king's son' (*mar šarri*), i.e., heir apparent or crown prince, and we know that the new year ceremony was not celebrated during Belshazzar's regency period.[19]

It has been argued that a Jew of Babylon might well refer to Belshazzar as 'king' since he was in direct control while Nabonidus was away and disliked by the Babylonians.[20] Of course, this is possible, though it does not say much for the precision of knowledge alleged for Daniel 5, since the Babylonian scribes never made that mistake. It also does not explain why the important new year festival could not be celebrated, as the 'Nabonidus Chronicle' makes clear. Are we to assume that a Jew of sixth-century Babylon would have been unaware of the importance of the new year celebration and the fact that Belshazzar's presence was not sufficient for it to go forward? Nor does the learned sixth-century writer seem aware that Nabonidus had returned from Tema and was *the resident* king of Babylon during the last year before its fall, regardless of how Belshazzar had appeared in the previous ten years. But these points can be overlooked for the moment since there is another problem of much greater magnitude.

Dan.5:30 says, 'That very night, Belshazzar, the Chaldean king, was killed.' It is now known that Babylon was taken by the Persian army without a fight.[21] One might still argue that perhaps Belshazzar alone resisted or that he was assassinated, unlikely but perhaps possible. But there is clear evidence that Belshazzar almost certainly *did not die at this time*. Our most important source, the 'Nabonidus Chronicle', is an unusual historical source. It is a part of the Neo-Babylonian chronicles about whose objectivity A. K. Grayson has written:

> Within the boundaries of their interest, the writers are quite objective and impartial ... Further, the authors have included all Babylonian kings known to have ruled in this period and there is no evidence that they have omitted any important events which have a bearing on Babylonia during their reigns. Every significant event known in the period from sources other than the chronicles ... which affects Babylonia is referred to in the chronicle.[22]

The 'Nabonidus Chronicle' is extant for the first years of Nabonidus' reign, despite some damage. Then, however, years twelve to sixteen are completely missing except for a few words, and the account becomes intelligible only with the last (seventeenth) year. At that point no mention is made of Belshazzar. In fact, all our known sources cease to mention Belshazzar after about 545 BCE (Nabonidus' fourteenth year). This may well indicate that he died between then and the conquest of Babylon though we cannot be sure. What we *can be sure of* is that he is not mentioned in the events of the seventeenth year and therefore was certainly *not killed* in that year. Remember that no important event is missing from the chronicle; the deaths of the queen mother and some important governors are recorded. It is inconceivable that Belshazzar's death would have been omitted except by a grave scribal lapse. In the present state of our knowledge it is much more credible that Dan.5:30 is wrong.

3. *Nebuchadnezzar's Madness*

One of the suggestions that fundamentalists consistently reject is that which sees Nabonidus as the figure behind the Nebuchadnezzar of Dan.4 and perhaps Dan.3. This theory was developed apparently as early as 1901, in light of the newly-discovered 'Verse Account of Nabonidus'.[23] A thorough exposition of it was made by the Assyriologist W. von Soden in 1935.[24] Basically, the theory argues that while no evidence has been found to substantiate a period of madness on the part of Nebuchadnezzar, we know from contemporary records that Nabonidus did take a course of action which was interpreted by the Babylonians as strange. Fairly soon after becoming king in a *coup*, Nabonidus left Babylon in charge of his son Belshazzar and made a 500-mile journey through the desert to the oasis of Tema (Tayma' in modern Saudi Arabia) where he spent the next ten years without returning to Babylon. Not only did he neglect his capital city, in the eyes of the Babylonians, but he committed gross acts of impiety by making it impossible to celebrate the important new year ceremony in honour of Marduk and by elevating another god (the moon god Sin) above Marduk the city god of Babylon.

Undoubtedly, Nabonidus had good reasons for the actions he took, perhaps partly religious but very possibly political. In any event the 'Verse Account of Nabonidus' shows the very unsympathetic view of the matter taken by the Babylonian inhabitants, particularly the priesthood of Marduk. Nabonidus is accused of committing an impious act by setting up the image of a strange deity (i 17–24; cf. Dan.3). His journey to Tema is presented in sarcastic terms. His actions are summarised, in contrast to the 'noble' actions of Cyrus, in this way: '(It was) he (who) stood up in the assembly to praise hi[mself]/(Saying): "I am wise, I know, I have seen (what is) hi[dden]/ (Even) if I do not know how to write (with the stylus), yet I have seen se[cret things]"' (v 8–10; cf. Dan.4:26–27).[25] Part of Nabonidus' derided 'claim of wisdom' is his many visions, which we also know of from Nabonidus' own inscriptions (cf. Dan.2 and 4).[26]

Thus, when the 'Prayer of Nabonidus' from Qumran (4QPrNab) was published in 1956, it naturally created a sensation. The king in it is Nabonidus and the setting is Tema. However, other features are strikingly reminiscent of Dan.4: (1) The king spends seven years in Tema; (2) he has an illness sent by God; (3) a Jewish wise man heals him; (4) he gives honour to the true God. 4QPrNab was concrete literary reality for what the hypothesis had postulated, confirming a remarkable scholarly prediction.

Although a number of fundamentalist writers correctly represent the development of the theory,[27] not all do. For example, Harrison writes:

> The discovery of a manuscript fragment in the fourth Qumran cave containing the "Prayer of Nabonidus" has given rise to speculation that the mental affliction described in Daniel 4 was wrongly attributed to Nebuchadnezzar, and should have been associated instead with Nabonidus.[28]

Similarly, Hasel incorrectly alleges, 'Several scholars have argued that the narrative of Nebuchadnezzar's madness is dependent on the "Prayer of Nabonidus" . . .'[29] 4QPrNab did not – as some have misleadingly implied – lead to the theory but simply gave it greater credence.

The basic fundamentalist response, however, is to argue that 'there are significant differences between Dan.4 and the "Prayer of Nabonidus" that cannot be overlooked',[30] which is to miss the point. Despite some of the misleading statements noted above, few would suggest that 4QPrNab is the source of Dan.4. What it illustrates is how the Nabonidus tradition came to be adapted in folk tradition: the ten year sojourn of Nabonidus in Tema has become seven years in 4QPrNab. A physical illness has become part of the tradition, along with a Jewish wise man who effects a cure and causes the true God to be praised by the pagan king. It shows how an original story of strange behaviour could become transmuted to one of physical illness, and the step from physical to mental illness would be an easy one in the development of the tradition. Nabonidus was not ill in Tema, but there were those who chose to interpret his actions as strange, irreligious, and otherwise suspect. 4QPrNab serves as concrete evidence of how a historical tradition of a Neo-Babylonian king could easily yield the folk tradition of Dan.4, serving as an example of one of the evolutionary stages that had already been postulated between the original Nabonidus tradition and Daniel.

If the Nabonidus connection is rejected, how is the difficult problem of Nebuchadnezzar's madness to be explained? Some of the attempts to find evidence for this are rather strange, as for example the arguments advanced by Harrison. He writes:

> A different tradition, as preserved by Eusebius, went back to Abyde-nus. . . . This tradition seems to be a somewhat garbled reflection of the

narrative in Daniel 4:31, but on the other hand it may have been preserved in such a form deliberately so as to conceal the presence of mental derangement and thus avoid an offense against propriety.[31]

The statement of Abydenus which Harrison refers to is as follows:

> And afterwards, the Chalaeans say, he [Nebuchadnezzar] went up to his palace, and being possessed by some god or other uttered the following speech: "O men of Babylon, I Nebuchadnezzar foretell to you the coming calamity ... There will come a Persian mule ... and will bring you into slavery." He after uttering this prediction had immediately disappeared.[32]

Apparently, Harrison thinks that Abydenus can preserve a garbled tradition of Nebuchadnezzar's madness, but it is still somehow impossible for Dan.4 to preserve a garbled tradition of Nabonidus' strange behaviour.

A further argument of Harrison's even found its way into the *Interpreter's Dictionary of the Bible*, where no source is listed for it.[33] He quotes an inscription which states that Nebuchadnezzar did not do any works of building or devotion for four years. Apparently, Harrison was only interested in supporting his preconceptions about Dan.4; at least he did not feel it necessary to check whether a translation done well over a century ago in the very infancy of cuneiform studies was still considered accurate by modern Assyriologists. If he had checked, he would have found that a completely different translation was already given at least as early as 1873, and there have been more recent editions and translations of the text.[34] Needless to say, current scholarship knows nothing of such a four-year hiatus in Nebuchadnezzar's reign. The inscription referred to by Harrison actually describes the many detailed buildings and works of devotion on the part of Nebuchadnezzar![35]

Hasel has advanced a similar argument, using a newly-published but fragmentary inscription:

> The accuracy of the biblical record of Nebuchadnezzar's insanity has been questioned.... A recent discovery, however, now provides historical information which appears to have direct bearing on Nebuchadnezzar's mental derangement.[36]

But the certainty of Hasel's statement is matched neither by the state of the text nor by Hasel's following comments (my italics):

It *is possible* that the subject refers to Nebuchadnezzar . . . If Nebuchadnezzar is the main actor in this text . . . *We may hypothesize* that the crown prince Evil-Merodach was forced to take over the government from his father . . . *If our interpretation* of this new cuneiform text *is correct*, we have for the first time extrabiblical contemporary historical evidence that corroborates and supports the account in Dan 4.[37]

Now, it is certainly legitimate to attempt to develop hypotheses and make sense of even fragmentary material. But one should also recognise that the use of uncertain and fragmentary material makes any interpretation tentative. Hasel does not bother to mention that the editor of the text gives a rather different overall interpretation:

> In the small portion that is preserved the main theme seems to be the improper behaviour of Evil-Merodach, particularly with regard to Esagil, followed by a sudden and unexplained change of heart and prayers to Marduk.[38]

But Hasel is not trying to make sense of a fragmentary inscription; he is trying to defend the historicity of Nebuchadnezzar's madness, and the slightest bit of evidence – however small or uncertain – is grist to his mill. He evidently finds it easy to hypothesise from obscure fragmentary texts but difficult to accept a theory based on such intelligible texts as the 'Nabonidus Verse Account' and 4QPrNab.

'Conservative' versus 'Liberal' Scholarship

An interesting study in itself is the rhetoric found in fundamentalist writings. On the whole, such writings are apologetic and often polemical as well, which is perhaps understandable since the authors obviously feel threatened by much scholarly work. What is strange, though, is the continual distortion of what scholarship is and how the scholarly process works. Unfortunately, many who would consider themselves scholars are as guilty of this as other writers, though their rhetoric is usually more restrained in their scholarly writings.[39]

In the popular writings one finds a constant reference to 'the critics', 'the higher critics' or 'higher criticism', 'liberal scholars', and the like. A frequent binary opposition is 'liberal scholars' versus 'conservative scholars', an opposition which represents one of the major misrepresentations found in fundamentalist writings attempting to be scholarly. There is no such thing as 'liberal' scholarship versus 'conservative' scholarship. Scholarship by its very nature is always liberal, and all scholars *by definition* are critics. That is, scholarship is a method of inquiring which implies being neither bound to dogma nor afraid to challenge the status quo. To be a scholar is to make judgments, to be a judge – *a critic*. All scholars have to challenge arguments, to weigh evidence, to exercise scepticism rather than taking things at their surface content. It requires independence.

There may be, and frequently are, different ways of weighing a set of data. Two careful and sincere scholars can in certain cases come to radically different conclusions, but the ideal is that all follow the evidence wherever it leads. The evidence may lead to conservative results, and it is no denial of the scholarly method to come to conservative conclusions *if* one has fully considered all the data and arguments. But those who talk of 'conservative' scholarship versus 'liberal' scholarship have already shown their ignorance about what the scholarly process consists of.

Yet do not writings by fundamentalists frequently exhibit a sceptical frame of mind, a necessary characteristic of scholarly thinking? The answer is that the scepticism of fundamentalist writers is completely uni-directional. It is *always* directed against any challenge to the credibility of the biblical text. It is simply the reverse of the coin, of which the other side is complete *belief* in the veracity of the Bible. It is not the scepticism of the scholar, which must be applied to all evidence, but the counterpart of religious faith. In the same way fundamentalists may advance new theories and attempt new understandings of the Bible, thus appearing to be engaged in the scholarly task. It is even possible to find one fundamentalist disagreeing with or even writing a critique of another. Nevertheless, this is always done within agreed limits: there can be no infringement of the inerrancy of the Bible in its original.

Does Critical Scholarship have an 'Antisupernaturalistic Bias'?

Gleason Archer has written 'The committed antisupernaturalist, who can only explain the successful predictions of Daniel as prophecies after the fulfillment, . . . is not likely to be swayed by any amount of objective evidence whatever.'[40] Of course, Archer does not admit that he and other fundamentalists also happen to be 'committed antisupernaturalists' when it comes to any writings or predictions outside the Bible. They are vehemently antisupernaturalist about the Quran, the Upanishads, the Gathas, the Mishnah, the book of Mormon, and any number of other religious writings not in their accepted canon.

It is not that the supernatural claims of other books have been considered; the fundamentalist is interested only in the supernatural claims of his particular Holy Book. This is made quite clear in Harrison's *Introduction*. He refers to 'the allegation that Daniel is replete with historical inaccuracies or errors, and that these are of a kind that a responsible author in the sixth century B.C. would not have committed or tolerated'.[41] He then goes on to spend pages and pages attempting to refute this 'allegation'. Later in his volume when he discusses the book of Tobit, however, Harrison is quite content with a blanket *allegation* (to use his language) about its historicity – 'the author was guilty of certain errors connected with the history and geography of the Near East'[42] – and a brief list of these errors (citing critical scholars!) without discussion. It is clear that he is uninterested in substantiating his claim that 'the book is completely unhistorical'.[43] Similarly, he deals only briefly with the historicity of Judith, being content with the statement that 'the author is guilty of a great many errors and anachronisms'[44] and a short account of these. Yet recent scholarship would see a historical core behind Judith, just as it does behind the tales of Daniel.[45]

However, we must not forget that some conservative Christians accept both Judith and Tobit as part of the inspired canon. Hugh Pope has written, with regard to the historicity of the book, 'Catholics with very few exceptions accept the Book of Judith as a narrative of facts, not as an allegory.'[46] He goes on to list the arguments in favour of the historicity, though he is candid that there are difficulties. In a similar vein Walter Drum has stated with regard to the Book of Tobit:

> Until recently there never was a question among Catholics in regard to the historicity of Tobias . . . With these and a few other exceptions, Catholic exegetes are unanimous in clearly defending the historicity of Tobias . . . Now the arguments against the historical worth of Tobias

are not at all solid; they are mere conjectures, which it would be most rash to admit. We shall examine some of these conjectures . . . Certain historical difficulties are due to the very imperfect condition in which the text has reached us.[47]

Thus, a conservative Catholic can use almost identical language about the historicity of Judith or Tobit that Harrison and other conservative Protestants use about Daniel. And their attempts at defence have very much the same flavour. On the other hand, Harrison and his fellow believers can use the normal language of critical scholarship about writings which they regard as non-canonical. This is all stark testimony to how the fundamentalist approach to scholarship is determined not by objective study but by preconceptions about what is inspired. Since fundamentalist Protestants do not accept the canonicity of Judith and Tobit, they are quite willing to accept the results of critical scholarship, whereas conservative Catholics find this difficult because they view the books as part of Holy Scripture. It is clear that the rhetoric about scholarship, historicity, and objectivity on the part of Harrison, Archer and others is so much sophistry. For them Daniel is known to be historically accurate from the start, not as the result of a neutral investigation. Critical study unhampered by such theological bias can find a historical core behind Judith just as it can behind certain of the tales in Daniel; both have historical remembrances but both are essentially unhistorical works of theology.

Conclusions

What I have attempted to demonstrate here is not that one way of understanding the book of Daniel is somehow *the* right one. On the contrary, scholarship is always pushing beyond today's *status quo*, probing, challenging, applying new data and new theory. What I have been trying to show is that – despite noises to the contrary – fundamentalism is incompatible with scholarship. Fundamentalism has already determined its conclusions; it is not seeking because it already knows the answer. If it has good evidence on its side which supports the Bible, it uses it. If it has little data, it twists and interprets what it has to support the Bible. If it has no evidence, it hypothesises that such will eventually be found. And of course no amount of contrary evidence is sufficient. Fundamentalism can *never* conclude that the Bible is wrong. Scholarship, on the other hand, recognises that any conclusion is always more or less tentative, that new data may require a revision of conclusions. New evidence can disprove a theory; it can disprove the historicity of the Bible as well as prove it. This the fundamentalist will not accept, no matter how much he may couch his arguments in the language of scholarship.

Scholarship combines theory with data to come up with results, sometimes more conservative and sometimes more radical. But the fundamentalist does not come sometimes to a more conservative conclusion and sometimes to a more radical conclusion when it concerns the Bible. He will always come to the most conservative conclusion possible. He may *appear* to be following the scholarly model but that is only an illusion. His 'theory' in the model already contains his conclusion, viz., that the Bible is somehow or other always correct. His model is really circular, in that he begins and ends with 'truth', while the data do not ultimately affect the conclusion.

The point is that scholars work with certain methods and certain presuppositions. These are known and accepted by all. Even fundamentalists accept them for writings other than their particular sacred literature. Perhaps in a hundred or a thousand years, scholarship will have changed drastically; perhaps much of what is done today will look wrong or at least very primitive. Nevertheless, one who wishes to deviate from the accepted methodology should make it explicit that he is doing so. Perhaps many fundamentalists assume that the vehicle used will make that clear, such as the use of a conservative journal or publishing house. For example, the *Journal of the Evangelical Theological Society* presupposes a fundamentalist approach, since all members of the Society must assent to a statement of belief of which the inerrancy of the Bible in the autographs is a central tenet. Similarly, the *Bibliotheca Sacra* is clearly fundamentalist in orientation, as a short perusal would demonstrate. On the other hand, while many of the articles in the *Andrews University Seminary Studies* are by believing Adventists, not all are by any means. Therefore, it seems only fair that writers should make clear their religious presuppositions instead of hiding them.

Certainly, a fundamentalist has a right to his beliefs, but he should declare them when they affect his scholarship. It seems to me a clear deviation from one's avowed religious faith to write an apologetic under the guise of scholarship. Unfortunately, some apparently are not even able to recognise their own lack of objectivity and evidently really believe that their religious apologetic should be taken seriously by scholars. For such individuals, there seems no hope. But it would be like a breath of fresh air to find a writer who wrote words along the lines of the following:

> By faith I believe that the Bible is correct on such and such a point, but I think that a scholarly case can also be made for its correctness. Of course, I am biased in this matter and therefore cannot evaluate the soundness of the arguments presented, but here is the argumentation for others to consider.

Professor Hanson throughout his career has pressed for a 'reasonable belief', one which denied the place of neither the intellect nor faith. He would have nothing to do with any personal religion which ultimately subordinated logic to belief. It is a pleasure to dedicate this essay to him.

Notes

1. James Barr, *Fundamentalism* (London, 1977).
2. For a discussion of the meaning of the term, see Barr, 1–10.
3. Among my writings were *The Source of True History* (unpublished M.A. thesis, Ambassador College, Pasadena, Calif., 1970); 'Evolutionists "Speechless" on the Origin of Language', *The Plain Truth* (Aug.–Sept. 1970) 28–32; 'Daniel – Battleground of Biblical Criticism', *Tomorrow's World* (Jan. 1971) 38–40; 'The Exodus', ibid. (April 1971) 28–30; 'The Tower of Babel', ibid. (July 1971) 17–18; 'The Computer looks at the Bible', *The Plain Truth* (Sept.–Oct. 1972) 33–6.
4. See Barr, pp. 128–32.
5. These sources include the following, which will be referred to only by the author's name unless a brief title is needed to distinguish between two publications by the same person: J. G. Baldwin, *Daniel* (Leicester, 1978); R. K. Harrison, *Introduction to the Old Testament* (Grand Rapids, 1969); G. H. Hasel, 'The Book of Daniel: evidence relating to persons and chronology', *Andrews University Seminary Studies* 19 (1981) 37–49; B. K. Waltke, 'The Date of the Book of Daniel', *Bibliotheca Sacra* 133 (1976) 319–29; D. J. Wiseman, 'Some Historical Problems in the Book of Daniel', *Notes on Some Problems in the Book of Daniel* (London, 1965) pp. 9–18; E. M. Yamauchi, *The Stones and the Scriptures* (Philadelphia/New York, 1972); idem, 'The Archaeological Background of Daniel', *Bibliotheca Sacra* 137 (1980) 3–16.

6. Harrison, p. 1111.
7. Baldwin, p. 42.
8. Yamauchi, *Stones*, p. 90.
9. Montgomery, *Daniel* (International Critical Commentary, Edinburgh, 1927) p. 2.
10. Wiseman, *Chronicles of Chaldean Kings* (London, 1956) p. 26 n.6.
11. Hasel, 47–9; Waltke, 325–6.
12. Harrison, p. 1112.
13. Yamauchi, 'Archaeological Background', 4.
14. Wiseman, 'Some Historical Problems', pp. 16–18; A. K. Grayson, *Assyrian and Babylonian Chronicles* (Texts From Cuneiform Sources, vol. 5: Locust Valley, NY, 1975) p. 99. In a review of Grayson in *Bibliotheca Orientalis* 34 (1977) 335–6, Wiseman indicates a change of mind since he there asserts that it must be 'Hatti'.
15. Wiseman, 'Some Historical Problems', p. 18.
16. E.g., Baldwin, pp. 77–8.
17. As recent commentaries will indicate, the origin of the statement in Dan.1:1 seems to be a misreading of 2 Chr.36:6–7. One is tempted to ask whether fundamentalists read the Bible which they so claim to revere, but of course they *do* read it. It is just that they do not see the problems because they do not expect any. In my early days as a student in critical scholarship, I was constantly amazed to be confronted by clear incongruities in passages with which I was very familiar.
18. R. P. Dougherty, *Nabonidus and Belshazzar* (Yale Oriental Series vol. 15: New Haven, 1929) pp. 199–200; for criticism of Dougherty, see W. von Soden, 'Eine babylonische Volksüberlieferung von Nabonid in den Daniel-erzählungen', *ZAW* 53 (1935) 88 n.1.
19. Dougherty, pp. 93–137; 'Nabonidus Chronicle' ii (Grayson, *Chronicles*, 106–8).
20. Yamauchi, *Stones*, p. 87.
21. 'Nabonidus Chronicle' iii 14–18; Berossos, *apud* Josephus, *C. Apion.* 1.150–3.
22. Grayson, *Chronicles*, pp. 10–11.
23. See the discussion in M. McNamara, 'Nabonidus and the Book of Daniel', *Irish Theological Quarterly* 37 (1970) 134.
24. von Soden (note 18 above) 81–9.
25. Translation that of Oppenheim in J. Pritchard (ed.), *Ancient Near Eastern Texts relating to the Old Testament* (3rd ed., Princeton, 1969) pp. 312–14.
26. Ibid., pp. 309–12.
27. Yamauchi, 'Archaeological Background', 7; Baldwin, pp. 116–18.
28. Harrison, p. 1117.
29. Hasel, 39.
30. Ibid., 40.
31. Harrison, p. 1115.
32. The fragment is preserved in Eusebius, *Praep. Evang.* 9.41, translation from

E. H. Gifford, *Eusebius, Preparation for the Gospel*, vol. 3 (Oxford, 1903) p. 484.

33. Harrison, p. 1115; 'Disease', *Interpreter's Dictionary of the Bible*, vol. 1. (Nashville, 1962) p. 851.

34. In *Assyrian Texts*, vol. 5 of *Records of the Past* (London, 1873) pp. 111–35, a very different translation is given by J. M. Rodwell, which shows that the inscription is actually a listing of Nebuchadnezzar's many building and other projects in Babylon.

35. The standard scholarly edition is S. Langdon (ed.), *Die neubabylonischen Königsinschriften* (Vorderasiatische Bibliotek, vol. 4: Leipzig, 1912) pp. 120–41.

36. Hasel, 41. The inscription is published in A. K. Grayson, *Babylonian Historical-Literary Texts* (Toronto, 1975) pp. 87–92.

37. Hasel, 41–2.

38. Grayson (note 36 above) p. 87.

39. An exception is the statement by K. A. Kitchen in his well-known work on Egyptology, *The Third Intermediate Period in Egypt* (Warminster, 1973): 'Discredited and gone forever are the foolish strictures of the arrogant Wellhausen' (p. 432 n.49).

40. Quoted by Waltke, 'Daniel', p. 329.

41. Harrison, p. 1112.

42. Ibid., p. 1210.

43. Ibid., p. 1212.

44. Ibid., p. 1215.

45. C. Shedl, 'Nabuchodonosor, Arpaksad und Darius: Untersuchungen zum Buch Judit', *Zeitschrift der deutschen morgenländischen Gesellschaft* 115 (1965) 242–54.

46. H. Pope, 'Judith', *Catholic Encyclopaedia* (London, 1910) 8.555.

47. W. Drum, 'Tobias', *Catholic Encyclopaedia* (1912) 14.752.

10

F. D. Maurice: Anticipations of a Synchronic Approach to Scripture?

Ieuan Ellis

The debate over 'Canonical Criticism' which has enlivened biblical studies recently has focused attention once more on that approach to the interpretation of scripture which may be termed synchronic, rather than the diachronic method of 'higher' or historical criticism. Whether this fresh interest will lead to a significant new movement, it is difficult to say. What is significant is the fact of the new ammunition which its supporters can command, drawn from developments in the field of literary criticism where encounter with the text itself (not its origins or evolution) is held to be all-important – the text in its wholeness, its thematic unity, its living quality as conveying the author's world of meaning.[1]

Michael Ramsey has shown in his book, *F. D. Maurice and the Conflicts of Modern Theology* (1951), how Maurice still speaks to our age. Maurice lived in a period when higher criticism was making its first confident assertions; did he also understand the Bible in a sense which may have anticipated the synchronic interest of today?

The answer seems to be that Maurice did direct attention away from purely historical questions, and that his actual practice of exegesis was frequently a holistic one, while he constantly spoke of the need to engage with scripture, not as an infallible document or a collection of proof-texts, but as the living utterance of Christ to the believer.

To develop this it is necessary, first, to look at Maurice's general concept of scripture. Maurice has often been described as a man of the Bible, or as a biblical theologian, but this description, as is so often the case with Maurice and his special gifts, has to be understood carefully. To both conservatives and radicals of his day, embroiled in the struggle over biblical authority, he seemed equivocal, engaged on his own quest. Evangelicals, indeed, dubbed him a liberal because he did not like the words 'inspiration' and 'infallibility', interpreted in their narrowest sense, and made his objections plain. When he used scripture in his *Theological Essays*, to propose a new understanding of the doctrine of everlasting punishment, it was Evangelicals who accused him of undermining biblical authority, and who applauded his removal from his chair at King's. Maurice, for his part, thought that the furore over *Essays and Reviews*, in 1860, was far more disturbing than the offending book itself: the fact that scriptural inspiration had to be defended in such a manner revealed the possibility of more actual atheism in the Church of England than he had imagined.[2]

For the liberals, Maurice failed to provide satisfactory evidence of his interest in biblical scholarship for its own sake – a monument like Jowett's commentary on Thessalonians, Galatians, and Romans, or A. P. Stanley's *Corinthians*, in which a self-consciously 'modern' approach to questions of apostolic authorship ruled, and in which German scholarship took pride of place. They also knew that he hated being called a liberal or Broad Churchman. It was not simply that he would not be allied with any sect or party in the Church; it was also that the Broad Churchmen, as he saw them, lacked a true interest in theology, and what Maurice seems to have meant by this was that they were too narrow in their biblical interests, so that the majesty and true meaning of scripture often eluded them.[3] So for the fighters of both parties, Maurice seemed strangely untouched by the concerns which dominated them.

Of course, Maurice was perfectly well aware of the critical issues in biblical study. Coleridge and Julius Charles Hare had introduced him to German literature, and he was familiar with the development of the Idealist tradition after Kant. He read German, not well but adequately enough to provide his own translations of Strauss, Schleiermacher and others, in his writings. Baur, Bunsen, Feuerbach, Fichte, Hegel, Lessing, Neander, and Schelling were among the authors whom he cited, and he had assimilated enough Kant to use him in his attack on H. L. Mansel. The select circle of English readers who knew and appreciated Schleiermacher certainly included Maurice. His *St. Luke*, translated by Connop Thirlwall in 1825, showed his negative side, with its interpretation of the nativity stories as beautiful but essentially unhistorical, and the theory that the gospels were not four independent witnesses of the life of Jesus but depended on a common source. But Maurice also referred to *Der christliche Glaube* and *Die Homilien über das Evangelium Johannis*, which suggested that Schleiermacher was a creative and 'Evangelical' theologian as well. As to French scholarship, Maurice gave one of the first English reviews of Renan's *La Vie de Jésus*, soon after it appeared in 1863, and his appraisal of this attempt to write a biography of Christ, untainted by supernatural belief, and using the gospels only as historical sources, is fascinating.[4]

The key to Maurice's understanding of scripture is his concept of revelation. After all, he wrote his most polemical book, in white heat, in answer to Mansel's Bampton lectures of 1858 (*The Limits of Religious Thought*) which propounded, he believed, the most dangerous teaching about the nature of religious faith. *What is Revelation?* was Maurice's attempt to set the matter right. Mansel, adapting Kant for his own purposes, contended that man could not know the Infinite, but that God had given us sufficient information to live by, which was 'regulative', and which formed a coherent body of truth.

Mansel's theory was intended as a defence of theism against the attacks of modern criticism. But for Maurice it meant that 'revelation does not reveal'. Mansel was doing 'a thousand times as much mischief as Mr Jowett', and his work was the prelude to atheism.[5] The Father could not thus leave his creatures in ignorance of himself. What a false doctrine, what a perversion of the truth! Revelation, Maurice answered, was not 'regulative', nor was it limited; indeed, it was universal, for God had willed that in Christ all men should come to knowledge of him. It was not to be sought for or discovered, for mankind was already constituted by it, in the fact that behind our world, and behind human society, lay the divine order itself, the kingdom of Christ which was the true pattern for all human relations, and the true form of the church, and into which we were to be incorporated. The basis for such universal revelation lay in the Trinitarian nature of God and in the love expressed in the Triune fellowship of Father, Son, and Holy Spirit. 'When we assert the doctrine of the Trinity, we do so because we believe it to be the grand foundation of all society, the only ground of universal fellowship, the only idea of a

God of love'. 'Become what you are' was Maurice's message to the men and women of his generation. This was no 'natural theology' in the old sense, for the traditional distinction from 'revealed theology' was unreal, in Maurice's eyes. The Incarnation, from his point of view, was also 'natural': the Father from eternity had created the human race in Christ, so that they should become aware of their sonship, and find in him the head of the whole race, and the 'root of humanity'.[6] And the Spirit, inspiring the church, ensured that the self-disclosure of God in Christ became known in increasing depth and meaning, as the divine society came to fuller and fuller expression in the life of mankind.

The place of scripture in this scheme of things followed quite logically from Maurice's premises. Scripture reflected the unity of mankind in Christ. He opposed all theories which set the Bible apart from the rest of human history and experience, for this too was constituted by the divine order. Scripture was concerned with the 'great commonplaces of humanity', and the interpreter found that it recorded 'those events in which one man has the same interest as the other.' 'The marvel of the history lies in the *absence* of the peculiar, the grotesque; in the homeliness of all the details; in the inherent littleness of the personages, who are the subjects of it.'[7] How, then, were the events recorded in the Bible connected with the wider revelation? It was to present a specific example of the whole history in which God was at work. 'I accepted the Bible as the interpretation of the history of mankind', said Maurice. Scripture was a key, a lesson book.[8]

This point of view enabled Maurice to integrate perfectly the Old Testament into his argument, and it is a strength of his approach that he gave so much weight to the Old Testament, and not simply as an introduction to the New. The Old Testament was fundamental because it showed the growth in an actual society, the community of Israel, of the knowledge of God, a knowledge not of religion (Maurice disliked the word), but of politics, economics, ethics, of the love of man for man, in all of which the kingdom of Christ was to be apprehended. The purpose of the Old Testament history was to 'exhibit facts which belong to other times as well . . . and laws and methods of a divine government which belong to all times.'[9] The revelation of God in Christ, which was the subject of the New Testament, again was not 'religious', for the New Testament was just as much the record of a society to witness to God, it was just as much a book of politics and the rest. 'If Jesus was the Word made flesh, if the order of the world was established by Him, then His acts upon earth would be done for the purpose of vindicating this order. By them He would claim it as His.'[10]

Convinced of this truth, Maurice insisted that scripture must be the basis of all theology. Theology which began from a series of abstractions, or which took a starting point other than scripture, was wrong. The Bible, in its wholeness, in all its integrity and consistency, was Maurice's agenda for theological activity. That was why he had little taste for the modern criticism which split up scripture into fragments and lost sight of the whole. The unitary nature of all experience must constantly be borne in mind. For that reason also Maurice did not spend time on theories of inspiration. The Bible did not need that sort of defence if the theological curriculum was as he saw it. Inspiration was not a strange anomalous fact, he said. 'It is the proper law and order of the world'. The inspiration of scripture was the Holy Spirit's work, but it was not separated from the rest of his activity. It was because the Bible was inspired in this manner, and not in the narrow dogmatic sense, that we were convinced of its truth, and in this the 'reason' (the faculty for understanding things divine) played its part.[11]

Undoubtedly, this approach gives Maurice's exegesis a range and interest all his own, and it enabled him to produce a flood of published works. It is also noticeable for its absence of strain and argumentativeness. Maurice could listen more easily to what the text was saying because he was free of the shibboleths of the theological left and right.

The function of history in Maurice's scheme of revelation was central, and it shaped his understanding of scripture. Maurice said repeatedly that his was an historical view of revelation. 'History is the subject with which, we believe, Theology stands in closest affinity.' 'We should not, under any circumstances, forsake the historical method, for the sake of introducing what is sometimes called a Course of Systematic Divinity.'[12] For God to reveal himself in a set of propositions or mere laws, or in some static representation, was unthinkable: the unfolding of the divine order must be universal, it must affect all the activities and energies of human life, and it must be progressive. In this historical interest Maurice was entirely a man of his time, and his criticism of the essentialism of the old metaphysics, or of the unhistorical outlook of many traditional writers, was as strong as the radicals'. Maurice would not have been so appealing to men like Westcott and Hort if he had not convinced them that, among other things, he had a profound historical sense.

The Bible dealt with 'facts', as Maurice said over and over again. Those who mistook his emphasis on eternal order as an ultimate disregard for facts were rebuked by him. If Jowett thought that the idea that a fact had occurred might be of the same use as the fact itself, then he was mistaken, Maurice told his son. And he quickly distanced himself from Colenso, who thought that he was adopting Maurice's principles in applying rigorous historical criticism to the Pentateuch but holding that the eternal truth which lay behind the Bible was not affected by this. That showed a disrespect for history which Maurice could not allow.[13]

None the less, before Maurice was an historian, or political thinker, or social theorist, he was a theologian. 'I have felt as a theologian, taught as a theologian, written as a theologian . . . all other subjects in my mind are connected with theology and subordinate to it.'[14] The reason for this emphasis should now be plain. The divine order itself, true to Maurice's Platonist and Johannine outlook, was not determined by history, though God chose to reveal himself in historical acts. Maurice could not have a simple linear understanding of history, so that the past remained in the past, and what came later must always be an improvement on what had occurred earlier. That point of view caused some liberals all kinds of difficulties, notably how one explained the definitive significance of Jesus if he belonged to an earlier stage in the development of the human race, and thus did not have the advantages possessed by later generations. The radicals who proclaimed that the historian must be the final arbiter, the judge of all matters, since he had the key to the interpretation of all reality, were anathema to Maurice. He disliked historical positivism, because it substituted the shadow for the reality. Historians, for their part, often had difficulty in understanding what Maurice meant by history and 'fact', and relations between them were uneasy. For Maurice, before history there was God, who chose history to reveal what he always had been, and would be, and to men of the present generation – those who were able to look at the events around them with the eye of faith and understanding – what he is. History, as it was handled by Maurice, emerged like this: 'a man will be enabled to teach History, so that his pupils shall feel that the past is really like the present; that the present cannot be viewed without the past; that the future lies in both; that there must be a point from which they are contemplated as one.'[15]

There are two consequences which follow from this, and which show how Maurice the theologian qualified Maurice the historian. They are:

(1) Given this belief in eternal order, Maurice did not see sufficiently the force of radical historical questioning of the Bible. He did not shout 'heresy' and fall about in a rage, like the traditionalists, as soon as problems about the evangelists' integrity, or the Pauline authorship of the epistles, or the Mosaic authorship of the Pentateuch, were raised. That was not Maurice's way. But he could not share the passionate conviction of the critics either. In practice, this meant that he was a conservative on a large number of matters: e.g. he accepted the raising of Lazarus, the walking on the water, the veracity of chapters 14 to 17 of the fourth gospel. It was not that Maurice thought that the questions were unimportant; they failed to shake his conviction of the overall historicity of the Bible. Scripture as the witness to the historical unveiling of the kingdom of Christ must be trustworthy, and, if this was the case, the historical reliability of individual events seemed less crucial to Maurice. Hence miracles did not engage his energies overmuch. If the whole divine order was miraculous, then miracles on earth were manifestations of it, and not violations of 'natural order'.[16]

(2) Maurice did not fully appreciate the difficulty which the higher critics felt about the task of recovering the words and emotions of the past. The liberals found this aspect of him most unsympathetic: Jowett and H. B. Wilson, editor of *Essays and Reviews*, spoke of a new sort of neo-Platonism, substituting one mysticism for another, and so dodging the historical problem.[17] But Maurice believed that the problem had been too much magnified. The effort of historical reconstruction, as he knew, could be attempted in various ways. Jowett seemed to have followed Schleiermacher in a species of intuitive hermeneutics, in which the reader tried to enter into the mind of the original writer as intensively as possible. A later theory, propounded by F. W. Farrar, treading in the footsteps of Renan, was an aesthetic or artistic recreation of the gospel events, so that the onlooker was drawn by the power of the description into an imaginative reconstruction of the scene with Jesus. Maurice avoided both these, and held that the unity of the human race, past, present, and future, in the Son of God – the Word 'from Whom all words have proceeded' – enabled us to bridge the chasm of the centuries, if we read the Bible with a real and not a conventional understanding. In his *St. John* he said that it did not need 'any effort of imagination to realize the

state of mind of an ordinary Jew, as he walked through the city of David', for the interpreter had only to 'realize the state of mind of an ordinary citizen of London, walking in our streets.'[18]

'No man was ever less of a purely historical critic', said Principal Tulloch of Maurice. 'He saw everywhere a reflection of his favourite ideas ... His vivid faith in the Divine – the strength of his root-convictions, amounting to a species of infallibility – made him see from Genesis to Revelation only the same substance of Divine dogma.'[19] Tulloch overstressed his case because he had not fully grasped the nature of Maurice's concern for history. But the remark about 'his favourite ideas' was shrewd enough: to elicit these in a scripture passage, to see their manifestation on the page and their relation to the whole, was bound to be more important for Maurice than a mere quest for origins or stages in the evolution of the material.

How may Maurice's principles be seen operating in practice? How did his understanding of revelation affect his exegesis? A number of his books would serve for illustration, but the clearest exposition of his approach is probably in a work published in 1854, *The Unity of the New Testament*. In this book, which takes up some of the themes raised earlier in his Warburton Lectures of 1846, Maurice tackles the relationship of the various New Testament writings to one another. As he does so, he seems to foreshadow some of the issues in the synchronic *v.* diachronic debate. *The Unity of the New Testament* has not usually been regarded as one of Maurice's major works, but it has a fresh importance today, and it illuminates the development of his mind in his middle period.

Maurice takes up an independent position at the outset, but one quite consistent with his concept of revelation, as we have seen it. The unity of the scriptures is that 'they have one common subject, that they refer to a living Person, that when considered in reference to Him they have a unity which we can discover by no collation of paragraphs.' If their centre was a living person and not a past event, then the question of their 'history' assumed a different complexion. He challenged the usual division of the New Testament which saw the synoptic gospels as the records of Jesus' life as the prophet of Nazareth, and the epistles and the Johannine writings as the witness to his divinity. The division was a false one, he said: whether it was accepted by traditionalists or radicals, it ended in the scepticism of Strauss or Baur. Maurice's argument was that this division obscured the unity of the New Testament in the person of Christ, but he was also implying that concentration on the historical issue (that the synoptics were earlier and the other writings later) lost sight of another, more vital, way of dealing with the authors. 'We have gone astray in the study of Scripture', he declared, 'not from excess of simplicity, but from excess of refinement, from looking to a distance for that which lies at our feet, from refusing to take words as they stand, and to believe that the writers meant what they say they meant.'

Any unprejudiced examination of the first three gospels would show that they accepted Jesus as the Son of God, and not simply the inspired prophet, just as much as Paul and the fourth evangelist. 'All the discourses and acts which they attribute to Him are simple and natural upon that hypothesis, unintelligible and incoherent upon any other.'[20]

Maurice's scheme was, first, a chapter in which he listed the features which the first three gospels had in common, and here he anticipated C. H. Dodd's *The Apostolic Preaching and Its Developments*, at least in implying that the synoptic framework was similar to the *kerygma* as outlined in the early Christian preaching. This kerygmatic interest (though Maurice did not, of course, use the word) was a guide to the synoptists' order of events. 'I do not profess to throw any light upon that chronology, but I am persuaded that the light must come where commentators have looked for it least, from the portions of the narratives which have the most evidently supernatural and celestial character.' Again, within the individual gospels, it was the author's objectives, rather than a straightforward historical interest, which explained the succession of his narrative, and which also explained why, in these respects, the gospels differed from one another. (Hence, a mere harmony of the gospels was avoided by Maurice: he called his method a 'synopsis'.) This could be admitted without doubting the veracity of the evangelists, or asking 'which was better?' 'With respect to the times, it seems quite clear that each Evangelist is always ready to sacrifice mere chronology to that order or succession of events which most revealed his purpose. In the short period of our Lord's ministry there are certain landmarks, such as the Temptation, the Transfiguration, the Entry into Jerusalem, which all observe. Within those landmarks they follow the bent and course of thought which the Spirit has given to each; they group events according to another than a time order. So far as we can see, it is a very simple and natural order'. The differences between Luke and the others in his description of the chronology of Jesus's journey to Jerusalem were vital to his objective, and 'a proof of how little the attempts to arrange the Gospels after the manner of the harmonists can help us to understand their real import, or appreciate the relation of different passages to each other.'[21]

Maurice developed his argument that each writer's purpose explained the characteristics of his gospel. One did not need to raise elaborate theories that the differences between them were due to their being 'Ebionite' (and therefore opposed to Paul, as in the case of Matthew) or 'Gentile' (as in the case of Luke), or that Mark was merely an abridger. Nor was it necessary to claim that they must be eye-witnesses or that they were written to present facts still unrecorded about Jesus. Their objective was 'to follow up those [facts] which were admitted, which had become the common-places of the Church's faith, in order that their full purpose might be brought to light, that they might be known in the length and breadth of their human and divine significance.' On these premises, one could then see why Mark did not think it necessary to include the Sermon on the Mount, the Lord's prayer, and much else; or why Luke's Sermon on the Plain was so much shorter than Matthew's Sermon on the Mount. Luke had not abridged Matthew, 'he has omitted precisely that part which conveys to us the object and design of St. Matthew which would have prevented us from perceiving his own.' Again, it was Mark's fidelity to his purpose (and not his 'primitivism') which was the reason for devoting so much space to the exorcisms and other works of healing. Nor was the fact that there were two feedings of the multitude in Mark accidental. Maurice did not allow that these were two versions of the same event, or that they were, again, evidence of Mark's poor quality as an author. He thought that this was a more satisfactory approach than the usual theories about Mark which (he added wickedly), in the end, might support the idea that Mark's was the first gospel.[22]

In looking at the gospels individually, Maurice was particularly interested in the manner in which their belief in Christ was demonstrated thematically. Matthew emphasised Christ's fulfilment of the law, and the Fatherhood of God. 'Observe how naturally this pervading feeling of the Evangelist's mind expresses itself in all his quotations, how at every turn in his Gospel, our Lord is bringing out the mind of the God of Abraham, and shewing it to be the mind of a Father.' He saw several strands in this general theme of fulfilment and followed them out in some detail in the various chapters. The nativity stories were not, he held, compilations of several inconsistent narratives. Matthew's postulates were that God did, indeed, promise that in the seed of Abraham all the nations of the earth should be blessed. 'Grant these postulates, enormously, absolutely incredible, postulates to a modern critic', and it was the consistency and not the inconsistency of Matthew that we felt. In this manner, also, Maurice sought to explain the difficulties over the prophecy 'He shall be called a Nazarene', which could not be found in any specific prophecy. It must mean that the evangelist, seized by the idea of fulfilment, referred to some general meaning which he traced through all the prophecies. Indeed, this passage explained, 'better than almost any other, what St. Matthew understood by the accomplishment of prophecy' – a typical Maurician way of turning a critical point in an unexpected direction.[23] Nonetheless, belief in the accomplishment of prophecy must be defined with some care:

> It is a very different thing to maintain that a prophecy may have a double or treble sense, where by double or treble you mean that what is true of one time may be even more clearly and emphatically true of another, just as ordinary historians have remarked that the same principles swayed the conduct of Charlemagne and of Napoleon, that even the facts of the history repeat themselves, and that the laws which govern those facts are brought out more completely in the latest facts than in the earlier; and to use words in a double sense, where by "double" we mean that the signification of them in the very same narrative or discourse is changed, so that it is at the pleasure of the interpreter to make them signify one thing in reference to one part of the subject and another in reference to another. To say that a prophet not only does, but that he must transgress the limits of a single event when he lays down a great law of the Divine mind, is to claim for him that very insight and foresight which his name implies; to say that he palters with words in a double sense, is nothing less than to call him a false prophet, to identify him with a heathen oracle.[24]

The singularity of Matthew's story of the tribute money was not an occasion to doubt it; rather, 'St. Matthew would be the Evangelist most likely to introduce such a conversation; it would accord with the whole purpose of his narrative; it would be a new illustration of the way in which our Lord came to fulfil all the purpose of the old dispensation, to substantiate the meaning of its forms, institutions, holy places.' Thus satisfied, Maurice did not linger over the miracle of the coin in the fish's mouth. Other alleged particularisms were solved by the same method. The final chapter was for him a perfect illustration of the evangelist's manner in keeping his purpose throughout the gospel closely in mind.[25]

In regard to Luke, Maurice anticipated later scholarship in insisting on the importance of the connection of the gospel with the Acts as indicating the objectives and unity of his narrative. What Luke promised was 'an *orderly* narrative, one that should exhibit the facts so coherently and harmoniously that the character which was disclosed by them, their relation to the past and present and future, might be more clearly and livelily apprehended.' Maurice naturally did not agree with 'modern critics' who thought that Luke had subverted the facts in his infancy narrative. '"How clearly", they exclaim, "we see not the purpose of an historian to tell facts, but of a theologian to bring out a certain artificial theory".' Maurice's reply was significant. 'Whether it is an artificial theory or the revelation of a Divine principle apart from which the facts in the life of Jesus of Nazareth would not mean anything or account for anything, is precisely the question at issue.'[26] Maurice's own convictions should now be so apparent that what he meant is obvious.

Again, he identified the themes which unified Luke's writing, and there were several: the new dispensation, the contrast between old and new, the work of Christ and the Spirit, and, interestingly enough, the position of woman in the kingdom of God. Not surprisingly, it was not the particularity of the miracle in Luke 7, the resurrection at Nain, which occupied Maurice's interest; it was Luke's reason for recording the event, which he thought was supplied by the words 'son of a widow'. 'In them I believe we discern the mind of St. Luke. If it is one leading character of the New Dispensation as distinguished from the Old, that it puts a more direct honour upon the woman, or, more strictly speaking, brings out the honour which was there latent and implied, St. Luke should certainly . . . exhibit that sign of the later time in connexion with the life of the Son of God.' So Maurice went on immediately to link this with Luke's story of the woman with the alabaster box of ointment in the house of Simon the Pharisee, and to refer both stories back to the point that he made about the Annunciation, when speaking of Luke's 'connecting the glory of the woman with the glory of humanity, by exhibiting her passive and receptive faith as the agent through which a real Divine energy makes itself effectual.' He absolved himself of any charge of being sentimental or fanciful: the conviction was there in Luke and only needed to be recognised.

The parables peculiar to Luke were important in revealing his purpose and explained their incorporation into his material; and a comparison of those that he shared with Matthew was a good exercise in arriving at 'a knowledge of the distinct objects and general design of the Evangelists'. Luke's account of the crucifixion differed, naturally, from the other evangelists. But his version was integral and must be seen as a whole, and his specific or unique aspects, instead of being regarded as breaks in the narrative or accidental additions to it, 'harmonize most strikingly with the structure and purpose of the Gospel, so that if the narrative of either of the other evangelists were substituted for it, we should feel, though we might not know why, a shock and jar in our minds.'[27]

Maurice discerned the same sort of organic principles at work in the epistles, and it is not necessary to follow him further in his exegesis. (He promised a work on the fourth gospel and the Apocalypse in a later volume.) He kept to his premise that the author must be allowed to speak for himself, and reveal his own design and intention, and not be interpreted by some alien external principle. Thus, Romans was not to be judged by an abstract theory of justification, because the exegete went first to the third chapter and saw everything preceding it as mere introduction. The 'simple reader' would perceive that Paul began at the beginning, and the epistle was really the manifestation of the righteousness of God. Maurice's remark on the authorship of Hebrews will not be unexpected. 'If it is contended that the Apostle Paul must have written formally about justification by faith, and would not have talked as he does in this Epistle, of kings, and priests, and sabbath-days, and the temple and the sacrifice, I protest against this objection as based upon a theory which contracts and misrepresents the purpose of all St. Paul's writings, and makes them ineffective for the defence of that vital truth, within the formal limits of which it seeks to confine them.' 'Whether the Epistle to the Hebrews is St. Paul's or not, it is necessary, I think, to complete the circle of thoughts into which St. Paul introduces us.'[28]

There is much material in Maurice's commentaries and sermons which would amplify these hints and suggestions, though, of course, nothing is worked out systematically. That was not Maurice's wont; nor would he have been a partisan if there had been a debate between synchronic and diachronic contenders in his day. However, his sympathies seem clear enough:

> Supposing these Gospels to be works of divine art, they should have characteristics answering to those which we recognize in works of human art, still more in nature itself. There is an arrangement of parts which we could not lose without losing the sense and meaning of the picture, or poem, or landscape that is presented to us, which it is worth while to mediate upon, which critics may often assist us in considering, but which, after all, comes out to us by very slow degrees, which we shall probably never be able to interpret rightly to others or to ourselves, though it may impart a method to our own minds and may make all we do and speak more clear and intelligible.[29]

Notes

I am grateful to the Revd Dr J. I. H. McDonald, of the University of Edinburgh, for his helpful comments on a draft version of this article.

The author of the writings cited below is F. D. Maurice unless otherwise stated.
 1. See e.g. Northrop Frye, *The Great Code: the Bible and literature* (London, 1983).
 2. J. F. Maurice, *The Life of Frederick Denison Maurice* (London, 1884) vol. 2, p.383 (hereafter cited as *Life*).
 3. *Life*, vol. 1, p.184.
 4. *Macmillan's Magazine* 9 (1863) 190–7, cf. *Life*, vol. 2, pp.461–6.
 5. *Life*, vol. 2, p.367, cf. *What is Revelation?* (London, 1859) pp.232–3 and *passim*.
 6. *The Kingdom of Christ* (London, 1838) vol. 1, p.61. *Sermons Preached in Lincoln's Inn Chapel* (London, 1891) vol. 2, p.215.
 7. *The Patriarchs and Lawgivers of the Old Testament* (London, 1885) pp.103–4.
 8. *Life*, vol. 2, p.494; cf. *Theological Essays* (ed. E. F. Carpenter) (London, 1957) p.172: 'The Bible is a book in which God is teaching His creatures induction by setting them an example of it.'
 9. *The Prophets and Kings of the Old Testament* (London, 1886) p.473.
10. *The Gospel of St. John* (London, 1885) p.64.
11. Cf. T. Christensen, *The Divine Order* (Leiden, 1973) p.157.

12. *Introductory Lectures delivered at Queen's College, London* (London, 1849) pp.25, 246.
13. *Life*, vol. 2, pp.410, 422–3.
14. *Moral and Metaphysical Philosophy* (London, 1886) vol. 2, p.ix.
15. *Introductory Lectures delivered at Queen's College, London*, p.24.
16. *Life*, vol. 2, pp.454–5.
17. E. Abbott and L. Campbell, *The Life and Letters of Benjamin Jowett* (London, 1897) vol. 1, p.262.
18. *The Gospel of St. John*, p.75; cf. *Lectures on the Apocalypse* (London, 1860) p.58: 'The spirit of a particular poem is that which awakens the poetical spirit in answer to it, and makes him feel that the thoughts and feelings of men who lived hundreds of years ago, and thousands of miles away, are his thoughts and feelings.' Maurice's statements here suggest another aspect of his approach to scripture. Our experience of the Word who encounters us in the Bible is a paradigm of our experience when reading all great literature, so that the emotions and convictions of the author become ours as well, and contribute to our self-understanding (cf. H.F.G. Swanston, *Ideas of Order* (Assen, 1974) pp.99–103). Again, Maurice seems to be insisting on a holistic approach: the text in its wholeness is the primary object of our study and thus self-understanding.
19. J. Tulloch, *Movements of Religious Thought in Britain during the Nineteenth Century* (London, 1885) p.276.
20. *The Unity of the New Testament* (London, 1854) pp.iii, 3, 11.
21. Ibid. pp.77, 244.
22. Ibid. pp.222–3, 245, 250.
23. Ibid. pp.178, 183, 191.
24. Ibid. p.133.
25. Ibid. pp.204, 221.
26. Ibid. pp.230–1.
27. Ibid. pp.246–7, 272, 300.
28. Ibid. pp.666–7.
29. Ibid. pp.241–2.

11

Old Testament Theology – A Non-existent Beast?[1]

R. N. Whybray

Each time I read the latest *Old Testament Theology* I find Lewis Carroll's *The Hunting of the Snark* running in my head. 'You may seek it with *Bund*', I mutter, 'you may threaten its life with a *Heilsgeschichte* . . .'. Is Old Testament theology a kind of snark? The failure of those hunters to find the snark was no doubt due, at least in part, to their inability to agree about the nature of the beast in question. But may it not also have been partly due to its non-existence? We shall never know. But does the hunt for an Old Testament theology perhaps offer a parallel?

1

The very use of the word 'theology' in connection with the Old Testament calls for an explanation. The *Shorter Oxford English Dictionary* defines theology as 'the study which treats of God, His nature and attributes, and His relations with man and the universe'. Is Old Testament theology, then, a particular kind of study of God which is to be found in the pages of the Old Testament, as one might speak of a 'Barthian theology'? Is it a particular branch of theology, like 'ascetic theology'? Or again, is it the whole of theology, seen from an Old Testament viewpoint?

In current usage 'theology' usually implies some sort of coherent body of teaching. Whether we speak of one man's theology or of a particular theological tradition such as 'Catholic theology' we are referring to bodies of teaching or of belief which take a creed, or a creed-like tradition, as their frame of reference. In other words they each have their

168

'centre'. This is also true of the two terms which would appear to resemble 'Old Testament theology' most closely, namely New Testament theology and biblical theology: both of these derive their coherence from the indisputable 'centre' of the person and work of Jesus Christ. Only in the case of Old Testament theology is there a problem of coherence, of a 'centre'.

It is therefore reasonable to ask whether it makes sense to use the word 'theology' in connection with the Old Testament at all – or at least in connection with the Old Testament as a whole. It may be useful to speak of particular 'theologies' within the Old Testament, such as that of the Deuteronomists or of Deutero-Isaiah. But taken as a whole the Old Testament has no central figure, nor is it given coherence by an identifiable creed. Even if it were possible, as was once the fashion, to point to *a basic series of events* from which the religion of the Old Testament took its origin,[2] it remains a fact that the authors of a number of Old Testament books were entirely unconcerned with those events.

Since the composition of the literature of the Old Testament spanned a period of a thousand years or so, and one which was marked by immense cultural, religious, social and political changes, its lack of theological coherence is hardly surprising. Ancient Israel undoubtedly cherished a number of enduring religious traditions, some of which persisted throughout its history; but this is not sufficient to justify the claim that the Old Testament provides the material for a theology.

The historical spread of the Old Testament suggests that it might be more realistic to compare it not with the New Testament, which was entirely composed within two or three generations, but rather with the whole body of Christian literature to the present day, whose time-span is, after all, only about twice as great as that of the Old Testament. Such a comparison may help to put the concept of an Old Testament theology into perspective. It would be possible to write a *history* of Christian literature; but who would attempt to write a *theology* of Christian literature? Yet Christian literature without exception has a 'centre' in Jesus Christ, a feature which the Old Testament lacks.

It may be objected that this analogy between the Old Testament and Christian literature is false because of the canonical status of the former. It may be argued that because the Old Testament is not merely the extant religious literature of an ancient people but a body of texts formed and selected in order to constitute a normative canonical corpus, it must *ipso facto* possess sufficient theological coherence to justify some kind of systematic treatment. In this connection it is perhaps pertinent to observe that up to the present time the stimulus for the writing of Old Testament theologies has come from an 'external' source: works of this kind have all been produced by *Christian* scholars. Jewish scholars, who might have been expected to find such a task useful and desirable, presumably have not believed that their scriptures lend themselves to such treatment, or that much would be gained by attempting it. Can it be otherwise with non-Jewish scholars? Unless we are to return to the earlier situation in which Old Testament theology was subsumed under the heading of 'biblical theology' and subjected to the Procrustean bed of a theological system imposed from without, canonical status cannot make the Old Testament more amenable to the construction of a 'theology' for Christians than it is for Jews.

These considerations have led me, over the years, to the conclusion, not that it would have been better if the numerous works published during the last fifty years with titles like 'The Theology of the Old Testament' had not been written – far from it! – but that their titles are misconceived and misleading. In so far as they succeed in illuminating aspects of the religion of the Old Testament, many of them are extremely valuable. Their authors have set out on voyages of discovery and have returned, in many cases, with a cargo of rich treasures; but none of them has found that mythical beast, 'Old Testament theology.'

2

This conclusion is not to be taken to mean that there are no proper or useful ways of studying the Old Testament as a whole. The remainder of this article will be devoted to exploring this question.

First of all it is necessary to rule out the traditional christological principle of interpretation, whereby the Old Testament is understood as looking forward to, or as in some way foreshadowing, the Christian dispensation. That this was the way in which the New Testament writers understood it, while of great importance for New Testament studies, is irrelevant for the interpretation of the Old Testament as a whole and as an historical phenomenon, for a number of reasons.

(1) With the exception of a few passages, the Old Testament is not

consciously 'looking forward' to an event beyond itself, and so cannot be said to foreshadow any Christian 'fulfilment'. To introduce the notion of 'Christian hindsight' is to introduce an external criterion which cannot explain the intention of the Old Testament writers.

(2) The christological principle is consequently inevitably radically selective in its application and so can only lead to an arbitrary treatment of the Old Testament.

(3) Since the christological principle, because of the narrowness of its perspective, to a large extent ignores both the thoughts and intentions of the authors of the Old Testament books and the existential beliefs of the ancient Israelites as a whole, it stands, however refined may be its application, under the condemnation merited by the traditional pre-critical method of interpretation: that it attempts to force the Old Testament into a mould which it was not intended to fit.

(4) It puts the cart before the horse. It has been said that the New Testament is a gloss on the Old. Whether there is truth in this or not, it is surely an absurdity to treat the Old Testament as a gloss on the New. To begin with the New Testament and to interpret the Old in its light is on a par with beginning with the rabbinical literature and viewing the Old Testament entirely in its terms.

In fact there is no single type of christological interpretation of the Old Testament. The New Testament itself testifies to the existence even at that early period of several different modes of interpretation; and most modern practitioners of the christological principle arbitrarily make a choice between these, rejecting the 'crude' proof-text method (such as the interpretation in John 19:36 – 'Not a bone of him shall be broken' – as predicting an incident at the crucifixion) and preferring more subtly 'theological' interpretations such as those of Paul or Hebrews. The grounds on which such a choice is made are not apparent. It would be better to admit frankly that the New Testament interpretation of the Old is not acceptable to modern biblical scholarship.

(5) The christological principle does not take the religion of ancient Israel seriously as a religion in its own right. It is regarded as the religion of Old Israel which has been superseded by that of the New Israel. Yet no 'neutral' scholar would accept, on religio-historical grounds, this claim of the Christian Church to be the 'new' or 'true' Israel.[3] Christian theologies of the Old Testament often give the impression that their authors are not really looking *at* the Old Testament but *through* it at something that lies

beyond it. For example. T. C. Vriezen, having first stated that 'The theologian must . . . be willing . . . to listen to the testimony of the Old Testament independently and with an open mind', asserts a few pages later that 'Jesus Christ stands at the end of Old Testament revelation as the man in whom God fully revealed His work in this world by Israel' and that 'The New Testament is the confirmation and the crowning of the Old.'[4] The same author in a work entitled *The Religion of Ancient Israel* treats the post-exilic period under the heading 'disintegration' and speaks of a 'renewal that came with Christianity.'[5]

The above considerations are by no means intended to imply that the study of the Old Testament is irrelevant to the Christian faith or to Christian theology. Their purpose is to make the point that the Old Testament can only be properly understood if it is studied independently. Only in this way can it be used in the service of Christian theology.

3

What, then, would be a valid treatment of the Old Testament as a whole? It could, of course, be argued that it is not a 'whole' at all: that it is not complete. From the historical point of view it is simply the literature of the earliest period of the history of a religion which has had a very long subsequent history. That this body of literature became normative for all later periods is a fact of great historical importance; but from the point of view of the historian of religions its marking off as a completed 'whole' as if what followed was of an entirely different character could, in the absence of a definite break in the continuity of the Jewish religion, be regarded as artificial.

Nevertheless, apart from the fact of canonisation, there are good reasons for regarding the Old Testament as a 'whole', as an object of study in its own right. The end of the Old Testament period does mark the end of an era in the development of the Jewish faith. Admittedly there is room for dispute about the meaning of the phrase 'the end of the Old Testament period'; equally admittedly, it could be argued that some other period such as the Babylonian exile or the time of Ezra marks a more definite watershed in the history of the religion of Israel.[6] It has also recently been shown that tendencies characteristic of the rabbinic period already appear in the Old Testament itself.[7] Nevertheless there is a strong case for believing that the instinct of the Jewish community, expressed in its definition of the canon, was a true one in purely historical and literary terms.

But in what sense is it a 'whole'? and by what method can its character as a whole be illuminated? The answer to the first of these questions is that in the Old Testament are comprised the only extant literary products of a particular stage in the development of a particular national religion. These are thus, despite their diversity, the primary evidence for a single phenomenon: the religion of Israel in its earliest stage.

About that religion modern scholars have generally asked two kinds of question: historical and structural. On the one hand, they have asked about its origin and development: about the forces, internal and external, which formed it and affected it at different times and which account for the diversity of its expression in the different strata of the Old Testament. On the other hand, they have enquired into the basically enduring qualities which, through a continuous tradition passed from one generation to the next, kept it identifiable as a distinct religion. The search for answers to these two kinds of question has led in modern times to the writing of two distinct kinds of book, each concerned with the Old Testament as a whole: Histories of the Religion of Israel and Theologies of the Old Testament.

These two approaches have generally been understood to be quite different from one another. But they are in fact only two aspects of the same undertaking. Confronted by these often perplexing documents from an alien culture there is fundamentally only one way in which we can reach a genuine understanding of them: we must attempt to put ourselves into the position of an ancient Israelite and to learn how he understood his commitment to the religion of Yahweh – or, in more popular parlance, we must try to discover what 'made him tick' as a servant of Yahweh.

But the undertaking clearly has two aspects. On the one hand, as the Israelites themselves recognised, there was a continuity of belief. 'Now make confession', said Ezra to the assembled people, 'to Yahweh the God of your fathers, and do his will' (Ezra 10:11). But a continuity of what? This is the question which the Theologies of the Old Testament have sought to answer. On the other hand, there is a very great variety in the ways in which this enduring and fundamental kernel of belief is expressed in the literature – a variety not entirely to be accounted for in terms of historical development, but pointing also to synchronic diversity of belief within different groups. Such diversity does not mean that the religion of Israel was a mishmash of essentially different religions; it means, on the contrary, that it was sufficiently vigorous and dynamic to be capable of adapting itself to new challenges and also of commending itself to different kinds of person. A better understanding of 'what made the ancient Yahwist tick' will only be achieved by the pursuit of both aspects of his religion outlined above.

4

The historical approach, in presenting us with a series of pictures of Israelite religion located in various situations which posed particular challenges to it, will at the same time contribute to an understanding of what it was which was challenged, in a way which an abstract systematic theology or a creed cannot do. It will be pursued free of presuppositions about the relative 'truth' of any particular version of Israelite religion in any period such as are displayed, for example, by Fohrer, who, in his *History of Israelite Religion*, despite a declared intention to avoid 'undertaking theological value judgements', later comments that 'Comparison reveals the superiority of the prophets' faith',[8] or by Vriezen's characterisation of the period after Nehemiah as 'disintegration'. On the other hand, due weight will be given – both positively and negatively – to those versions of Israelite religion which are the product of serious theological thought.

In one sense the Deuteronomists or Deutero-Isaiah can tell us more about the nature of Israelite belief than other Old Testament writers because they are more comprehensive, drawing together and bringing to light the mutual relatedness of various older traditions, and because their theology is presented more directly and more sharply than elsewhere. But, on the other hand, one must consider to what extent these theologians were typical of their own generation. It is not always to the theologian – however practical his intentions may be – that one goes to discover what were the truly characteristic beliefs of a people.

There is also a danger that the religion of Israel may be defined too narrowly. For example, the wisdom literature has frequently been almost or completely ostracised from works supposedly dealing with the Old

Testament as a whole. This is true of Clements' quite recent *Old Testament Theology*,[9] and also of Vriezen's *The Religion of Ancient Israel*. The reasons generally given for this omission are (1) that wisdom is 'profane' in character; (2) that it is a foreign borrowing; (3) that it does not witness to Israel's historical traditions; and (4) that much of it is 'not theological' but rather 'the wisdom of experience' (von Rad's phrase). Yet – and this is a point of great importance which has been ignored in most studies of the theology of the Old Testament – there can be little doubt that any reader with no previous knowledge of the Old Testament would, after a first reading, *pronounce Job and Ecclesiastes to be the most 'theological' of all its books* on the very rational grounds that they are entirely devoted to serious discussion about God and man and the relationship between them.

The arguments generally put forward in defence of the omission of the wisdom books from consideration are inadequate. (1) Even those sayings in Proverbs which do not mention God are 'profane' only by a very narrow definition of that word; (2) the fact that some parts of these books bear the marks of foreign influence does not mean that wisdom thought was not an integral part of the religious thought of at least one section of the Israelite people; (3) their exclusion from consideration on the grounds of their failure to refer to Israel's historical traditions merely shows that Israelite religion has been too narrowly defined in terms of those traditions; and (4) their rejection as 'non-theological' makes a questionable assumption about the meaning of theology.[10]

The reference to foreign influence on Israelite religion raises a further question about the way in which the historical approach should be pursued. If the intention is to study the various forms assumed by Israelite religion through the centuries, nothing should be excluded on account of its foreign origin provided that it was understood at the time as being part of that religion. References to the deliberate practice by Israelites of another religion altogether – for example, of Baalism in an overt form – are of course to be excluded, since such religions were not forms of the national religion. But everything which was subsumed under the worship of Yahweh must form part of our series of pictures showing, as far as may be possible, what it was like to be a Yahwist at various times and in various circumstances. The distinction may sometimes be hard to draw; but it is necessary to make the attempt.

Most important of all for the historical approach is the relating of the different versions of Israelite religion to their historical backgrounds. To discover 'what made the Yahwist tick' it is necessary to discover what were the pressures on him, what the temptations which faced him, what the cultural, political and social atmosphere in which he lived. For religious belief is not only a matter of following a religious tradition, nor on the other hand is it just a matter of receptivity to new ideas. It is also a matter of relating the religious tradition which one has received to the facts of individual and corporate life.

5

The other approach, which is concerned with the 'what' of tradition – with that which, transmitted through the generations, constituted the particular identity of the Israelite religion, and without which it could not have survived – brings us back to the question of the *Mitte*, the 'centre', which has been the subject of so much recent discussion.[11] But as Westermann rightly pointed out,[12] this question of the 'centre' may be an inappropriate question, to which no meaningful answer can be given. To say that the centre is God would be true but tautologous: it would simply be to assert that the Israelite religion was a religion. To say that the Old Testament, or the Israelite religion, is centred on a particular kind of God is also inadequate, since God was perceived very differently at different times and by different worshippers. To take, as it were, either a lowest common denominator or a highest common factor would be to misrepresent most, if not all, of the actual conceptions of God to be found in the Old Testament.

Like many other religions, the religion of Israel was a mixture of diverse and even contradictory elements *which, however, constituted a unity in the minds of those who practised it*. It was the service of 'the God of our fathers'. It was, probably, a mixture of elements from various sources from the very beginning; and it continued to absorb further new elements throughout its history. It is true that certain religious leaders are represented by hindsight as having stood for a 'pure' Yahwism, like Joshua with his 'Choose this day whom you will serve . . ., but as for me and my house, we will serve Yahweh' (Josh. 24:15) or Elijah with 'If Yahweh is God, follow him; but if Baal, then follow him' (1 Kgs.18:21); but these are the pious oversimplifications of a later age. They do, however, point to the fact that the gradual changes which occurred in the course of history remained unperceived by the majority, who believed, throughout their lives, that they were worshipping the same Yahweh that their fathers had worshipped.

We cannot point to any one of these stages of development and affirm that *this* was the true religion of Israel on the ground that in some way it bears the marks of maturity or of completion: that the teaching of a Deutero-Isaiah, for example, represents what is truest and best in it. If we are to find and describe the nature of the Israelite religion we must include in that description *all* its substantial manifestations.

6

A completely adequate description of ancient Israelite religion is clearly an impossibility. We should not, however, abandon the attempt to achieve it. It is significant that such attempts have been made with regard to other ancient religions which are now dead; and the results, whatever those who actually practised those religions would have thought of them (this we shall never know!), have been successful, at least to the extent that they help the student to make some sense out of what might otherwise seem to be a meaningless collection of unrelated beliefs and practices. The distinguished Egyptologist Siegfried Morenz, for example, attempted in his *Egyptian Religion* 'to see Egyptian religion as the faith of the Egyptian people', and set himself as his main task 'to seek out the piety of the Egyptian believer within the dominant phenomena of his religion'.[13] Despite difficulties far greater than those which face the student of ancient Israelite religion, Morenz succeeded in conveying to the reader something of 'what made the Egyptian worshipper tick'; but it is significant that he was unable to pick out from Egyptian religion any one 'centre' of belief. His success was due to three things: he did not indulge in speculation which went beyond the ascertainable facts; he did not attempt to impose a system on his material; and he approached his subject with sympathetic imagination. Instead of trying to find a single 'centre' he picked out a number of features which, because they appear to have been prominent in all periods, he called the 'dominant phenomena'. This did not mean that other features were ignored; it simply meant that as far as the evidence went these phenomena occupied a more prominent place in the religious life of the ancient Egyptian than did others. They 'served the need of the pious man.'[14]

H. H. Rowley in his *The Faith of Israel* approached the Old Testament in a similar way. He eschewed the singling out of 'one key idea in terms of which to construct the whole, such as the covenant, or election, or salvation, partly because I think no one of these, or even all together, adequate, and partly because it is of the essence of the Old Testament to deal not so much in abstract ideas as in ideas which are embodied in concrete history.' He preferred to expound, one by one, 'those elements of Israel's distinctive faith which, incipient at first, were developed in her history, and . . . those ideas and practices which, even though of older or alien origin, were accepted permanently into her faith and made its vehicle.'[15] He made no systematic attempt to show how these were related to one another; yet their coherence emerges naturally in the course of his exposition.

Morenz and Rowley, dealing with very different materials, demonstrate how a religion can constitute a real unity and yet comprise a number of quite distinct and not necessarily logically connected dominant features. In the case of the religion of Israel its very survival is sufficient proof both of its identity and of its essential unity.

7

Has the study of the nature of the religion of ancient Israel reached the point of exhaustion? One might well imagine that there is nothing new to be said on the subject. Yet Claus Westermann has shown quite recently how easy it is to miss, or at least greatly to underrate, significant features of it. He is the first fully to appreciate – though due credit must be given to the pioneering work of Pedersen[16] – that the experience of God's continuing *blessing* (*Segen*) in daily life was as much part of Israel's religious experience as redemption (*Rettung*) and must be given equal status with the latter in any balanced treatment of Israelite religion as a whole.[17] Samuel Terrien has also recently pointed to a somewhat similar and equally neglected feature of the Old Testament in his *The Elusive Presence*.[18] This shift in emphasis away from the dynamic towards the static and enduring marks an important advance towards a true understanding of what it meant in Old Testament times to be a servant of Yahweh.

These somewhat wide-ranging comments on the problem of the best approach to the study of the religion of ancient Israel and of the Old Testament are not intended to do more than to express a personal view. This is a kind of study in which, to return to Lewis Carroll – this time to the caucus-race in *Alice's Adventures in Wonderland* – all may take part, and all can have prizes.

Notes

1. This is a revised and shortened version of my Presidential Address to the Society for Old Testament Study, delivered in January 1982.
2. See e.g. G. E. Wright, *God Who Acts: biblical theology as recital* (Studies in Biblical Theology, 8), (London, 1952); G. von Rad, *Old Testament Theology*, vol. 1 (Edinburgh and London, 1962) pp. 105–28 (ET from *Theologie des Alten Testaments*, vol. 1, Munich, 1957. The 6th ed. was published in 1969). For a critique see B. S. Childs, *Biblical Theology in Crisis* (Philadelphia, 1970).
3. A sociological explanation of the reasons why the claim was made could be given in terms of the concept of 'cognitive dissonance'. For a popular account of this concept see R. P. Carroll, *When Prophecy Failed: reactions and responses to failure in the Old Testament prophetic traditions* (London, 1979) and in particular pp. 125–6, 216 for its application to the early church.
4. T. C. Vriezen, *An Outline of Old Testament Theology* (Oxford, 1958) pp. 10, 18 (ET from *Hoofdlijnen der Theologie van het Oude Testament*, Wageningen, 1949).
5. Idem, *The Religion of Ancient Israel* (London/Philadelphia, 1967) pp. 263, 273 (ET from *De godsdienst van Israël*, Arnhem, 1963).
6. E.g. G. Fohrer, *History of Israelite Religion* (London, 1973) p. 359 (ET from *Geschichte der israelitischen Religion*, Berlin, 1968) refers to the reforms carried out by Ezra as 'a new religion . . . in the making'.
7. See especially J. Weingreen, *From Bible to Mishna: the continuity of tradition* (Manchester, 1976).
8. Fohrer, pp. 23, 289.
9. R. E. Clements, *Old Testament Theology: a fresh approach* (London, 1978). Rather more attention is paid to wisdom by C. Westermann, *Elements of Old Testament Theology* (Atlanta, 1982) (ET from *Theologie des Alten Testaments in Grundzügen*, Grundrisse zum Alten Testament: Das Alte Testament Deutsch, Ergänzungsreihe, 6, Göttingen, 1978) and by W. Zimmerli, *Old Testament Theology in Outline* (Atlanta, 1978), (ET from *Grundriss der alttestamentlichen Theologie*, Theologische Wissenschaft, 3, Stuttgart, 1972), especially pp. 155–66, though Westermann still denies it a proper place in Old Testament theology (see e.g. *What does the Old Testament say about God?* (Atlanta/London, 1979) pp. 99–100). Cf. also W. Zimmerli, 'The Place

and Limit of the Wisdom in the Framework of the Old Testament Theology',
SJT 17 (1964) 146–58 = J. L. Crenshaw, ed., *Studies in Ancient Israelite
Wisdom* (New York, 1976) pp. 314–26 (ET from 'Ort und Grenze der
Weisheit im Rahmen der alttestamentlichen Theologie', *Les Sagesses du
proche-orient ancien* (Paris, 1963) pp. 121–37 = W. Zimmerli, *Gottes Offen-
barung: gesammelte Aufsätze zum Alten Testament*, Theologische Bücherei,
Altes Testament, 19 (Munich, 1963) pp. 300–15).

10. Cf. J. Barr, *Old and New in Interpretation: a study of the two Testaments*
(London, 1966) pp. 65–102.

11. See *inter alia* von Rad, pp. 111–12; R. Smend, *Die Mitte des Alten Testaments*
(Theologische Studien, 101, Zurich, 1970); G. F. Hasel, 'The Problem of the
Center in the OT Theology Debate', *ZAW* 86 (1974) 65–82; W. Zimmerli,
'Zum Problem der "Mitte des Alten Testaments"', *EvT* 35 (1975) 97–118.

12. Westermann, *Theologie*, p. 5.

13. S. Morenz, *Egyptian Religion* (London, 1973) pp. xiv, 4 (ET from *Ägyptische
Religion*, Die Religionen der Menschheit, 8, Stuttgart, 1960).

14. Ibid., p. 4.

15. H. H. Rowley, *The Faith of Israel: aspects of Old Testament thought* (Sprunt
Lectures, 1955; London, 1956) pp. 20, 19.

16. J. Pedersen, *Israel: its Life and Culture* (4 vols in 2, London and Copenhagen, 1926, 1940), especially vols 1–2, pp. 182–212 (ET from *Israel* vols 1–2,
3–4, Copenhagen, 1920, 1934).

17. C. Westermann, *Blessings in the Bible and in the Life of the Church*
(Philadelphia, 1978), (ET from *Der Segen in der Bibel und im Handeln der
Kirche*, Munich, 1968); *Theologie*, 88–101; *What does the Old Testament say
about God*?

18. S. Terrien, *The Elusive Presence: toward a new biblical theology* (Religious
Perspectives, vol. 26, New York, 1978).

12

'Joseph and Asenath' and the Eucharist

Barnabas Lindars SSF

'The bread of life' is a phrase that is familiar to readers of John 6, and 'the cup of blessing' is used by Paul in 1 Cor.10:16, but both these phrases occur, along with other similar expressions, in the Jewish Hellenistic romance of *Joseph and Asenath*. This book was first brought to the attention of New Testament scholars by G. D. Kilpatrick in 1952.[1] It then came into discussion of the Qumran meal, known from the recent discovery of the Dead Sea Scrolls, which was also attracting the interest of New Testament scholars in connection with the Jewish background to the eucharist.[2] However, its contribution to the solution of the problems of eucharistic origins was not decisive, so that the interest which it had at first aroused declined. I. H. Marshall, in his recent *Last Supper and Lord's Supper* (1980), draws attention to the quasi-eucharistic language found several times in the book, but dismisses it as far too obscure to tell us anything about the historical basis of the Christian meal.[3] In his *The Eucharist in Bible and Liturgy* (1983) Kilpatrick himself takes up the position of his 1952 article and develops it further.[4] But, as will be shown below, his theory is questionable, and he scarcely appreciates the real value of *Joseph and Asenath* for the New Testament. There is, indeed, an unsatisfied need to look at the matter from a broader perspective.[5] In what follows it will be shown that the romance has many points of contact with New Testament issues, and that its evidential value for the primitive eucharist, though more limited than at first supposed, is by no means negligible.

The story is based on the information in Gen.41:45 that Pharaoh gave to Joseph as his bride Asenath, the daughter of Potiphera (Pentephres), the priest of On (Heliopolis). This very brief notice is built up into a long plot with many fantastic details. The chief issue is the conversion of Asenath to Judaism in order to marry Joseph. This is effected by the archangel Michael, who appears to Asenath in response to her prayer. This is the central scene of the book, and is important for understanding the author's purpose. In the first place it enhances the impression, already evident in the book, that Asenath, and not Joseph, is the real focus of interest. The privilege of embracing the Jewish religion is far more important than the custom for a woman to accept her husband's religion would imply. It is represented as the discovery of the true faith by an Egyptian woman brought up in idolatrous worship. Secondly, Michael confers on her a new symbolic name, City of Refuge (15.7[6]),[6] because she is the model for all those who repent and seek refuge in the Most High God. This might suggest a directly propagandist aim, to win converts to Judaism. But it must be pointed out, thirdly, that Michael's response to Asenath never at any point touches on the Law and its obligations. Jewish religion is referred to only by means of symbols. The details of life under the Law are passed over in silence. It would seem, then, that the author has deliberately played down this aspect of Judaism, so as to avoid reference to anything unpleasant or burdensome. This may well be to reassure Egyptian women, who are alarmed at the implications of marrying Jews. Thus the purpose of the book should probably be regarded not as propaganda for Judaism in general, but as an effort to welcome Egyptian women in mixed marriages, and to encourage them to accept their husbands' faith with joy and conviction.[7]

This assessment of the purpose of the book also decides the date when it is likely to have been written. It clearly belongs to the time when proselytising activity in the Diaspora was at its peak, around the turn of the era, and certainly before the fall of Jerusalem in A.D. 70. This was not realised when the book was first published by Batiffol in 1889.[8] He thought of a Jewish work of the fourth century A.D., subsequently heavily christianised, with Joseph as a type of Christ and many sacramental allusions. That the Jewish original must belong to the earlier date was recognised by Brooks[9] and Aptowitzer,[10] but both still thought of Christian alterations and interpolations. Kilpatrick, however, insisted that a Christian interpolator would have gone further and incorporated explicit reference to Christ. This is always true of interpolated Jewish works. The text must be accepted as it stands as a Jewish work, and the theory of Christian alteration must be abandoned. This view is now generally accepted by scholars.[11] We must therefore look at the passages which appear to have a sacramental ring, to see whether they can be interpreted in terms of Judaism in New Testament times and how they relate to the author's aim.

The first passage comes when Joseph arrives at Heliopolis on his tour of Egypt in the first of the seven years of plenty, and enters the house of Pentephres. His fame has gone before him, and Pentephres has already suggested to his daughter that she should marry him, though she has refused numerous suitors, including the son of Pharaoh himself. Asenath, however, is not willing to consider this upstart foreigner, but when Joseph arrives she sees him from an upper window and is deeply smitten by him. Entering the courtyard in his chariot, he is comparable to the sun in the sky. She even refers to him as 'the son of God' (6.3,5[6,2]). When she meets Joseph, Pentephres encourages her to kiss him, but Joseph refuses to allow it.

> 'It is not fitting', he says, 'for a man, who blesses with his mouth the living God and eats the blessed bread of life and drinks the blessed cup of immortality and is anointed with the blessed oil of incorruption, to kiss a foreign woman, who blesses with her mouth dead and dumb idols and eats from their table the bread of strangling and drinks from their libations the cup of deceit and is anointed with the oil of destruction' (8.5).[12]

Not surprisingly, Asenath is ready to burst into tears at this rebuff. Full of sympathy, Joseph lays his hand on her head, and prays for her conversion:

> 'O Lord, the God of my father Israel, the Most High, the Mighty One of Israel, the one who gives life to all things and has called [them] from darkness to light and from error to truth: do you, O Lord, bless this virgin, and renew her with your Spirit, and refashion her with your secret hand, and revitalise her with your life, and let her eat your bread of life, and let her drink your cup of blessing, and number her with your people whom you have chosen before all things came to be, and let her enter into your rest which you have prepared for your chosen ones, and let her live in your eternal life for the time of eternity' (8.9[10–11]).

From a Christian point of view, attention at once falls on the bread and the cup and the oil, all said to be blessed, and each provided with an interpretative noun – life, immortality, incorruption – suggesting sacramental significance. Brooks, assuming Christian influence, naturally thought of the eucharist and confirmation. Seeing that Asenath is a convert to a new faith, a reference to initiation is not out of place, though obviously, if communion and chrismation are meant, they are in the wrong order.

Kilpatrick, however, as we have seen, denied any Christian influence, and was disposed to see allusion to a Jewish cultic meal, which included anointing with oil as part of the ceremony. More will be said about this later. If a special Jewish meal is indicated here, it would certainly be a valuable addition to our knowledge of Jewish meals which form the background to the eucharist.

The question then arises whether the meal implied here can be identified with the Qumran meal, for which rules are laid down in the Manual of Discipline, and also in the Messianic Rule when the Messiahs are present. This issue was examined by K. G. Kuhn. He thought that, as the meal is evidently confined to the initiated, there might be a connection. But in the Qumran Community only men are admitted to membership. He therefore suggested that the background to *Joseph and Asenath* should be sought in the Therapeutae, an Egyptian Essene sect which was open to women, according to Philo, and might have had a similar meal.[13] Although Delcor has argued for a connection with the Therapeutae,[14] this cannot be regarded as at all probable, because of the total omission of any reference to observance of the Law, which is scarcely conceivable in a work emanating from this sect, and also because the whole book is concerned with marriage, and a mixed marriage at that, whereas the Therapeutae prized celibacy in the same way as Qumran. Moreover, according to Josephus, the Essenes expressly forbad the use of oil, regarding it as a dangerous luxury.[15] A further point is that *Joseph and Asenath* is in no way concerned with the contemplative life, which Philo regards as the most attractive feature of the Therapeutae.

Noting these points, R. Schnackenburg, in an article in the Kuhn *Festschrift*,[16] insisted that the search for a special kind of meal was a mistake. Joseph does not refer to an actual meal, and no such meal is described later when Asenath's conversion is complete. The expressions are symbolical, referring to the religious values of Jewish faith, as can be seen clearly from the larger context of Joseph's prayer for Asenath's conversion. But Schnackenburg went too far in denying that there is any reference to a meal. J. Jeremias had already asserted against Kilpatrick that, as the references to bread and wine are indeed used symbolically to denote Jewish religion more generally, only the common Jewish meal could be intended.[17] This opinion has been endorsed in the studies of C. Burchard.[18]

One of the strong points in the view of Jeremias is that it suits the contrast with the description of Asenath's present position as a pagan. Her blessing of the dead and dumb idols and eating the bread of strangling and drinking the cup of deceit and anointing with the oil of destruction are all aspects of her normal everyday life as a pagan. They can be said to typify the pagan's religious life. And Joseph's point is that they are incompatible with the corresponding aspects of Jewish religious life. In so far as these descriptions refer to specific ceremonies, it is because they can be regarded as typical facets of the religion as a whole. Thus they are not exclusively symbolical, for they do refer to actual ceremonies in a vague way. But they are introduced as symbols of the religion as a whole, which is the real point at issue. Precisely because Jewish meals are controlled by the prescriptions of the Law, it can be assumed that, by seizing this aspect of Jewish life as typical, the author intends to imply that the convert will live under the Law without actually saying so.

Moreover the reference to the meal locates Jewish religion primarily in the home. This meets the situation to which the book is addressed, as it is in the home that a proselyte woman will chiefly experience her new religion. But this should not blind us to the fact that a meal together is a normal way in which a specialist group expresses its common life. There is much to be said for the view that the Qumran meal is the ordinary family meal in this way, though it is for the fully fledged members of the community only and has no kinship basis. It is also significant that the novices are excluded, so that it is confined to a specially accredited group. In the same way there is much to be said for the view that the eucharist is the normal meal of the Christian community when it is gathered as a community, in contrast with meals at home, where not all members of the household may be Christians. However it must be said that the situation presupposed in *Joseph and Asenath* neither supports nor precludes such specialised gatherings of particular groups.[19]

Another point which is likely to have struck the reader is that Joseph's words to Asenath bear a remarkable resemblance to Paul's argument in 1 Cor.10:14–21. Joseph himself could have said, 'You cannot drink the cup of the Lord and the cup of demons. You cannot partake of the table of the Lord and the table of demons.' Here there is exactly the same connection between confession of faith and liturgical participation. Christianity demands a complete break from the worship of pagan gods, just as in the case of Asenath, and the community gathered for the eucharist defines the church as a distinct body. From this point of view the church is the company of those who bless with their mouth Jesus as Lord and eat the blessed bread of life and drink the blessed cup of immortality and are anointed with the oil of incorruption. The eucharistic assembly is central to Christian social definition, and to speak of participation in it is to speak vividly of adherence to Christian religion as a whole.

So far we have looked at the symbolism of Joseph's words only in a general way. In order to prepare for a more detailed analysis we may look first at the continuation of the story. After Joseph's prayer for her Asenath goes up to her room, suffering from a violent conflict of emotions, and Joseph takes leave of Pentephres, promising to return a week later. Asenath's distress is brought to an end by the appearance of Michael at the end of seven days of mourning and penitential exercises.[20] Michael announces that her name has been written in the 'book of the living' from the moment she began her penance (15.4[3]), and assures her that 'from today you will be renewed and refashioned and revitalised and eat the blessed bread of life and drink the blessed cup of immortality and be anointed with the oil of incorruption' (15.5[4]). He also promises that she will marry Joseph, who is due back on this very day. It is at this point that he gives her the symbolic name of City of Refuge, then undertakes to inform Joseph of her conversion, and tells her to put on her bridal attire in readiness to meet him. However, Asenath insists that first the unknown messenger must have refreshment, as in the story of Gideon in Judg.6:11–24 (which is no doubt the author's literary model for what follows).[21] As she goes to the cupboard Michael tells her to bring a honeycomb, but she knows there is none there. However, miraculously she finds one. Then Michael shakes her head with his hand and says:

Blessed are you, Asenath, because there have been revealed to you the unspeakable mysteries of the Most High, and blessed are all who are joined to the Lord God in repentance, because they will eat of this honeycomb. For this honeycomb is the spirit of life. The bees of the paradise of delight made it out of the dew of the roses of life which are in the paradise of God. And all the angels of God eat of it and all the chosen of God and all the sons of the Most High, because this is the honeycomb of life, and whosoever will eat of it will not die for the time of eternity (16.14[7–8]).[22]

Here we may pause to observe that the honey is clearly symbolic of the heavenly manna which supported Israel in the wilderness. It is compared to dew, and it is the food of angels.[23] The manna is said to taste of honey in Exod.16:31.

Then Michael shares a piece of the honeycomb with Asenath. As soon as she has eaten it, he says, 'Behold, you have eaten of the bread of life and have drunk of the cup of immortality and have been anointed with the oil of incorruption' (16.16).[24] He mentions her future glory, and how she will be 'as a walled metropolis for all those who take refuge in the name of the Lord God, the king of the ages.' This is further demonstrated by the honeycomb, as bees come out of it and swarm all over Asenath, and some attack her, but she is completely unharmed.[25] Then Michael dismisses the bees, and (as in the Gideon story) fire comes out of the table and consumes the honeycomb. When Asenath's seven maidservants have been called in and blessed by Michael as the first to take refuge in her, he returns to heaven in a chariot of fire.

It is thus clear that there is no attempt to describe a ceremony of initiation any more than there is to describe a meal. Just a taste of the life-giving heavenly manna embodied in the honeycomb is enough to warrant the statement that she has already eaten the bread of life, etc. Without either initiation or meal, Asenath has reached the point where her conversion is complete. Her share in the honeycomb has set the seal of divine approval on her repentance and denotes her acceptance into the Jewish people.

It follows that the repeated references to bread and wine and oil are to be explained by their symbolic value. We do not need to argue whether they fit a known Jewish meal, incorporating blessings not only of bread and wine but also of oil.[26] Of course these things do figure in Jewish meals, but they have been chosen for their symbolic value in relation to Jewish religion as a whole. The choice of these three elements in particular invites comparison with the numerous passages in the Old Testament where corn, wine and oil are grouped together to typify God's blessings on his people in an agricultural setting, e.g. Deut.11:14. This sense of blessing finds expression in rejoicing, especially in the meals which accompanied the sacrifices in old Israel. The three elements are combined in what may be an allusion to such a meal in Ps.23:5: 'You have prepared before me a table in the presence of my enemies; you have anointed my head with oil; my cup is brimming over.' There is thus an interaction between symbolism and actuality. Bread and wine and oil symbolise the joy of participation in Jewish faith, and this joy is experienced in the meals in which they are blessed and used. It is to be observed that not all the references in *Joseph and Asenath* include all three elements. The oil is omitted in Joseph's prayer, quoted above (8.9[11]), and again when Asenath tells him of her experiences on his return (19.5).[27] There is room for variation, because the symbolic value is primary and there is no direct reference to precise ceremonies.

But the symbolism goes further than this. The three elements are defined as vehicles of life, immortality, and incorruption. This is reminiscent of the language of the Greek mystery cults. Michael actually tells Asenath that to her have been revealed 'the unspeakable mysteries of the Most High' (16.14[7]). Through eating the honeycomb, in which is 'the spirit of life', she has been admitted to the knowledge of God and granted participation in a life-giving religion. It is on this basis that Kilpatrick has argued that the author is referring to a Jewish meal which has been influenced by the mystery cults.[28] But it is necessary to distinguish between the use of the language of the mystery cults and adoption of their presuppositions and beliefs. Preoccupation with immortality is certainly characteristic of these cults, which claimed to release their clients from the inexorable wheel of fate. This was achieved through participation in an enactment of the myth of a dying and rising god, in which the initiant is reborn as a divine being. The author of *Joseph and Asenath* must surely have had some knowledge of the mysteries of Osiris and Isis, which embodies a mythic pattern of this kind.[29] Indeed the description of Asenath in her new radiance after her conversion (18.9–11[7])[30] may owe something to the hymns in praise of Isis. But her conversion is effected by the divine response to her prayers and penitence, and not by any enactment of a dramatised myth either in an initiation rite or in a sacred meal.

Nevertheless a connection with the language of the mysteries can be accepted, because the concepts of immortality and incorruption represent the religious aim of the people for whom the book is written. We can see this in another product of Egyptian Jewry of roughly the same period, the Wisdom of Solomon, though here the debt is not to the mystery cults but to Greek philosophy: 'For God created man for incorruption, and made him in the image of his own eternity' (Wisd.2:23).

This use of the religious concepts valued in other traditions is characteristic of the frontier situation of Diaspora Judaism. Though there can be no compromise with regard to faith and worship, Judaism can be made attractive and meaningful only if it fulfils the existing aspirations of the people. So also the fourth gospel requires a provenance in Hellenistic Judaism, in spite of its many Palestinian features, because of the substitution of 'life' or 'eternal life' for 'the kingdom of God' in the underlying tradition.[31] It is thus no accident that the fourth gospel shares 'the bread of life' with *Joseph and Asenath*. Similarly, when Ignatius calls the eucharist 'the medicine of immortality', this should not be taken to imply a quasi-magical property of the eucharist.[32] The phrase already existed as the designation of a particular remedy, popularly attributed to the skill of Isis herself. But Ignatius uses it metaphorically to denote the spiritual benefit of participation in the eucharist, specified in the context as communion with the risen and victorious Christ.

The real meaning of these references to immortality in *Joseph and Asenath* can be deduced from Joseph's prayer for Asenath's conversion, which has already been quoted. He begins by addressing God as 'the one who gives life to all things and has called them from darkness to light and from error to truth' (8.9[10]).[33] This at once indicates the religious categories of the author's understanding of Judaism. Life, light and truth belong together, just as they do in the Dead Sea Scrolls and other literature of this period. This is confirmed by Joseph's action when Asenath meets him on his return. After her description of her conversion there is no longer a barrier, and so, we are told, 'Joseph kissed Asenath and gave her the spirit of life; and he kissed her a second time and gave her the spirit of wisdom; and he kissed her a third time and gave her the spirit of truth' (19.11[3]).[34] The final phrase (πνεῦμα ἀληθείας) is of course reminiscent of the Two Spirits doctrine at Qumran and actually occurs several times in John 14–16 as a designation of the Holy Spirit. These spiritual gifts are available to Asenath because of her participation in Jewish faith. Here the author uses words which are at home in his own religious tradition. This must be set in the scales against his use of the language of the mysteries with regard to the bread and wine and oil.

After this opening address, Joseph's petitions for Asenath enlarge the range of reference still more. He prays God to bless her and to renew her, using three virtually synonymous phrases for the divine act of renewal. There seems no point in this repetition, unless it is to achieve an artistic balance with the three life-giving elements, though (perhaps also for artistic reasons) only the bread and the cup are mentioned in what follows, with the concept of life only once ('bread of life' and 'cup of blessing'). Seeing that life, immortality and incorruption are also virtually synonymous, they can be taken as expressions of the renewal for which Joseph prays, and this must be understood in the spiritual and moral sense implied by his address to God.

But this is not the whole matter. Joseph's prayer concludes with another triad of petitions, balancing the first three for renewal. These are to include Asenath in the chosen people, to admit her to the rest (κατάπαυσις) that is prepared for them, and to live in the eternity of God.[35] The concept of the chosen people carries with it the covenant idea, here located in the predetermined plan of God. The 'rest' belongs to the future, and so is an eschatological concept. Joseph's words at this point have a striking parallel with Hebrews 4, where the promise of rest is deduced from Ps.95:11, using κατάπαυσις, and this is correlated with the fact that God 'rested' (κατέπαυσεν) on the seventh day of creation. So 'there remains a sabbath-rest (σαββατισμός) for the people of God' (Heb.4:9). But neither in *Joseph and Asenath* nor in Hebrews is the rest merely future. It is already available to Asenath, because her new religion brings her into fellowship with God who is eternal (the third item in the triad), and it is already available to the readers of Hebrews, because Jesus has led the way to the promised land which the Israelites had forfeited through disobedience. There is an interchange of eschatological and timeless concepts which suggests the three items of this final triad – membership in the chosen people, the coming rest, and the eternity of God – are again to be considered virtual equivalents. Asenath is renewed, gains the secret of immortality, and enters the company of those who have life in God.

It can thus be seen that the use of phrases reminiscent of the mystery cults is a kind of top-dressing, while the fundamental religious concepts remain those of Jewish religion. In line with a general tendency in the Jewish Diaspora, eschatological concepts are played down without being denied. There is no suggestion that Asenath has gained a magical substance which releases her from the limitations of mortal existence or protects her from inexorable fate. It is only in a very generalised way that the benefits of Judaism can be expressed in the language of the mysteries. Unlike Christianity, Judaism does not have a dying and rising Lord to invite comparison with the myths of dying and rising gods which were central to many of these cults. Even if Asenath can be likened to Isis, there is no hint of the search for the dead Osiris and the joy of finding him.

These thoughts on the meaning of 'the bread of life' in *Joseph and Asenath* can lead us to consideration of the meaning of the eucharist, in distinction from the question of historical origins. We can suitably start with John, the only book in the New Testament where the phrase occurs. It comes twice in the discourse of John 6, each time as a predicate of Jesus himself: 'I am the bread of life' (6:35,48). But these should be seen in relation to other similar statements in the same chapter: 'The bread of God is that which comes down from heaven and gives life to the world' (33); 'I am the bread which came down from heaven' (41); 'I am the living bread which came down from heaven' (51); 'This is the bread which came down from heaven, not such as your fathers ate and died; he who eats this bread will live for ever' (58). The contrast is with the manna in the wilderness, which in *Joseph and Asenath* is represented by the honeycomb as a symbol of immortality. Here too immortality is the religious concept which is meaningful in John's circle. Though the discourses of the fourth gospel reflect debates with the unbelieving Jews, they are conducted in a milieu which has the marks of Hellenistic Judaism, and may well be located in the Diaspora. This is supported by the traditional connection of the fourth gospel with Ephesus.

In the Bread of Life discourse of John 6 the manna is not only a symbol of immortality. It is also a symbol of the spiritual nourishment of the Law. This has been shown in detail by P. Borgen, who found parallels both in the writings of Philo and in the later Jewish midrashim.[36] It is thus presupposed in the discourse that the Jews identify the Law with the divine Wisdom, which nourishes the soul in the same way as the manna gave physical sustenance to the Israelites in the wilderness. The symbolism of food and drink for Wisdom is found already in Ecclus.24:21,[37] almost certainly alluded to in John 6:35, and the claim that it is embodied in the Law follows a few verses later (Ecclus.24:23ff.). Thus the correlation of Wisdom and the Law is already explicit in the Palestinian tradition. It seems less certain that the manna was used in connection with these ideas in Palestinian Judaism, to judge from the evidence collected by B. J. Malina.[38] In fact it entails allegorisation of the manna story in Alexandrian style, and thus a setting in the Diaspora is perhaps to be preferred.

But does this have any bearing on the eucharist? The above interpretation of the discourse in terms of Wisdom and the Law (often referred to as the sapiential interpretation) has been held to be incompatible with the sacramental interpretation. Bultmann excludes the manifestly eucharistic section (John 6:51b–58) as an interpolation by an 'ecclesiastical redactor', bent on bringing John into line with catholic practice.[39] The omission of the institution of the eucharist in John's account of the Last Supper is held to support the view that John was opposed to the sacraments. But it must be objected that this is a false opposition. Our study of *Joseph and Asenath* has shown that the language of food and drink can denote participation in Jewish faith at the same time as referring to actual meals in which this faith is experienced. The sapiential interpretation of John 6 is right and is to be accepted, but it does not exclude the sacramental interpretation. John's choice of theme has been prompted not only by the symbolic use of the manna tradition in Jewish thought, but also by the church's practice of the eucharist.

It thus seems permissible to make use of John 6 as a guide to one aspect, at any rate, of the meaning of the eucharist in a predominantly Hellenistic Jewish congregation of Christian believers outside Palestine. In the eucharist they 'eat the flesh of the Son of man and drink his blood' (John 6:53) in the sense that the bread and wine, blessed in the context of a commemoration of the death of Jesus, using his own words at the Last Supper, are symbolic of the faith which they profess. Attention is fastened on the life-giving effect of this faith, because this is the aspect which is religiously meaningful to them. Ignatius' 'medicine of immortality' is an entirely appropriate metaphor for the eucharist from this point of view.

Joseph and Asenath helps us to understand the rise of the language and metaphors used in connection with the eucharist in a Hellenistic Jewish Christian setting. But in a negative way it may also point the way to more primitive ideas. Joseph's prayer for Asenath correlates eschatological and timeless concepts, and this is also true of John 6:39–40. It also suggests that a Jewish meal – not necessarily a special meal distinguished from ordinary daily practice – is an occasion when Jews are conscious of their identity as the people of God. Though the covenant is not mentioned, it is presupposed. Both in Qumran and in Christianity there is a meal with eschatological overtones, in which the members are aware of their special identity as the covenant people. The variations between 'covenant' and 'new covenant' in the eucharistic texts show differing emphases in the meaning of the eucharist.

The eschatological thrust is clearly a feature of the earlier meaning of the eucharist. After recording the tradition of the institution of the eucharist in 1 Cor.11:23–25, which he may well have received from the Jerusalem church, Paul adds his own comment: 'For as often as you eat this bread and drink the cup, you proclaim the Lord's death until he come' (26). Thus a present activity, participating in the eucharist, has both a past and a future reference. The primitive kerygma is presupposed. Jesus, who 'died for our sins according to the scriptures' (1 Cor.15:3), has been raised to the right hand of God in readiness for his coming as God's representative at the end of the age, which Paul still holds to be imminent. Thus the consistent eschatology of the primitive preaching is retained without the tendency to rewrite it in timeless concepts which we can see in both *Joseph and Asenath* and John. That it belongs to the earliest days is suggested by the *marana tha* ('Our Lord, come!') invocation, quoted by Paul from the Aramaic-speaking church in 1 Cor.16:20.[40]

The references to past and future necessarily imply a vivid sense of Christ's present Lordship. Those who have been pledged to him by baptism acknowledge his lordship in heaven and pray for his speedy return. It is significant that the *marana tha* invocation is direct address to Jesus himself. This practice, at the centre of the church's common life, must have had a powerful influence on the development of christology.

With regard to the meal itself, the value of *Joseph and Asenath* is that it shows how religious ideas of central importance may be attached to any Jewish meal. There is thus no intrinsic reason why the eucharist should not be any Christian meal. It is defined only by membership. It is the common meal of the covenant people of God. The meaning of the meal is expressed in the eucharistic words which accompany the blessing of the bread and of the cup. Kilpatrick is probably right in regarding the words of institution, not as the blessing as such, but as part of the 'charter story' of the rite, providing the link between the commemoration of the death of Christ and the meal in which it is expressed.[41] But inevitably special significance attaches to the blessing of the bread and of the wine, so that the way is prepared for these to be separated from the rest of the meal, as Paul recommended to the Corinthians on account of abuses (1 Cor.11:34).

On the other hand, the common meal cannot explain the words of institution themselves. As the words are basically a simple self-identification on the part of Jesus with substances used at the meal, they lack the meaning required for them to serve as commemoration of his death, unless the meal itself has a special character to make it appropriate for the purpose. As the breaking of the bread is the signal for the start of the meal, the words over the bread may be taken to identify Jesus with the meal as a whole, not just with the bread as such. Similarly the blessing of the cup at the end ('after supper', 1 Cor.11:25) identifies Jesus with the whole meal retrospectively, but this time with more obvious symbolism in relation to his certainty of death. These identifications are difficult to elucidate if the Last Supper was the common meal, because it has no charter story to define its meaning. On the other hand, if the Last Supper was the Passover, as the Synoptic Gospels require (and probably Paul, cf. 1 Cor.5:7), the meal was laden with meaning which Jesus could relate to his premonition of death, and so indicate the sacrificial intention with which he faced the danger to his life. It is in the context of the Passover Haggadah that Jesus' self-identification with the bread and wine at a meal makes sense, and the repetition of his words in the subsequent eucharistic commemoration of his death is explained.

In conclusion, the main points treated above may be briefly summarised, and a couple of further items from this intriguing story of *Joseph and Asenath* may be added because of their relevance and interest.

First and foremost, the Jewish meal can be used to symbolise Jewish faith and the benefit which it confers. This is true also of the Christian eucharist. The meal references do not relate to a particular meal, nor to rites of initiation. The common meal, whether in the home or in a special group, is central to religious self-definition, and may thus be used as a symbol of the religion as a whole which is professed by the participants. By the same token it can be used to denote differentiation from pagan religion, which also has its meals effecting social definition.

Bread, wine and oil, used in various types of meal, have broader significance as symbols of God's providence in general. This is filled out in the frontier situation of Diaspora Judaism with language borrowed from the mysteries, which express the religious values and aspirations of the people. This is similar to the sapiential aspects of the Bread of Life discourse in John 6, in which the manna tradition symbolises the Law as the embodiment of Wisdom and is applied to the fulfilment of the Law in Christ.

At the same time the benefit of the Jewish religion is expressed in *Joseph and Asenath* with the Jewish concepts of light, life and truth as gifts of the Spirit, as in Qumran and in John. Asenath after her conversion can be compared to the charismatic community of the primitive church. Membership of the covenant people is implied, as in the eucharist. A trace of eschatological language furnishes an interesting link with Hebrews, but the transmutation of eschatology into timeless concepts is more prominent. On the other hand, this supports the contention that the eschatological orientation is primary, as evidenced for the eucharist by the *marana tha* invocation.

While *Joseph and Asenath* supports the view that the eucharist was the common meal of the Christian community, it gives no help towards deciding the setting in which the words of institution, commemorative of the death of Jesus, were first given. It has been argued above that the traditional connection with the Passover is still the best explanation.

The first of our additional points follows the reunion of Joseph and Asenath, when he kisses her and confers on her the threefold gifts of the Spirit. She then invites him in for a meal, but first she insists on washing his feet (20.1–5[1–3]). Joseph objects that it should be done by a servant, but she persuades him that it expresses the unity between them. The similarity to John's Last Supper narrative in John 13:1–20 is quite striking.

Our second point is the rich use of language which must be taken into account in the development of christology. We have already seen that Asenath compared Joseph on his first arrival to the sun and called him 'the son of God'. Then, when all is ready for the marriage, Pharaoh (whose permission is required, to accord with Gen.41:45) comes to perform the ceremony, and says to Asenath, 'He is the firstborn son of God, and you will be called the daughter of the Most High' (21.4[3]). Afterwards Asenath sings a psalm, in which she gives thanks that she has become 'the bride of the firstborn son of the Great King. . . . And he has given me to eat the bread of life and to drink the cup of wisdom' (21.20–21).[42]

Notes

1. G. D. Kilpatrick, 'Living Issues in Biblical Scholarship: the Last Supper', *ExpT* 64 (1952) 4–8.
2. Cf. K. G. Kuhn, 'The Lord's Supper and the Communal Meal at Qumran', *The Scrolls and the New Testament*, ed. K. Stendahl (London, 1958) pp. 65–93.
3. I. H. Marshall, *Last Supper and Lord's Supper* (Exeter, 1980) pp. 26–7.
4. G. D. Kilpatrick, *The Eucharist in Bible and Liturgy* (Cambridge, 1983) pp. 59–68.
5. This also applies to the much more detailed study of H.-J. Klauck, *Herrenmahl und hellenistischer Kult* (Neutestamentliche Abhandlungen, N.F. 12; Münster, 1982) pp. 187–96.
6. Chapter and verse numbers are those of C. Burchard for his English translation in *The Old Testament Pseudepigrapha*, vol. 2 ed. J. H. Charlesworth (London, 1985) pp. 177–247. For quotations I have made my own translation from Burchard's Greek text published in *Dielheimer Blätter zum Alten Testament* 14 (1979) pp. 2–53. This differs considerably from the shorter Greek text used by M. Philonenko, *Joseph et Aséneth* (Studia Post-Biblica 13; Leiden, 1968), which has been used by D. Cook for the English translation in *The Apocryphal Old Testament*, ed. H. F. D. Sparks (Oxford, 1984) pp. 466–503. Figures in square brackets refer to the verse numbers in this edition where they differ from those in Burchard.
7. So A.-M. Denis in an oral communication. The suggestion does not appear in his *Introduction aux pseudépigraphes grecs de l'Ancien Testament* (Studia in Veteris Testamenti Pseudepigrapha, vol. 1; Leiden, 1970) pp. 40–9. It should be noted that Joseph is mindful of his father's warning to beware of marrying a foreign woman (7.5[6]).
8. P. Batiffol, 'Le Livre de la Prière d'Aseneth', *SP* 1–2 (Paris, 1889–90) 1–115. This was the first critical Greek text. A Latin text and a Greek fragment had been published by J. A. Fabricius in 1723 and a German translation of the Latin by R. Akibon in 1850 (for details, see Philonenko, pp. 16 and 26).
9. E. W. Brooks, *Joseph and Asenath* (Translations of Early Documents, Series 2, Hellenistic-Jewish Texts vol. 7: London, 1918), based on Batiffol's text.

10. V. Aptowitzer, 'Asenath, the Wife of Joseph: a Haggadic Literary-Historical Enquiry', *HUCA* (1924) 239–306.
11. Cf. Kuhn, p. 75, and notes, pp. 261–2; Philonenko, p. 100; Denis, p. 44.
12. The short text omits from the first sentence 'of life . . . blessed oil', possibly by homoeoteleuton. This is one of several instances where Philonenko has been compelled to supplement the short text from the long text, because the sense absolutely requires it. It is not possible to argue that the short text preserves the Jewish original without Christian interpolations, as supposedly Christian features are frequently found in the short text. In his *Untersuchungen zu Joseph und Aseneth: Überlieferung – Ortsbestimmung* (Wissenschaftliche Untersuchungen zum Neuen Testament 8) Tübingen, 1965, C. Burchard distinguished four text traditions, of which three are variant forms of the long text. The task of establishing the best text is thus complex and problematical. Burchard's text differs from that of Batiffol, though both use forms of the long text.
13. Philo, *On the Contemplative Life* 3.32; 8.68. Essene origin had already been proposed by P. Riessler, *Altjüdische Schrifttum ausserhalb der Bibel* (Augsburg, 1928) pp. 497–538 (translation), pp. 1303–4. (notes).
14. M. Delcor, 'Un roman d'amour d'origine thérapeute: Le Livre de Joseph et Asénath', *Bulletin de littérature ecclésiastique* 63 (1962) 3–27.
15. Josephus, *Jewish War* 2.123.
16. R. Schnackenburg, 'Das Brot des Lebens', *Tradition und Glaube* (*Festschrift K. G. Kuhn*; Göttingen, 1971) pp. 328–42.
17. J. Jeremias, 'The Last Supper', *ExpT* 64 (1952) 91–2.
18. In a seminar paper at the meeting of *Studiorum Novi Testamenti Societas*, Leuven, 1982.
19. The Pharisaic *ḥabūrāh* provides another example of a religious meal of a specialised group. It is now recognised, against Lietzmann, that this word denotes the group, and the meal is simply the common meal of the regular meetings of the group (usually Friday evening). Cf. Marshall, p. 20; J. Jeremias, *Jerusalem in the Time of Jesus* (London, 1969) pp. 251–2.
20. On his first appearance Michael is 'in every way like Joseph' (14.9[8]). He is thus Joseph's counterpart, bringing the inward religion of which Joseph is the outward bearer. He causes Asenath to eat the bread of life, etc., for which Joseph had prayed, but afterwards Asenath can say in her hymn of praise that Joseph has given her the bread of life (21.21 – not in the short text).
21. Other Old Testament theophanies may also have played a part, e.g. Abraham and the three angels (Gen.18) and the annunciation of Samson (Judg.13). The literary affinities of *Joseph and Asenath* with the Hellenistic romance have also suggested influence of Greek magical texts, in which a demon visitor (δαίμων πάρεδρος) in human form visits and eats with the person who is seeking spiritual enlightenment, cf. Philonenko, p. 97. However Old Testament models are surely more important, as witness the episode in the concluding part of the story, where Benjamin slays the son of Pharaoh with a sling like David and Goliath (27.1–3).

22. The short text omits the following: 'mysteries'; 'For this honeycomb is the spirit of life'; 'and all the chosen . . . life.'
23. Cf. Exod.16:13–15; Num.11:7–9; Ps. 78:23–25.
24. Omitted in the short text.
25. Before calling forth the bees Michael appears to make the sign of the cross on the honeycomb, leaving a mark as of blood. This appears to be a magical practice rather than a Christian feature, cf. Philonenko, p. 189.
26. Philonenko, pp. 91–3, adduces such Jewish evidence as there is for such a meal, but decides that it is too tenuous. He therefore suggests a meal, not attested elsewhere, influenced by the symbolic value of corn and wine and oil in the Old Testament, but actually embodying features of the sacred meal of the mystery cults.
27. 'A man came to me from heaven, and gave me bread of life, and I ate, and cup of blessing (ποτήριον εὐλογίας, cf. 1 Cor.10:16), and I drank.' This is a further piece omitted from the short text (cf. n. 24), possibly both deliberate, because of the discrepancy between what is said and what is actually done.
28. Kilpatrick (1952) connects it with meals at initiation ceremonies. In his more recent book (1983) pp. 59–68, he modifies the suggestion, though he notes the influence of the mysteries. Though Philonenko's text omits the word μυστήρια (cf. n. 22), he actually translates ἀπόρρητα ('unspeakable things') by 'mystères' and argues strenuously for the influence of the mystery cults.
29. By New Testament times Osiris was merged with Apis to form Sarapis. For description of the mystery and its wide ramifications, cf. J. G. Griffiths, *The Conflict of Horus and Seth* (Liverpool, 1960; rev. 1980); id., *The Origins of Osiris and his Cult* (Supplements to Numen 40: Leiden, 1980); id., *Apuleius of Madauros, The Isis-Book (Metamorphoses, Book XI)* (Études préliminaires aux religions orientaux dans l'empire romaine 39: Leiden, 1975).
30. Another defective passage in the short text, cf. Cook in Sparks (1984) p. 492, n. 8. According to the long text, Asenath has ordered water to wash her face, but when she sees her reflection she decides not to risk washing off her new beauty! Is there perhaps an allusion here to proselyte baptism?
31. It is, of course, a mistake to distinguish too sharply between Palestinian Judaism and the Hellenistic Judaism of the Diaspora. Since the work of M. Hengel, *Judaism and Hellenism* (London, 1974), it has been increasingly recognised that Palestine belongs to the Hellenistic culture region.
32. Ignatius, *Eph.* 20.2. For the reference to Isis cf. Bauer-Arndt-Gingrich, *A Greek-English Lexicon of the New Testament* (Cambridge, 1957) 862a.
33. Philonenko, p. 158, sees here traces of a liturgy for the admission of proselytes. The language of renewal in this context obviously does include the concept of initiation. Thus the symbolism is important not only for the eucharist but also for the theology of baptism, cf. H. C. Cavallin, 'Leben nach dem Tode im Spätjudentum und im frühen Christentum: I. Spätjudentum', *Aufstieg und Niedergang der römischen Welt* 2.19.1, ed. W. Haase (Berlin, 1979) pp. 240–345.
34. Again the short text is defective, and says only that 'they embraced one another for a long time and received new life in the spirit.'

35. The short text of 8.9[10–11] is not only deficient (supplemented by Philonenko to some extent from the long text) but also changes the sense. Instead of 'And number her with your people whom you have chosen before all things came to be,' the first clause is omitted and the second reads 'her whom you have chosen before she was begotten,' thus destroying the artistic balance with the following petition on rest. The final item of the triad on eternity is omitted altogether.
36. P. Borgen, *Bread from Heaven* (*NovTSup* 10; Leiden, 1968), p. 114.
37. Cf. also Isa.55:1–2. The quotation of Isa.54:13 in John 6:45 may well reflect the use of Isa.54:9–55:5 as a *sēder* reading along with the *haphtārāh* Exod.16 in the synagogue, cf. A. Guilding, *The Fourth Gospel and Jewish Worship* (Oxford, 1960) p. 63.
38. B. J. Malina, *The Palestinian Manna Tradition* (Arbeiten zur Geschichte des späteren Judentums und des Christentums vol. 7: Leiden, 1968) is particularly concerned with the Palestinian Targumim.
39. R. Bultmann, *The Gospel of John* (Oxford, 1971) p. 219.
40. Cf. also *Didache* 10.6. Like 'amen', this seems to be a primitive liturgical item which was to some extent carried through unchanged into the Greek-speaking communities. For the invocatory form cf. Rev.22:20, 'Amen. Come, Lord Jesus.' For recent discussion cf. Klauck, pp. 358–63.
41. Kilpatrick (1983) pp. 69–80.
42. The psalm is missing from the short text, cf. n. 20 above.

13

The Old Testament and Christian Charismatic/Prophetic Literature[1]

John W. McKay

Over the past twelve years I have been deeply impressed by similarities between the prophetic writings and utterances of the Charismatic Movement and those of the Old Testament. It would, of course, be rash to draw facile comparisons between the two sets of literature, partly because they are separated by well over two thousand years, partly because the Charismatic Movement is strongly biblical in orientation and therefore inevitably employs prophetical modes of expression that reflect biblical modes to some considerable degree. None the less, the comparison still seems worthwhile, and it suggests some fascinating possibilities.

One way of trying to bridge the historical gap is by surveying the records of Christian prophetic movements through the centuries, and such study does reveal a remarkable continuity of ethos and theological attitude, suggesting that the kind of comparisons drawn on the following pages are at least permissible. The field is such a vast one that it is impossible to outline here,[2] and, since it is relatively unfamiliar territory to most biblical scholars, the scope of this article is necessarily limited to one or two introductory remarks and to a few examples of ways in which the reading of Christian prophetic literature can shed a little extra light on some aspects of Old Testament study. For this purpose I have chosen three topics of fairly general interest that do not require a detailed acquaintance with the primary sources: first, the nature of some of the story-materials in the Old Testament; second, the problem of the relationship between prose and verse in some of the Old Testament prophetic books; and third, the question of the setting of some of the Old Testament prophetic teaching.

Traces of charismatic Christianity can be found in most ages of the church's history, but there have been certain periods that have witnessed remarkable outbursts of charismatic activity resulting in the appearance of powerful, evangelistically-minded movements and churches. The earliest of these after New Testament times was, of course, the end of the second century, which saw the growth and flowering of Montanism. Prophetic/charismatic religion flourished again in the thirteenth and fourteenth centuries in the wake of Joachim of Fiore's eschatological teaching, particularly on the fringes of the Franciscan movement and in certain circles among the Rhineland mystics. In the sixteenth century there were various manifestations, notably the charismatic group known as the Zwickau Prophets, which made its presence strongly felt at Wittenberg in the early days of the German Reformation. In Britain there has been an almost continuous charismatic presence of some description since the beginning of the eighteenth century when the French Prophets first came to London. They were followed in the second half of the century by the Shakers in the Manchester area, though they removed themselves to America in 1774 because of persecution. The 1820s and 1830s witnessed the rise of Irvingism and the establishment of the Catholic Apostolic Church, and there were spontaneous outbursts of charismatic activity associated with the revival movements of the later nineteenth century. But none of these bears comparison with the phenomenal growth of the Pentecostal Churches and most recently of the Charismatic Movement in this century.

Not all of these movements have left written records of their utterances and teachings. The earlier ones tend to be known mainly through the writings of their critics or protagonists, but some movements in post-Reformation times have left a great deal of first-hand written material, that is, apart from the present-day Pentecostal and Charismatic Movements. Among these are the French Prophets and the Irvingites who merit a fuller word of introduction here.

The French Prophet movement originated in the mountain regions of Southern France at the end of the seventeenth century after the revocation of the Edict of Nantes. Catholic persecution of the Huguenot community was harsh, but was countered by guerrilla-style resistance from prophet-inspired armies that are known to history as the Camisards. One effect of the wars was the flight and exile of thousands of Huguenot families to sympathetic settlements all over Europe. Many found their way to London, amongst them a number of the prophet-soldiers who continued to foster their charismatic activites and won a considerable following among the English population as they went on their missionary journeys up and down the land. They flourished during the first two decades of the century, but traces of their existence are still to be found even later. They left behind them a large amount of published literature, some of it in the form of apologia, some of testimonia, some of a historical or autobiographical nature, some of it collections of oracles and utterances.[3]

The Irvingites are perhaps better known today and require less introduction. They came into being as a result of a Pentecostal-style revival among Scottish Presbyterians in the Glasgow area and in London in the late 1820s. Their theologian, apologist and leader in the early days was the minister of the Scotch Kirk in London, Edward Irving, after whom they were nicknamed, but he died soon after the movement became established, and in the 1830s his followers formed themselves into what became known as the Catholic Apostolic Church. Again they have left an extensive literature, though not so much of it is prophetic, for, as the Catholic Apostolic Church developed, its charismatic zeal abated fairly rapidly and its interests became thoroughly ecclesiological.[4]

Now, after these brief introductions, let us turn our attention to the Old Testament.

Old Testament Stories viewed as Charismatic Literature.

'Story' has recently become fairly popular as a technical designation for some of the narratives in the Old Testament. Comparisons have been freely drawn between Old Testament stories and modern European and American novels and short stories. To take but one example: in a recently published essay J. B. Vickery compares the Samson story with short stories and other writings by Bret Harte, Sherwood Anderson, Mark Twain, William Faulkner, J. F. Power, Samuel Beckett and John Barth, while he compares Samson himself with Robin Hood, Rob Roy and Jesse James.[5] This is perhaps a fairly exaggerated illustration to choose, and Vickery does himself admit to some embarrassment about drawing such comparisons in view of the very different attitudes in the Bible and in the modern literature to divine activity in human affairs.[6]

For myself, the fact that the Bible is essentially about God's action in history and in the lives of men, whereas the modern novel or short story is not, introduces some scepticism about the value of such comparisons at all. On the positive side, they do encourage us to adopt a holistic approach to the biblical narratives which is a welcome antidote to the almost destructive fragmentary approach of some older scholars. What follows here is in no way intended to detract from this current tendency, but may be regarded as supplementary to it.

It seems to me that many of the Old Testament's stories have much closer modern counterparts among the very popular charismatic biographies and autobiographies that are currently for sale in our religious bookshops. These represent a type of literature that can be found among the depositions of most prophetic movements. Today they come from the Charismatic Movement, but there are plenty of older examples from the Pentecostal, Irvingite, Shaker, French Prophet and other such movements. They vary immensely in content, but they are written precisely to highlight the transforming activity of God in the life of an individual, a community or a church. Usually they begin by describing conditions of religious decadence, moral decline, lukewarm faith, ineffective ministry, or something similar. They then proceed to describe how the gospel about the empowering of the Holy Spirit was relayed by an evangelist, preacher, prophet, or whoever, and this leads on to an account of divine irruption in the form of a Pentecost-style outpouring of the Spirit, accompanied by various supernatural phenomena such as tongues, prophecy, vision, healing, or the like. The final outcome is generally a success story, of a life or a ministry transformed by the power of the Spirit, of a dramatic increase in supernatural activity, of healings, conversions, growing churches and so forth.[7]

One of the best examples of this sort of writing in the Old Testament is the story of Samuel's life and ministry. Typically, the story is set in a context of moral and political decadence, which is highlighted by the behaviour of the priests at the sanctuary at Shiloh (1 Sam.2:17, 22–25). The need for revival is evident, but 'the word of the Lord,' we are told, 'was rare in those days' (3:1). Our hope is focused on the hero, Samuel, but he, though from a devout home, was being trained by a priest with a pretty ineffectual ministry. Then we read the account of the visit by a 'man of God' who comes speaking God's prophetic word about the situation and it is immediately followed by the story of Samuel's night vision (2:27–3:18) – a sequence that corresponds well with the pattern of today's stories about baptism in the Holy Spirit consequent upon the preaching of the gospel. Thereafter 'Samuel was established as a prophet of the Lord' (3:20), and although we only get a few glimpses of his subsequent ministry, we learn from them that he became the leader of a revival that spread through the land (3:19–4:1; 7:3–17) and that he became something of a national figurehead. But, more important for our purposes, we discover that he became the head of a prophetic movement, something like the equivalent of a modern charismatic church, and that it was through the activity of this prophetic group that Saul, the first king of Israel, himself became a charismatic (10:5–13; 19:18–24). As the story continues, we find that Saul and Samuel split up and that Saul's spiritual endowment went sour (15:34–35; 16:14–23). In the end we find him seeking the guidance of a witch, in desperation that God no longer speaks to him (28:3–25). Tension between charismatic Christianity and spiritualist or magical arts is again a common feature in today's literature. To the present-day charismatic there is something very contemporary about the atmosphere in some sections of 1 Samuel.[8]

If space allowed, something similar could be remarked about the Patriarchal narratives, or some of the stories in Kings. The reader of charismatic biographies ceases to be surprised by tales about conversations with God or with angels, such as we find in Genesis, or by stories about miraculous events that scholars would tend to dismiss as legendary, such as we find in the catalogue of Elijah's and Elisha's miraculous exploits (1 Kgs.17–2 Kgs.9). Material like that is of the very essence of the charismatic story.[9]

One Old Testament book that is full of stories about charismatics is, of course, Judges. But since these are mainly tales about military heroes, they find no good parallels in the literature of most Christian charismatic movements. However, there are plenty of excellent parallels in the stories of the Huguenot prophet-armies, which are replete with accounts of Spirit-inspired guidance in planning battle-strategy, or escaping enemy ambush, or selecting suitable troops. Reading their records is very much like reading the book of Judges. Although we do not find Samsons there, we do find plenty of Gideons and Jephthahs. For example, Gideon's angelic vision, his testing of God's will with the fleece, and his reduction of the troops to the number of those dedicated to his holy war (Judg.6 and 7) all find excellent counterparts in the French records. The

Huguenot prophets ascribed their victories, not simply to God being on their side, but to the direct intervention and leading of the prophetic Spirit. So much so that it is said of one of their commanders, Jean Cavalier, that he would not lead his troops into battle unless and until he and his men were persuaded that they had received direct and explicit instruction from the Spirit, whether in visions or prophetic utterances.[10] The charismatic Judges of the Old Testament and the Camisard commanders would, I am sure, have understood each other very well indeed.

More could be written about stories of men like Moses, David, Solomon and, of course, some of the later prophets, but sufficient has been said to support the general contention that some of the Old Testament writings should now be viewed as charismatic literature, charismatic biography, charismatic history, charismatic legend, and the like.

Prose and Verse in Prophetic Books.

The relationship between the prose and verse utterances in the prophetic books of the Old Testament presents a perennial problem.[11] In any single book they purport to come from the one prophet, but scholars have often suspected them to be from different people. For instance, questions are raised about the authenticity of the prose 'remnant-sayings' in Isaiah, or passages in Jeremiah like the Temple Sermon in ch.7 and the New Covenant teaching in ch.31. But equally, at the other end of the prose/poetry spectrum, there are doubts about those parts of the prophetic books that are recognisably of a psalmodic quality, such as the psalm in Hab.3, or the acrostic material in Nahum 1 or the hymn of creation fragmented and scattered through the book of Amos (4:13;5:8;9:5–6). Whilst almost every scholar seems happy to admit the authenticity of most prophetic verse oracles, there is widespread doubt about allowing the same verdict for prophetic prose teaching and prophetic psalm writing.

In discussing this subject it is worth remembering that it is not always clear when we are handling prose and when verse in Hebrew prophecy. To take a few striking examples: most scholars would probably describe Ezek.18, on the doctrine of individual retribution, as a passage that is written in very turgid, legalistic prose, but the NIV prints much of it as

verse; and the NIV does the same with the New Covenant passage in
Jer.31:31–34, which most scholars would again want to regard as prose
material; similarly, the prayers and prophecies of Amos in 7:1–8:7 are set
out in verse in the RSV, but in prose in the NEB. Clearly, the borders
between prophetic prose and prophetic verse are not always easily
drawn. Perhaps the main reason for this is that prophetic verse, whilst it
is frequently discerned to have a parallel structure, is often defined as
verse only because of its apparently metrical or rhythmic style. Prose, on
the other hand, is distinguished for the most part by the absence of any
particularly striking metrical or parallel structure. But occasionally we do
come across what looks like an odd parallelism in a prose section and
some prose material does have a certain rhythmical quality about it.

The same ambiguity of style is very much a mark of modern charismatic prophecy also. There are utterances that are unquestionably in
prose form and others quite surely in verse, but perhaps the vast majority
are in what might be described as poetic prose, that is, they have some
sort of rhythmic quality, though they lack rhyme and the steady metre
that is found in most English poetry. I have chosen three examples to
illustrate this fact: the first, from a present-day charismatic, is almost
psalmodic; the second, spoken by George Macdonald of Port Glasgow in
the early days of Irvingism, is more akin to the poetic oracles of the Old
Testament in style; and the third, from a collection of prophecies by John
Lacy, one of the English leaders of the French Prophets in London, is the
most prosaic.

Reach out, O Holy One,
Come close to me,
    e'en from the shore of eternity.
Roll back the eternal billows,
    The dark storms of earthly passions;
    in the grips of these we are.
Time stretches forwards, backwards, and never stands still.
But still Thou art, and still Thou, Creator blessed, wouldst
    have us.
Not as the world bequeathes do Thou
    Thy everlasting peace, Thy promise of Thy presence.
Everlasting, never ending, the Alpha and the Omega.
    And so our soul has found its anchor, its rest in Thee.[12]

The Lord he is God.
At his word the nations shall tremble.
His voice shall be heard;
   his glorious voice;
   the voice of the Lord full of majesty.
Behold he cometh.
The Lord God shall blow the trumpet,
   and come with the whirlwinds of the south.
Oh, the coming of the glorious King;
   coming in his own and his Father's glory.
He comes to destroy sin.
   So be ye holy.[13]

Oh ye hard hearted and unbelievers, fear, fear, fear. I am the Lord of the whole earth, who am come down to visit iniquities; to pull down and to destroy; to purge away all hypocrites. I call you this day to repent. Choose. Own or deny. . . . O ye sheep of my flock; oh come, come, come to your shepherd, who calls you from all the ends of the world. O ye sheep of Israel, ye lost wandering sheep come, come to your shepherd, your Lord, who was crucified by you. He comes to call you. O don't harden your hearts as your fathers.[14]

Reading Christian prophetic utterances such as these one frequently has the awareness of passing from metrical to non-metrical structures, of being in a sort of twilight area between poetry and sermonic prose. Space permitting, further examples could be provided to show that the same fluidity exists in the prophecies of any one movement, and where sufficient materials exist to draw on, in the utterances of single prophets. The inference is clear, that we perhaps tend to draw too sharp lines of demarcation between prose and verse in the Hebrew prophetic books and that such distinctions can only be of limited value in discussing questions of authorship and authenticity.

Let us now consider the place of psalms in the prophetic books. Probably the most vivid example is in Hab.3, and for the present we shall limit the discussion to it. Broadly speaking, there are two main views about this poem: one that it is a later addition to the book, whether by the prophet himself or by someone else, and had no major part in the prophet's original message, a conclusion that finds some support in the observation that the Qumran Commentary on Habakkuk does not include it; the other that it does have a significant part to play, but since it is a psalm, that part was probably in some kind of liturgical setting, possibly on some occasion like the New Year Festival when the whole book would have been recited or dramatically enacted in the context of a celebration of the power of Israel's God over the nation's enemies, who were seen as the embodiment of the evil chaotic forces in creation.[15] But, in the light of what can be learned from studying more recent charismatic activity, there is another possible way of looking at this chapter, and indeed the whole book.

Prophetic persons in other ages have always had a marked propensity to hymn-composition. Today's Charismatic Movement has stimulated a considerable outpouring of new hymns and songs, as did the Pentecostal Movement, the Irvingite, the Shaker, and every other that has left its records for us to examine. But what is particularly significant for our purposes is the content of many of these songs. Almost every religious revival, be it Pentecostal or other, can claim its own hymnody. The evangelical movements tend to produce songs about forgiveness, cleansing, righteousness, salvation, sanctification and the like; and the ecclesiastical, liturgical and more catholic movements produce songs about the eucharist, the church, the beauty of worship and so forth. A large number of charismatic songs focus on the more visionary aspects of Christianity, celebrating Christ's resurrection, ascension and continuing presence in the Spirit, and rejoicing in disclosures of him in these aspects of his being. They are often very personal, sometimes speaking in the first person singular rather than in the communal plural, singing of revelatory experience, or personal blessing, or awareness of Christ's intimate presence, or occasionally looking for the renewal of such things. They are the songs of men and women who have longed for and sought some kind of prophetic experience similar to that of many of the ancient prophets like Isaiah or Ezekiel. And having received the vision, they find it an entirely natural matter to turn the vision into song.[16]

Of course, the present-day Charismatic Movement is by no means unique in composing such hymns. Other prophetic groups have left us further examples, as also indeed have the mystics. But that is not the main point of interest here; it is similarities with the psalm of Habakkuk that is our primary concern. Certainly the style of such hymns is generally very different from that of Habakkuk's, as also is the symbolism which reflects very diverse cultural contexts, but the celebration of the personal vision that has been sought after and longed for, the themes of God's majesty in his appearing and the prophet's consequent security and rejoicing are indeed entirely comparable in both. The immediate conclusion we can draw from this observation (rather than comparison) is that a priori there is no good reason for treating the psalm in Hab.3 as secondary, but rather the converse, particularly if it can be shown to form an integral part of his theme on its own merits.

In Hab.1:2–4 the prophet is seen pleading with God for an answer to the problem of injustice among his people. In 1:5–11 he receives the answer that God is raising up the Babylonians who will sweep through the land to execute his wrath against that injustice. Habakkuk protests that that means invoking even greater violence to suppress the present wrongs, which seems a merciless solution (1:12–17). However, realising he does not properly appreciate what God is trying to tell him, he sets himself to wait for fuller illumination (2:1). In reply he receives a revelation which he is told to commit to writing (2:2). We are not informed at this point how it came or what it said, but only that it spoke of things that were yet to come and that would find fulfilment in due course (2:3). At its heart, however, there lay a clear assurance that God's wrath would certainly be executed against the wicked, but that in the midst of all the fury that would entail 'the righteous will live by his faith' (2:4). There is a tremendous profundity in that statement that goes beyond the scope of this paper to analyse, but its message is basically the same as Paul's in Rom.8:35–39, that no matter what we go through in life or how God desires to deal with our environment, nothing can separate us from his love and life, and that we receive and stand in that assurance by our faith and by that alone.

On the basis of this revelation Habakkuk is able to enunciate with unshaking conviction a series of woes on those who deal unjustly, declaring their fate with the full assurance that his new insight has brought him (2:4–20), but scattered through these are some precious glimpses of the immensity of his vision which has carried him into realms of understanding that reach out far beyond the immediate knowledge of the imminent judgment that is coming with the Babylonians, into the wider vista of God's ultimate purposes for man (2:4,14,20).

Then we come to ch.3 which, far from being an irrelevant extra or a special composition for a liturgical drama, celebrates, after the manner of some of the hymns of later mystics and charismatics, the actual vision

Habakkuk refers to in 2:1–3. It starts with a reminder of his reaction to his first revelation in ch.1 by recalling how he pleaded with God to remember mercy in the midst of his wrath (3:2), and then it goes on to recount how God revealed himself in all his warlike power and majesty (3:3–15). The vision is clearly like Job's, in as much as it offers no philosophical solution to the problems of suffering and injustice, and its effects are equally astounding. First comes a Job-like response of awe and the acceptance that God knows what he is doing, even if the prophet himself has not been able to understand all its implications (3:16), and that is followed by one of the greatest statements of faith and assurance in the whole Bible, entirely comparable with that of Paul in Rom.8 mentioned above: 'Though the fig tree do not blossom, nor fruit be on the vines ... yet will I rejoice in the Lord ...' (3:17–19). It is the profundity of insight this vision brought that is the basis for the equally profound statement in ch.2 that 'the righteous will live by his faith'.

The conclusion from these observations is surely that the book of Habakkuk is to be read as the deposit of a prophetic person who, in seeking God's answer to the problems of life, found it in a vision of God himself, and in the strength of the spiritual satisfaction thus received, like so many other prophets and mystics in Christian history after him, told of his vision and new-found faith in the traditional forms of the hymnody of his day. The book is thus, in its own way, a kind of charismatic's spiritual autobiography. It does, of course, include material that gives us some notion of what this man was preaching to his contemporaries about social and ethical matters, but its greater concern is to relate how he found his solution to the problems of his times in a vision of the presence of God. The true climax of the book is thus not ch.2, v.4, about the righteous living by his faith, as so many commentators maintain,[17] influenced no doubt by traditional Christian usage ever since the day Paul cited that verse as the text for his message to the church in Rome (Rom.1:17), but the end of ch.3, where, in the wake of his revelation, the prophet rejoices in the Lord and joys in the God of his salvation. Or perhaps we should say that the book has two climactic points, because 2:4 expresses in theological language the assurance that ch.3 expresses in song, or, to put it another way, ch.3 gives the content of the revelation that enabled Habakkuk to make the statement in 2:4. The fact that ch.3 is not placed between 2:1 and 2:2 is quite unimportant, for it is a totally independent creation. It is like a second version of what is told in chs 1–2, but this time told in song. Hence it seems entirely unnecessary to invent elaborate theories about literary structure or about cultic usage to explain the nature of this particular book. It is quite simply something like a charismatic's diary.

Other psalmodic materials in the prophetic books would have to be approached in different ways, but there are plenty of other hymnic modes used by charismatic groups for wider comparisons to be made possible. My only desire here is to appeal for a readier willingness to look at the possibility that such materials, like some of the prophetic prose, are not necessarily secondary or even that their presence in the writings of prophetical men should engender any surprise on our part at all.

The Setting of the Prophets' Teaching.

We have grown accustomed to thinking of the Old Testament prophets as men who, whilst they sometimes addressed their oracles to individuals, as Isaiah addressed Ahaz (Isa.7), or Amos Amaziah (Amos 7:10–17), for the most part probably spoke out in the market square or in some public place of assembly and who perhaps also gave oracles in some kind of cultic setting. We then go on to think of their followers, disciples, circle of admirers, or some close inner group finding their utterances so striking and memorable that they seek to cherish and preserve them at first in oral form and then in writing for their own edification and for the benefit of the wider circle of their contemporaries and for posterity. Now it is not intended here to undermine or detract from this picture in any way, but only to supplement it with some suggestions that present themselves as a result of my studies in Christian prophetism.

From the beginning Christian prophecy has found its most natural home in the Christian assembly. History has left examples of prophets who had a public ministry, such as the wandering prophets described in Origen's *Contra Celsum*, men who are said to have circulated in Syria and Palestine in the third century prophesying outside temples, and in various cities and army-camps up and down the region.[18] In later times we may think of men like Savonarola who had a very public ministry. But in Acts the prophet Agabus gave utterance in the church at Antioch (11:27–28) and at a house-meeting in Caesarea (21:8–11), and when Paul discussed prophecy in 1 Cor.14, it was entirely in the context of the gathered church. Perhaps the fullest picture we have of the operation of early Christian prophecy is in the 11th Mandate of *The Shepherd of Hermas*, where we read:

> When the man who has the divine Spirit comes into an assembly of righteous men who have faith in the divine Spirit and the men of that assembly offer prayer to God, then the angel of the prophetic Spirit that is allotted to him will fill the man and he, now filled with the Holy Spirit, will address the congregation, speaking whatever the Lord wishes him to speak. This is how the Spirit of the Godhead will show himself.[19]

Now when we come down to later Christian times we find the same pattern prevailing. We see it in the early thirteenth century among the followers of a certain Amalric of Bena in and around Paris.[20] We see it again at the time of the Reformation among the Zwickau Prophets, and we find the same pattern among the French Prophets, the Shakers, the Irvingites, the Pentecostals and the Charismatics. A similar setting is not unknown among the Old Testament prophets as well. For example, we find Ezekiel sitting in his house with the elders of the exiled community at Tel Abib, prophesying to them (Ezek.8:1;11:24–25; cf.33:31). Isaiah had a number of disciples and it must be assumed that they met together from time to time (Isa.8:16), as Elisha and his followers (2 Kgs.4:38ff.) or Samuel and his prophets did (1 Sam.19:20). We are actually informed that Samuel and his troop prophesied when they met together, though it is not exactly clear what that means in the setting. Of course, we cannot always tell what went on at such gatherings in Old Testament times, but observation of later Christian practice is suggestive and it seems worth pursuing some of the suggestions it throws up.

The following discussion is mainly limited to the example of the French Prophets, because they alone of all Christian prophetic movements actually made a point of collecting and publishing their prophecies, somewhat after the fashion of the Old Testament prophets.

They prophesied mainly at their assemblies. Though there are instances of prophesying in public, they preferred to address outsiders through preaching and evangelism. But when they came together and their prophets prophesied, there were frequently those present who were uncommitted and who became convicted by hearing the prophetic word. Most of their leading personalities testified to having been converted to the movement in that kind of way. But by and large, their utterances were intended for the admonition, encouragement and edification of their own members.

The prophecies themselves were usually in the form of sermonettes, condemning spiritual lassitude, moral abuses, social disorders and the like, and urging repentance, holiness and commitment. The judgment and the wrath of God played a prominent part in their teaching, as also did the theme of the blessing of the faithful. But what is particularly interesting is that, although the prophecies were usually spoken at the assemblies, many of them were actually addressed to church leaders, politicians, or to the populace in general. Of course, we are not to imagine that it was often that churchmen or statesmen were present, though that was certainly the case at times.[21] But what did happen was that stenographers regularly took down the prophets' sayings in writing as they were spoken, partly so that the faithful could cherish their words, partly so that they would ultimately reach a wider audience than that present at the meeting:

> There were several men, English and French, who sat at a table, taking down in writing what was spoken, and afterwards read it to the assembly present. Those who took down in writing what was spoken, if it was in French, translated it, and read it in English to those present, and if desired, would write out copies of what was spoken and give them to the persons so desiring.[22]

Many of these prophecies were later published in massive volumes for the benefit of any who cared to plough their way through them. The book titles are also interesting: for example, *Prophetical Warnings of Elias Marion, heretofore one of the commanders of the Protestants that had taken arms in the Cevennes, or discourses uttered by him in London under the operation of the Spirit and faithfully taken in writing whilst they were spoken.* Occasionally the oracles contained in these books were uttered in private, in the presence of one other person who took them down, or at a very small gathering of two or three people. It is interesting to note that, although this has not been a common practice in other prophetic movements, it has occasionally been done, as, for instance among the Irvingites, as the following example illustrates. It describes an event that took place during a eucharistic celebration at one of the great festivals:

After the Celebration and before the Communion anthem, I became aware of a voice proclaiming loudly from one of the benches occupied by the officiating clergy. An underdeacon had hurried forward armed with notebook and pencil ready to take down in shorthand the message which was being uttered. I could make nothing of what was being said ... (but) I still remember something of the awe and the apprehension which came upon me.[23]

In this instance the message was given in tongues, but the method of transcription is not unlike that used by the French Prophets. The Catholic Apostolic underdeacon was clearly doing something he had done many times before and following what appears to have been customary practice in his church. Today the tape recorder has largely taken over from pencil and paper at charismatic meetings, but the prophecies thus collected are not often published, except occasionally in a journal or news-sheet, depending on how important its content is reckoned to be for the readership.

One cannot but recall how Isaiah on one occasion instructed his disciples to take down his words in writing on the spot, as soon as they had been spoken (Isa.8:1,16), or how Baruch took down Jeremiah's oracles as he uttered them (Jer.36:4,32). Publication in the eighteenth century was by means of the printing press, but perhaps the ancient counterpart is to be seen in the public reading of Jeremiah's scroll at the Temple (Jer. 36:4–8), or the transmission of his message to foreign ambassadors visiting Jerusalem (Jer. 27:3), or the carrying of his words by messenger so that they could be read out aloud in Babylon (51:60–64). Of course we cannot draw exact parallels and must be careful about jumping to conclusions on the basis of comparisons like these, but they do encourage us to speculate that the Old Testament prophets may have uttered their sayings much more often among their friends in private than we have hitherto suspected; and that they may have had them immediately written down as they were spontaneously uttered, that is rather than having them carefully composed and then studiously learned and edited over a protracted period of time; and that they may have followed this procedure to ensure that the teaching of the Spirit would be made available to a wider audience. In view of these considerations it may sometimes be legitimate to think once more in terms of written oracles without becoming too deeply involved in discussions about tradition schools, oral processes and editorial arrangements and additions.

Nothing that has been written here demands the abandonment of methods currently employed among biblical scholars for studying the literature of the Old Testament, but some of it does suggest that it may be legitimate to regard much more of the Old Testament as first-hand deposit than is often admitted today. By looking at the sort of literature that has been produced in Christian prophetic circles, we have seen that biographical, testimonial literature magnifying the operation of the supernatural has been a popular mode of communicating the charismatic gospel, that prophetic style fluctuates freely between poetry and sermonic prose, and that the assembly has been the regular setting for prophetic utterances to be heard and taken down in writing (or on tape), so that they could then be relayed to the outside world. We have also looked briefly at the possibility that all three findings have relevance for Old Testament study. But the final impressions this study leave with me are, firstly, that much more of the material contained in the Old Testament prophetic writings, be they oracular or biographical, belongs to original compilations than I had hitherto been willing to credit, and, secondly, that a guide to understanding the spiritual mind of the Old Testament prophets may well be found in the continuing practice of prophecy evinced in charismatic movements throughout history and today.

Notes

1. This article is an edited version of a paper read at the summer meeting of the Society for Old Testament Study at Hull University in July, 1982. It was my privilege and pleasure to serve under Anthony Hanson in the Theology Department in Hull University for thirteen years. It is therefore with the warmest gratitude and appreciation that I offer this contribution.
2. There is no book covering this field properly, but much helpful information can be gleaned from R.A. Knox, *Enthusiasm* (Oxford, 1950), R.M. Jones, *Studies in Mystical Religion* (London, 1919), G.B.Cutten, *Speaking with Tongues, historically and psychologically considered* (New Haven, 1927).
3. Whilst the literature is extensive, most of it comes from the eighteenth century and is not easily available, but see Knox, *Enthusiasm* pp.365–9, J. Symonds, *Thomas Brown and the Angels* (London, 1961), pp.13–42. From the eighteenth century the most detailed historical account in English is S. Keimer's *A Brand Snatch'd from the Burning* (London, 1718), which is

largely reprinted in D. Hughson, *A Copious Account of the French and English Prophets* (London, 1814).
4. Mrs M.O. Oliphant, *The Life of Edward Irving* (London, 1862), A.L. Drummond, *Edward Irving and his Circle* (London, 1937), P.E.Shaw, *The Catholic Apostolic Church* (New York, 1946), H.C. Whitley, *Blinded Eagle* (London, 1955), G. Strachan, *The Pentecostal Theology of Edward Irving* (London, 1973).
5. J.B. Vickery, 'In Strange Ways: the story of Samson,' *Images of Man and God: Old Testament short stories in literary focus*, ed. B.O. Long (Sheffield, 1981).
6. Ibid., pp.58–9.
7. E.g., D. Bennett, *Nine O'Clock in the Morning* (Eastbourne, 1971), D.J. du Plessis, *The Spirit Bade Me Go* (Plainfield, New Jersey, 1972), M. Harper, *Bishop's Move* (London, 1978), G. Pulkingham, *Gathered for Power* (London, 1973), D. Shakerian, *The Happiest People on Earth* (London, 1977).
8. See especially chs. 1–3, 7, 9–13, 15–16, 19, 28.
9. While this observation is purely literary and makes no judgment about historical value, it is true that most charismatics have little difficulty in crediting the historicity of such biblical materials because they are able to draw parallels between them and what they know from their own experience of the activity of the Spirit.
10. To get the true flavour of Camisard enthusiasm it is necessary to return to contemporary sources, the best of which are in John Lacy's *A Cry from the Desert* (London, 1707), a collection of eye-witness testimonies about the operation of the prophetic gifts. E.g., we read:

> When the inspiration said 'March, fear not, obey my command, do this, do that, nothing could ever dissuade from it; if the Spirit had strengthened me with those good words, 'Fear nothing, my child, I will preserve and stand by thee,' I rushed into the midst of the enemy as if their hands had been paper and I were sheltered in steel (p.70–1).

We discover that on one occasion as the troops were lined up before battle one, Solomon Couderc,

> under the operation of the Spirit, walked with his eyes open, intentively viewing every man, from one rank to another, and received secret intimations whom he ought to reject among them. He drew these out of the line and ordered them apart to a place assigned them. These poor people obeyed with tears in their eyes (pp.86–7).

Again we read:

> It was only by the inspirations and their repeated orders that we began the war for the enjoyment of our holy religion. They alone chose our officers and commanders, and by them did they steer. They taught us the discipline of war. They instructed us to bear the first fire of the enemy on our knees, and to make our attacks upon them with loud chant of psalms for terror. They changed our fearful temper into that of lions, and made us perform gloriously. Our inspirations instructed us to deliver our brethren out of

prison, to know and convict traitors, to shun ambushes, to discover plots and to strike down persecutors (pp.97–8).

11. Note that we are only concerned here with the prose utterances of the prophets, not with biographical notices and narratives in the prophetic books.

12. Unpublished; taken from a private collection of contemporary prophetic sayings in my possession.

13. R. Norton, *Memoirs of James and George Macdonald of Port-Glasgow,* (London, 1840) p.164.

14. *The Prophetical Warnings of John Lacy, Esq.* (London, 1707) p.7–8.

15. For a summary of the various views about the structure of the book of Habakkuk, see O. Eissfeldt, *The Old Testament: an introduction* (Oxford, 1966), pp.416–23; G. Fohrer, *Introduction to the Old Testament* (London, 1970) pp.451–6; R.K. Harrison, *Introduction to the Old Testament* (London, 1970) pp.931–8.

16. Particularly popular song books used in Charismatic circles include *Songs of Fellowship* (Eastbourne, 1981 and 1983), and *Worship the King* (Eastbourne, 1984), which include many songs of personal renewal. Some excellent and even more strongly personal examples are found in earlier ages among the writings of the mystics, such as Richard Rolle, St John of the Cross, and Madame Guyon.

17. So S.R. Driver, *Minor Prophets II*, Century Bible (Edinburgh, 1906) pp.61–4; W.O.E. Oesterley and T.H. Robinson, *An Introduction to the Books of the Old Testament* (London, 1934) pp.397–8; H.H. Rowley, *The Growth of the Old Testament* (London, 1950) p.119; B.W. Anderson, *The Living World of the Old Testament* (London, 1958) pp.322–3; N.K. Gottwald, *A Light to the Nations* (New York, 1959), pp.348–52; E.J.Young, *An Introduction to the Old Testament* (London, 1960) pp.271–3.

18. *Contra Celsum* 7.9.

19. In the context the author is attempting to give some guide-lines for distinguishing between true and false prophecy. He argues that the false prophet will tend to operate outside the circle of the church, the true prophet within it.

20. For translations of original sources on the Amalricians, see W.L. Wakefield and A.P. Evans, *Heresies in the High Middle Ages* (New York and London, 1969) pp.258–63; J.B. Russell (ed.), *Religious Dissent in the Middle Ages* (New York, London, Sydney, Toronto, 1971) pp.83–4.

21. John Wesley gives an interesting account of a visit he paid to a French prophet meeting in 1739; see the entry in his *Journal* for 28 February of that year.

22. Keimer, *A Brand*, pp.6, 9.

23. Whitley, *Blinded Eagle*, p.75.

14

Lyricorum Poetarum Optimus: Pindar in Philo of Alexandria

J. L. North

Anthony Hanson has been tireless in his study of the reworking of the Old Testament in the New Testament. This article deals with another instance of the same phenomenon, the redeployment of an ancient 'scripture' (Irmscher (see note 22), p. 297, speaks of Pindar *'als moralische Autorität'*), and it is offered to Anthony in gratitude for his encouragement and intuitive scholarship.

Philo's well-known admiration for and indebtedness to his Greek philosophical predecessors were already observed by early Christian writers. Where he could speak of τὸν μὲν οὖν τῶν Πυθαγορείων ἱερώτατον θίασον (*Prob.*2), Clement of Alexandria could speak of ὁ Πυθαγόρειος ... Φίλων (*Strom.*1.72.4; 2.100.3); and where he could praise ὁ ἱερώτατος (s.v.l) Πλάτων (*Prob.*13), Jerome could quote the Greek jingle ἢ Πλάτων φιλωνίζει ἢ Φίλων πλατωνίζει ... *tanta est similitudo sensuum et eloquii* (*De viris inl.* 11).[1] But outside the area of philosophy Philo's admiration is qualified. On the one hand, we still have a eulogy of Greece, quoted from *Provid.* 2.109–10 (H-L pp. 344 ff.) by Eusebius, *Praep. Ev.* 8.14.66–68. On the other, there is the faint praise of *Sacr.* 78–79. In this last passage there is a reference to the poets (τὸ ποιητικὸν γένος), and while a passage like *Provid.* 2.40–41 (H-L pp. 268 ff.) represents one point of view, the other instances of this phrase (*Opif.* 133, 157; *Agr.* 41; *Jos.* 2; *Spec. L.* 2.164), itself, I think, ambiguous in form and intention, reflect Philo's uncertain attitude towards the poets and are probably another example of Philo's indebtedness to Plato; the phrase itself is borrowed from Plato, *Tim.* 19d5; *Leg.* 682a3.

Amongst these poets we must number Pindar since the Philonic corpus mentions him by name five times and once Philo calls him the best of the lyric poets.[2] In the absence of any reference to Philo in the review of Pindar's *Nachleben* in W. Schmid, *Geschichte der griechischen Literatur*,[3] and with only one in part three (*'Nachwirkung'*) of E. G. Schmidt's collection (see note 11), I shall make a start, however tentatively, to examine the role of Pindar's poetry in Philo.

At the end (161–174) of the section on φιλανθρωπία (51–174) in *Virt.*, Philo speaks of the arrogance of the great. He has already (162) quoted the maxim τίκτει γὰρ κόρος ὕβριν,[4] and begun to discuss Deut.8:11 ff., on the proper stewarding of one's blessings. Turning to the question of punishment (171) Philo says that only God[5] can punish the arrogant; firstly, because only he is in a position to do this, and, secondly, 'every braggart, full of senseless thinking' and 'considering it right to advance beyond the limits of man's nature', in Pindar's words, 'supposes himself to be οὔτε ἄνδρα οὔτε ἡμίθεον ἀλλ᾽ ὅλον (s.v.l.) δαίμονα' (172), and so he must be punished by the One whom he challenges. The words I have left untranslated have been differently assessed. Older editors regarded them as a quotation; e.g. T. Bergk (4th ed. Leipzig, 1878) registered them as frag. 280, and O. Schröder, who doubted their authenticity (Leipzig, 1923, p. 389 note) considered them to be inspired by the proverb μηδὲν ἄγαν (p. 487) and compared two more of Pindar's formulations of it, at *Isth.*5.11–14:

κρίνεται δ᾽ ἀλκὰ διὰ δαίμονας ἀνδρῶν.
δύο δέ τοι ζωᾶς ἄωτον μοῦνα ποιμαίνοντι
    τόν ἄλπνιστον, εὐανθεῖ σὺν ὄλβῳ
εἴ τις εὖ πάσχων λόγον ἐσλὸν ἀκούῃ.
μὴ μάτευε Ζεὺς γενέσθαι·

and at a passage which Schröder cryptically abbreviated as *'interpp O V extr'*, which I take to refer to *Olym.* 5.23–24:

ὑγίεντα δ᾽ εἴ τις ὄλβον ἄρδει,
ἐξαρκέων κτεάτεσσι καὶ εὐλογίαν προστιθείς,
    μὴ ματεύσῃ θεὸς γενέσθαι.[6]

B. Snell (Leipzig, 1953, p. 291) also thought that the words were an allusion, possibly to *Olym.*2.2:

τίνα θεόν, τίν' ἥρωα, τίνα δ'ἄνδρα κελαδήσομεν;

In *Aet.*117–131 Philo is rehearsing Theophrastus' summary of four (Stoic) arguments in favour of the view that the world was created and could be destroyed. The second argument (120–123) is that the falling of the sea level, exemplified in the emergence of the island of Delos, was an indication that in due time there would be no sea left at all, and then no earth or air, only fire. The Stoics had found proof of this in Pindar's address to Delos (121), which assumes that the island's existence was due to the retreating sea: διὸ καί Πίνδαρος ἐπὶ τῆς Δήλου φησί·

Χαῖρ', ὦ θεοδμάτα, λιπαροπλοκάμου παίδεσσι

Λατοῦς ἱμεροέστατον ἔρνος,

πόντου θύγατερ, χθονὸς εὐρείας ἀκίνητον

τέρας, ἄν τε βροτοὶ

Δᾶλον κικλήσκουσιν, μάκαρες δ' ἐν 'Ολύμπῳ

τηλέφαντον κυανέας χθονὸς ἄστρον.

Philo goes on: θυγατέρα γὰρ πόντου τὴν Δῆλον εἴρηκε τὸ λεχθὲν αἰνιττόμενος. Editors have classed this as a fragment (33b Snell), but Carl Siegfried regarded it as an allusion to 'Ol. 6, 101', which must be the alternative versification for *Olym.*6.59 with its reference to Δάλου θεοδμάτας.[7] I shall return to these two passages (and to the next one) later on.

The Armenian version of *Provid.* contains the last three references to Pindar, for only one of which is there a Greek original extant.[8] On p. 97 of J. B. Aucher's *editio princeps* (Venice, 1822)[9] Philo quotes the opening lines of a poem on a recent eclipse of the sun (which editors catalogue as *Paean* 9 (frag. 109 Schröder, where there is a valuable note, = frag. 52k Snell)), introducing the passage with words which Aucher rendered into Latin *lyricorum poetarum optimus Pindarus* (pp. 96–7 = 2.80 H-L p. 308). This is a part of *Provid.* that Eusebius unfortunately did not excerpt, although 'Greek Philo' later does refer back to it (Aucher p. 110 = 2.100 H-L p. 332 ap. Eus. *Praep. Ev.*8.14.50), ὃ καὶ Πίνδαρος ᾐνίξατο (cf. αἰνιττόμενος above), and Dionysius of Halicarnassus, *Demosthenes* 7 (*Opuscula* vol. 1 p. 142 H. Usener–L. Radermacher), quotes the Greek both for these first lines and for another 24 or so, and *P. Oxy.* vol. 5 (London, 1908) §841 pp. 73 ff., 107 ff., provides yet more. These additional sources are particularly valuable in that the Armenian translator, not too unreliable for Philo, has barely understood Pindar.[10]

The third mention of Pindar in 'Armenian Philo' (Aucher p. 120 = 2.113 H-L p. 350) appears to be an error in that Philo, or his nephew Alexander whom he is reporting, has attributed to Pindar a line that really belongs to Simonides. Aucher's Latin, which was confirmed by F. C. Conybeare, reads: *Pro honore itaque, ut dixit olim Pindarus, silentium laetabundus suscipiam.* D. L. Page provisionally reconstructed the Greek so: ἔστι καὶ σιγᾶς ἀκίνδυνον γέρας. Alexander uses the quotation elegantly to concede defeat in his debate with his uncle.[11]

In addition to these five certain references to Pindar, scholars have assigned six other passages or phrases in Philo to Pindar. As Wolfson[12] recognised, such attributions must inevitably be conjectural, but it is an activity worth attempting and may well contribute to our reconstruction of the survival of Pindar in Philo. Schröder (p. 488) surmised that behind the mistaken attribution we have just noted Philo or Alexander had been trying to recall the following authentic words of Pindar (frag.180 line 2): ἔσθ' ὅτε πιστότατα σιγᾶς ὁδός. Siegfried (*Philo*, p. 37) noted as parallel to ἄτρυτοι πόνοι at *Ebr.*21 the expression in *Pyth.*4.178 ἄτρυτον πόνον. The phrase was clearly a favourite with Philo (though it does not occur in Plato), found at *Det.*19; *Conf.*92; *Fug.*173; *Spec.L.*2.60.260; *Praem.*27. The fact that the phrase is also found amongst the fragments of Philo's Stoic contemporary and, probably, fellow-countryman and opponent, Chaeremon, suggests that there may be a nearer source, if we need to look for a source at all (ap. Porphyry, *De Abstinentia* 4.8, Nauck p. 240 = Schwyzer p. 47 = van der Horst p. 20).[13] Snell (p. 367) proposed that the particular version of the story of the immortality of both of the Dioscuri found in *Leg.*84 is indebted to *Nem.*10.76. This does look probable; cf. E. M. Smallwood ad loc. (Leiden, 1961, p. 196). On p. 1183B of an edition of Philo's works published in Frankfurt in 1691 (a reprint of the 1640 Paris edition, which in turn combines the Geneva and Augsburg editions of 1613 and 1614) David Hoeschel adds in the margin against a phrase in a section of a work we now identify as *Spec.L.*2.87, μὴ πάντα, φησι (sc. Moses), ἴσθι τοῦ κέρδους, a reference to Pindar, *Pyth.*3.54, ἀλλὰ κέρδει καὶ σοφία δέδεται. Pindar is speaking of the σοφία or medical skill of Asclepius, and of how even it could be bribed. Philo is giving a second reason for observing the sabbatical year. Man should not be enslaved to gain and periodically should willingly forgo a field's produce. It is not clear whether Hoeschel thought that Philo was quoting or alluding to Pindar, or whether the note in the margin was regarded as a parallel to the sentiment in the text. Notice that even if there is a reference to Pindar here, Philo still attributes the saying to Moses. Elsewhere Philo speaks about slavery to gain, at *Spec. L.* 4.3: κέρδους παρανομωτάτου δοῦλον. In the section titled 'Sachweiser zu Philo' in the seventh volume (Breslau, 1964) of the German translation of Philo, Willy Theiler (p. 389) has suggested two new examples of possible borrowings from Pindar. In *Plant.* 127 ff. Philo appears to be referring to that version of the story about the birth of the Muses (repeated a century later by Aelius Aristides περὶ ῥητορικῆς 420 (Behr *LCL* p. 534)) which traced the birth to the request of the gods to Zeus. But, where Aristides attributes the story to Pindar, Philo speaks simply of παλαιὸς ... λόγος. Both Schröder (p. 395) and Snell (p. 196) register it as a fragment (31), but, in fact, not a single line is extant; the passage they quote from Aristides is, rather, a testimonium. But the passages from *Plant.* and Aristides are very similar, though with some interesting differences, and Philo may well have an unknown Pindaric rendering of the myth in mind. However, whether or not Pindar is in mind, Hesiod, the 'canonical' source for the story of the birth of the Muses, seems to be excluded, *inter alia*, by νόσφιν ἀπ᾽ ἀθανάτων (*Theogony* 57). Secondly, under the rubric 'Unbekannte Dichter' Theiler (ibid.) hazarded the guess '(Pindar?)' for *Prob.* 42, where Philo describes those who love God and are loved by him as πανάρχοντές τε καὶ βασιλέες βασιλέων, again a phrase rather vaguely introduced by καθάπερ οἱ ποιηταί φασι. Colson (*LCL* vol. 9 p. 35 note b) identifies the hapax πανάρχων as the reason for Philo's reference to 'the poets'.

As a seventh possibility I would suggest that *Migr.* 126 not only is a reminiscence of *Pyth.* 4.286–287, but also shows how Philo or his source understood what is a crux in the Pindaric text. Pindar is writing of his friend Damophilus, who is never indecisive:

οὐδέ μακύνων τέλος οὐδέν· ὁ γὰρ καιρὸς πρὸς
ἀνθρώπων βραχὺ μέτρον ἔχει.
εὖ νιν ἔγνωκεν. θεράπων δέ οἱ, οὐ δράστας ὀπαδεῖ.

The pronoun νιν must refer either to καιρός or to the truth of the maxim at the end of the previous line. In either case the meaning thus far is the same, but to what does οἱ refer and who or what is the subject of ὀπαδεῖ? Is καιρός the servant of Damophilus or Damophilus the servant of καιρός? A. B. Drachmann's edition of the *Scholia Vetera*, vol. 2 (Leipzig, 1910) pp. 167–8, shows that both interpretations were current.[14] Philo at *Migr.*126 is speaking of the mischief of human ἀκαιρίαι in obscuring ἀρετή, and of its rectification by ὁ δὲ ὁπαδὸς θεοῦ καιρός. I suggest that Philo or his source is familiar with the fourth *Pythian* and with that interpretation which sees καιρός as the servant of Damophilus, but now it is God who is said to be served by καιρός, over against the view that Philo combats elsewhere, that καιρός is a god.[15] καιρός does have a role within human history, but it is a subordinate role (cf. Plato, *Leg.*709b). Another way of pre-empting this pagan position is to say that God himself is καιρός (*Mut.* 264–266 with Colson's note).

The three passages which are definitely attributable to Pindar are insufficient to explain Philo's encomium – *lyricorum poetarum optimus* – or to suggest a single trend behind or a single source for Philo's choice, if such were thought necessary; but the physical geography in the two certain quotations is clear (*Aet.* 121: oceanography; *Provid.*2.80.100: eclipses) though surprising, in that we might have expected that it would be rather those features of Pindar's thought that had already impressed Dionysius of Halicarnassus (εἴνεκα . . . μάλιστα δὲ τῶν εἰς σωφροσύνην καὶ εὐσέβειαν καὶ μεγαλοπρέπειαν ἠθῶν, op. cit., vol. 2 p. 205) which would have most attracted Philo. But not chiefly so. As we have seen, at *Aet.*121 Philo appears to be repeating Stoic interpretations of certain ἱστορίαι about Rhodes and Delos, with lines from Pindar which may or may not have stood in Theophrastus' own report of these Stoic views.[16] The Stoics saw in the poetry an allusive (αἰνιττόμενος) confirmation of their science. In his reply (138–142) Theophrastus neatly counters the ἱστορίαι of Rhodes and Delos with the ἱστορία of Sicily and with Plato on Atlantis (141), and counters a Stoicised Pindar with a couplet from an unknown poet (140).

As we have already noted, the 'enigmatic' quality that Theophrastus or Philo had seen in the Stoic use of Pindar, Philo himself notes in the second definite quotation, *Provid.*2.80.100. In 99–100 he is discussing the Stoic doctrine of the usefulness of ἐπακολουθήματα or 'secondary consequences' and (100 fin.) illustrates it from eclipses. They occur because of the movements of other, primary, phenomena, the sun and the moon, and yet can still themselves be useful in that they presage (μηνύματα) the deaths of kings and the destruction of cities (themes which in fact are suggested only in the sequel to the lines quoted in 80, in

Dionysius of Halicarnassus) and Pindar's poetry hints at this (ἠνίξατο). In both places Pindar's physical geography yields religious philosophy αἰνιγματωδῶς.[17] The doctrine that Philo illustrates in 100 was briefly mentioned in 79, and there the usefulness of eclipses, questioned by Philo's nephew and interlocutor Alexander in 71, is said to consist in this: if one knows the cause of eclipses, one appreciates the *firmitas* and *constantia* of the universe. But in addition, in 80, Philo sees in the phenomenon of an eclipse, quoting Pindar, a means of recalling someone alienated from philosophy (Alexander?) back to it (and to Judaism?), because (81) if he realises that it is God who is ultimately responsible for eclipses and not demons, who might otherwise be suspected, he is free from fear to pursue true philosophy.[18]

As for the source or sources of these quotations,[19] while Theophrastus may be the source at *Aet.*121, for both of them[20] we may be able to posit as an intermediate source another natural scientist, the Stoic Posidonius. In fact, Willy Theiler's posthumous and maximising edition of the Posidonius fragments (Berlin, 1982) includes the whole of *Aet.*117–150 as frag. 310![21]

That leaves us with *Virt.*172 and the braggart's pretensions to divinity. Cohn in his German translation (vol. 2, Breslau, 1910 p. 363 note 1: 'eine offenbare Anspielung') and Reiter in his edition of the Greek text at *Leg.*75 were of the view that Philo had the Emperor Gaius in mind. Colson (*LCL* vol. 8 p. 269 note b) considered this proposal 'rather unnecessary even if it can be verified chronologically', and in her commentary on *Leg.*75–117 E. M. Smallwood (Leiden, 1961) nowhere makes reference to *Virt.*172. However *Leg.*75, οὐκέτι ἠξιόυ μένειν ἐν τοῖς τῆς ἀνθρωπίνης φύσεως ὅροις, does echo *Virt.*172, ὑπὲρ τοὺς ὅρους τῆς ἀνθρωπίνης φύσεως βαίνειν ἀξιῶν, rather neatly. We have seen how Theophrastus could counter one ἱστορία with another, and one poet with another. Is it too much to see in Philo's use of Pindar in *Virt.*172 the circumspect countering of one pagan's blasphemous claims with the rebuke of another pagan, one of antiquity's great moralists?

But, overall, Pindar clearly does not have the importance of other Greek poets (Homer (cf. note 2), Hesiod, the tragedians) and certainly not the Academy or the Stoa in the provision of content or form to Philo's thought. I suggest that the reason lies in the schools. Philo's Hellenistic predecessors and contemporaries were interested in Pindar mainly as a source of mythology, geography[22] and linguistic curiosities.

The extant texts suggest that it was an ancient science that could be developed into religious philosophy and a pagan morality that could be prudently deployed against a pagan emperor that Philo found in Pindar.

Notes

1. Cf. Eusebius, *Hist. Eccl.* 2.4. fin. Is the first part of the jingle an elaboration of Numenius' question, τί γάρ ἐστι Πλάτων ἢ Μωυσῆς ἀττικίζων; (ap. Clem. Alex., *Strom.* 1.150.4; in the collection of the Numenius fragments made by É. des Places (Paris, 1973) pp. 51–2)? For this E. H. Gifford compares Dio of Prusa, *Or.* 10.23–24: νομίζεις τὸν Ἀπόλλωνα ἀττικίζειν ἢ δωρίζειν; cf. id., *Or.* 11.22–23, in his edition of Eusebius, *Praep. Ev.* (Oxford, 1903) vol. 4 p. 389. The scholiast on Plato *Leg.* 625a speaks of οἱ Στωϊκοὶ πλατωνίζοντες (C. F. Hermann, vol. 6 (Leipzig, 1892) p. 373). On the whole question see the essay of M. Alexandre, 'La culture profane chez Philon', in the volume emerging from the Lyon-Colloque, *Philon d'Alexandrie* (Paris, 1967) pp. 105–29; Mireille Hadas-Lebel's edition of *De Providentia I/II*, vol. 35 (Paris, 1973) in the Lyon series *Les Oeuvres de Philon d'Alexandrie* (henceforth H-L), pp. 24–33; *Jewish Writings of the Second Temple Period* (Assen, 1984), ed. M. E. Stone, pp. 254 ff. (P. Borgen); for further bibliography, *Aufstieg und Niedergang der römischen Welt* 2.21.1 (Berlin/New York, 1984), ed. W. Haase, pp. 67–70 (E. Hilgert) and, for Jerome and Philo, pp. 745 ff. (H. Savon).
2. *Provid.* 2.80 (H-L (whose capitulation I follow throughout, not F. H. Colson's in *LCL* vol. 9) p. 308). Philo anticipates the well-known passages in Quintilian 8.6.71 and 10.1.61, *novem vero lyricorum longe Pindarus princeps*; cf. *Provid.* 2.15 (H-L p. 228), *apud probatissimum laudatissimumque poetarum Homerum*.
3. In *Handbuch der Altertumswissenschaft* 7.1.1 (München, 1929) pp. 615–21, esp. pp. 618–19.
4. Found in Solon frag. 6 and Theognis 153 (M. L. West, *Iambi et Elegi Graeci ante Alexandrum cantati* vol. 1 (Oxford, 1971) p. 181, vol. 2 (1972) p. 125 with note). H-L p. 235 note 2 lists other places where Philo uses the maxim; add *Post.* 145. Pindar uses it at *Olym.* 13.10. Cf. M. Harl, 'Recherches sur l'origénisme d'Origène', in *SP* vol. 8 (1966) pp. 373–405, esp. pp. 376–83.
5. Philo expresses another view at *P. Oxy.* vol. 11 (London, 1915) 1356 p. 14 lines 34 ff., p. 18.
6. Curiously Philo quotes μηδὲν ἄγαν only once, at *Spec. L.* 2.83.
7. *Philo von Alexandria als Ausleger des Alten Testaments* (Jena, 1875) p. 138.
8. This reference to Pindar is not found in G. Mayer's *Index Philoneus* (Berlin/New York, 1974) since *Provid.* was not included in Mayer's base

text, the *editio minor* of Cohn-Wendland-Reiter (Berlin, 1896–1915), and so not indexed.

9. Aucher's Latin is now much more accessible in H-L. The editor has taken only the slightest liberties with Aucher's Latin. The most recent assessment of 'Armenian Philo' known to me is A. Terian, *Philonis Alexandrini de Animalibus* (Scholar's Press, Chico, California, 1981; *Studies in Hellenistic Judaism* 1), where of course he mentioned Aucher and discusses the characteristics of the translation into Armenian, pp. ix–x, 9–14, 57–60.

10. See Schröder, H-L p. 308 note 2, and Colson, *LCL* vol. 9 p. 546, but cf. pp. 449–50.

11. *Poetae Melici Graeci* (Oxford, 1962) frag. 77 p. 299 = frag. 66 Bergk. As Philo appears to allude further to this line at *Sobr.*37; *Det.*42, in addition to *Mos.*1.285, we can supplement Page's testimonia (= Bergk's) and R. Stoneman, '*Fidele silentium*: a Pindaric motif in Horace', an essay in *Aischylos und Pindar* (Berlin, 1981), ed. E. G. Schmidt, p. 262. The *Provid.* passage would have assisted Stoneman in his further argument as to how the line could be considered Pindaric (pp. 262 ff.). For Alexander's use of the line, already a favourite with Augustus, cf. W. Bousset, *Jüdisch-Christlicher Schulbetrieb in Alexandria und Rom* (Göttingen, 1915) pp. 138–9, and, for his literary and philosophical achievements, V. Burr, *Tiberius Iulius Alexander* (Bonn, 1955) pp. 18 ff., 92–5, 112. M. Hengel, in *Judaism and Hellenism* (London, 1974) vol. 2, p. 173 note 33, appears to misrepresent Bernays when he says that Bernays regarded Alexander as the author of Ps.-Aristotle, *De Mundo*. J. Bernays, *Gesammelte Abhandlungen* vol. 2 (Berlin, 1885) p. 278 ff., must mean that Alexander was the addressee.

12. H. A. Wolfson, *Philo*, vol. 1 (Cambridge, 1948) p. 94, note 37.

13. Perhaps it is no more than one of those 'rhetorische und poetische Floskeln' to which P. Wendland drew attention, *Die hellenistisch-römische Kultur in ihren Beziehungen zu Judentum und Christentum* (Tübingen, 1907), p. 115 note 6 (= (1972) p. 205 note 2), regarding Philo's biography of Moses; but cf. E. Schwartz, *RE* 3 (Stuttgart, 1899) col. 2027 lines 19–20, 'auf litterarische Beziehungen zwischen Philo und Ch.[airemon] darf nicht geschlossen werden', and H.-R. Schwyzer, *Chairemon* (Leipzig, 1932), pp. 79–80, with parallels between *Cont.* and Chaeremon, frag. 10. Add to these the specialised use of ὀνειρώττειν in the same fragment (Schwyzer p. 46 line 5 = van der Horst p. 20 line 11) and in *Spec.L.*1.119. But note the greater caution expressed by P. W. van der Horst in his edition of the fragments (Leiden, 1984) p. 56.

14. The general verdict of scholars favours the second view; cf. W. Headlam, *Journal of Philology* 30 (1907) 299–300; A. C. Pearson, *Classical Quarterly* 18 (1924) 154–5, presents the best case I know for the former interpretation.

15. *Post.*121–123; *QG.*1.100 (*LCL* Suppl. vol. 1, pp. 67–8; vol. 2, p. 193). I find it difficult to agree with Barthélemy's suggestion (as reported in *JTS* n.s. 28 (1977) 540) that it was the Pythagorean identification of ὁ καιρός and Athena or the Hebdomad which Philo is attacking in his reference to those who deify καιρός in *QG.*1.100. Apart from his laudatory reference to the

Pythagoreans already noted, Philo himself mentions the Pythagorean identification of the Hebdomad with Athena (*All.L.*1.15) and with ὁ ἡγεμὼν τῶν συμπάντων (*Opif.*100), neither time critically (μυθεύοντες in the former passage means no more than 'in the language of myth') and in the latter approvingly – see the reference to the Pythagorean Philolaus at the end of the paragraph. I realise that Philo does not use καιρός in the two passages, but in view of the Pythagorean equation of καιρός and the Hebdomad, we can assume that it is in the background of these reports of similar Pythagorean identifications.

16. H. Diels, *Doxographi Graeci* (repr. Berlin/Leipzig, 1929) p. 108 and Colson, *LCL* vol. 9 p. 177, believed that Philo added the Pindar quotation to his source; cf. P. Wendland's 'poetische Floskeln' (see note 13 above), O. Regenbogen's 'blümige Zusätze' (*RE* Suppl. vol. 7 (Stuttgart, 1940) col. 1540 lines 2–3; cf. ibid. col. 1539 lines 40–41) and K. Reinhardt's 'Anklänge, Reminiszenzen, Ornamente, Ausfüllungen', quoted by Mühl (see note 21 below) p. 35. Then the awkward question has to be faced, would Philo have bothered to document a view he thought mistaken? How far would he go in identifying with doctrines he did not accept? Colson, vol. cit., pp. 269 note a, 13 note e, cf. p. 174, thought Philo could accommodate quite considerably. D. T. Runia, 'Philo's *De Aeternitate Mundi*: the problem of its interpretation', *Vigiliae Christianae* 35 (1981) 105–51, sets, *passim*, this accommodation within the requirements of the literary genre to which *Aet.* belongs.

17. Cf. ἀλληγορικῶς and αἰνιγματωδῶς with their cognates in A. B. Drachmann's edition of the *Scholia vetera*, vol. 3 (Leipzig, 1927) pp. 360, 378; R. M. Grant, *The Letter and the Spirit* (London, 1957) pp. 120–3; *Der Kleine Pauly* vol. 4 (Stuttgart, 1972) s.v. 'Rätsel'. Pindar himself was aware that his poetry would always need interpreters, *Olym.*2.85–86:

    ἐς δὲ τὸ πᾶν ἑρμανέων
    χατίζει [sc. ὠκέα βέλη].

18. Cf. *Spec.L.*4.147 for the contrast between the sunlight of piety and superstition.

19. None of the quotations or allusions we have listed is found amongst Plato's reminiscences of Pindar; cf. É. des Places, *Pindare et Platon* (Paris, 1949), ch. 14, 'Pindare chez Platon: les citations expresses'.

20. This may be the case for the other examples of Philo's interest in physical geography adduced by R. Arnaldez in his edition of *Aet.* (Paris, 1969) p. 158 note 1: *Post.*144; *Plant.*24.

21. See vol. 1 pp. 233–8 and, for the justification, vol. 2 pp. 129–200. For other possible links between the two see M. Mühl, 'Zu Poseidonius und Philon', *Wiener Studien* 60 (1942) 28–36. Cf. frags.228, 123–126 (Edelstein-Kidd (Cambridge, 1972)) for Posidonius' own views on the phenomena referred to in *Aet.*121 and *Provid.*2.80.100. Cf. frag. 246 line 28 for more geography Posidonius took from Pindar.

22. Cf. note 21 and Schmid (note 11 above) p. 618 note 1, though, as we have seen, Dionysius of Halicarnassus and Quintilian found more. Similiarly Pindar seems to have been largely neglected by earlier Christian writers

except Clement of Alexandria; cf. Nicole Zeegers-van der Horst, *Les Citations des Poètes grecs chez les Apologistes chrétiens du IIe Siècle* (Louvain, 1972) pp. 32, 40; R. M. Grant, 'Greek Literature in the Treatise *De Trinitate* and Cyril *Contra Julianum*', *JTS* n.s.15 (1964) 267 ff.; J. Irmscher, 'Pindar in Byzanz', an article in Schmidt (see note 11), pp. 296–302; G. Glockmann, *Homer in der frühchristlichen Literatur bis Justinus* (Berlin, 1968) pp. 3–17; C. Datema, 'Classical Quotations in the works of Cyril of Alexandria', in *SP* vol. 17 (1982) pp. 422–5. Unfortunately Datema does not list the specific references to Pindar, though they must be somewhere there in his statistics. It does not help that half of Datema's notes have gone missing in the printing of his article! However, the third *Pythian* 55, 57–58, which deal with the greed and punishment of Asclepius, were frequently quoted, by Athenagoras *Leg.*29, by Clement of Alexandria *Cohort.*2.30.1, by Eusebius of Caesarea *Praep.Ev.*3.13.19 and by Cyril of Alexandria *C. Julianum* ·6 (*MPG* 76.805D–808A) (references from Schröder p. 197, but modified). Athenagoras, alone, begins his quotation with line 54, that Hoeschel (see p. 221 above) has detected in Philo. Eusebius and Cyril speak of Pindar as μελοποίος, no doubt the original of the Armenian behind Aucher's *lyricorum poetarum*, though, according to Mayer's *Index* (see note 8 above), it does not occur in 'Greek Philo'. Are these quotations in four Christian writers alone sufficient to justify C. N. Cochrane's contention about Pindar, 'one who still, in the fourth century after Christ, ranked as among the most reputable of the "ancient theologians"' (*Christianity and Classical Culture* (New York, 1940) p. 372)? A Polish scholar has traced a similar variation in the Latin response to Pindar, with the second and third centuries AD appearing to neglect the poet: M. Brożek, 'De scriptoribus Latinis antiquis Pindari laudatoribus et aemulis', *Eos* 59 (1971) 101–7 (my knowledge of this article is secondhand).

List of Contributors

C. K. Barrett	Professor Emeritus of Divinity, University of Durham.
Ernest Best	Professor Emeritus of Divinity and Biblical Criticism, University of Glasgow.
Otto Betz	Professor of New Testament, University of Tübingen.
F. F. Bruce	Emeritus Professor, University of Manchester; formerly Rylands Professor of Biblical Criticism and Exegesis.
Ieuan Ellis	Senior Lecturer in Theology, University of Hull.
Birger Gerhardsson	Professor of Exegetical Theology, University of Lund.
Lester L. Grabbe	Lecturer in Theology, University of Hull.
Barnabas Lindars SSF	Rylands Professor of Biblical Criticism and Exegesis, University of Manchester.
John W. McKay	Director of Studies, Roffey Place Christian Training Centre (Bethany Fellowship), Horsham, West Sussex.
J. L. North	Barmby Lecturer in New Testament Studies, University of Hull.
Wendy E. Sproston	Department of Theology, University of Hull.
Margaret E. Thrall	Formerly Reader in Biblical Studies, University College of North Wales, Bangor.
R. N. Whybray	Professor Emeritus of Hebrew and Old Testament Studies, University of Hull.
Max Wilcox	Professor of Biblical Studies, University College of North Wales, Bangor.

Index of References

Old Testament

Genesis

11:26	49n.10
11:31–12:5	41
12:1	107, 129n.29
12:4	41
15:5	112n.25
15:6	93, 112n.25
18	197n.21
22:1–2	123
22:12	129n.34
22:16–18	122
23:16–20	41, 127n.6
25:32	130n.49
33:19–20	41
41:45	181, 196
46:27	50n.13
48:22	116
49:29–32	41, 127n.6
49:33	116
50:2	124
50:13	41, 116
50:24–26	114–30 passim

Exodus

1:5	50n.13
1:6	116
2:11	43
3:16–17	119, 121
4:22–23	6
4:28	128n.25
4:31	119, 121
7:7	42
13:8	22n.12
13:19	114–30 passim
16	199
16:13–15	198
16:31	187
21:1–11	6
21:2–6	22n.5
21:26–27	22n.5
23:20–21	43
30:11–16	11

34	xii
34:28	36

Leviticus

6:2–5	73
19:20	22n.6
25:10	22n.6
25:39–55	6
25:42–43	6, 17
26:11–17	6
26:13	6

Numbers

11:7–9	198

Deuteronomy

6:10–25	6
8:11 ff.	219
10:22	50n.13
11:6	111n.18
11:14	188
15:12	22n.5
15:12–18	6
15:13	22n.5
15:18	22n.5
18:15	44
28	7, 80
32:33	48, 50n.23

Joshua

23	7
24:15	176
24:32	41, 114–17, 119

Judges

3:7–8	7
3:41–42	7
6–7	204
6:1–2	7
6:4	111n.18
6:11–24	186
10:6–8	7
13	197n.21
13:1	7

Ruth

1:12	111n.18

230

New Testament

Apocrypha, Pseudepigrapha, and Other Jewish Literature in Greek

Early Christian Writers

Classical and Ancient Near Eastern Writers

Index of Modern Authors

An asterisk indicates merely the first reference to an author in the notes on the page cited.

DATE DUE

DEMCO 38-297